THE PRINCE

broadview editions
series editor: Martin R. Boyne

THE PRINCE

Niccolò Machiavelli

edited by Jason P. Blahuta

translated by Manuela Scarci

broadview editions

BROADVIEW PRESS
Peterborough, Ontario, Canada

Founded in 1985, Broadview Press remains a wholly independent publishing house. Broadview's focus is on academic publishing; our titles are accessible to university and college students as well as scholars and general readers. With over 800 titles in print, Broadview has become a leading international publisher in the humanities, with world-wide distribution. Broadview is committed to environmentally responsible publishing and fair business practices.

Library and Archives Canada Cataloguing in Publication

Title: The prince / Niccolò Machiavelli ; edited by Jason P. Blahuta ; translated by Manuela Scarci.
Other titles: Principe. English
Names: Machiavelli, Niccolò, 1469-1527, author. | Blahuta, Jason P., 1971- editor. | Scarci, Manuela, 1957- translator.
Series: Broadview editions.
Description: Series statement: Broadview editions | Translated from the Italian. | Includes bibliographical references and index.
Identifiers: Canadiana (print) 20230596363 | Canadiana (ebook) 20230596398 | ISBN 9781554813605 (softcover) | ISBN 9781770489219 (PDF) | ISBN 9781460408520 (EPUB)
Subjects: LCSH: Political science—Early works to 1800. | LCSH: Political ethics.
Classification: LCC JC143 .M3713 2024 | DDC 320.1—dc23

Broadview Editions
The Broadview Editions series is an effort to represent the ever-evolving canon of texts in the disciplines of literary studies, history, philosophy, and political theory. A distinguishing feature of the series is the inclusion of primary source documents contemporaneous with the work.

Advisory editor for this volume: Michel Pharand

Broadview Press handles its own distribution in Canada and the United States:
PO Box 1243, Peterborough, Ontario K9J 7H5, Canada
555 Riverwalk Parkway, Tonawanda, NY 14150, USA
Tel: (705) 482-5915
email: customerservice@broadviewpress.com

For all territories outside of Canada and the United States, distribution is handled by Eurospan Group.

Broadview Press acknowledges the financial support of the Government of Canada for our publishing activities.

Canadä

Cover design and typesetting: George Kirkpatrick

Broadview Press® is the registered trademark of Broadview Press Inc.

PRINTED IN CANADA

For my parents, Jenny and Lawrence

*Without your continued love and support
I would never have journeyed so far.*

Contents

Acknowledgements

Jason P. Blahuta (Editor)

There are several persons I need to thank for their invaluable help in developing this book. First, the incredible editorial staff at Broadview Press, especially Stephen Latta and Michel Pharand for their help and patience. I am also grateful to Andrew Slivchack for generating the map of Renaissance Italy used in this edition, as well as the anonymous reviewers who provided several constructive comments. I would also like to express my gratitude to the students who have taken my senior seminar on Machiavelli over the past two decades and whose inquisitiveness and passion are a constant source of encouragement and inspiration. As always, I am indebted to my wonderful wife Michelle for her love and support in this, and every other project, I undertake.

Kirsty Jane Falconer (Translator of Appendices B – I)

I am profoundly grateful to the staff of the manuscript room of the Biblioteca Ariostea, Ferrara, who furnished me with a peaceful and beautiful place to work as well as setting "my" Machiavelli edition aside for the duration of the project. My friends Nicola Rebagliati, Hilary Ely, and Josephine von Zitzewitz provided valuable moral and practical support, as did Rosa and Frida.

Introduction

Niccolò Machiavelli (1469–1527) is one of the most misunderstood and maligned authors in history. This stems mainly from three things. First, Machiavelli was an intellectual provocateur of the highest order. He had to be, given his personality, the undesirable position he found himself in when he began to write, and the competition to be heard. Second, *The Prince* is often read in isolation from Machiavelli's other writings. Machiavelli created a wide-ranging corpus that included political treatises, histories, plays, a novella, poetry, transcriptions of Roman works, and personal correspondence; in these often-overlooked works he expounds and develops his various ideas about politics. To read *The Prince* without taking these works into consideration is to take the ideas presented in *The Prince* out of context. Third, Machiavelli neither lived nor wrote in a vacuum, but at the nexus of a remarkable range of intellectual, cultural, and political traditions and influences. While Machiavelli is not merely the effect of the convergence of these influences, ignorance of his circumstances inevitably leads to underappreciating and overstating his originality and significance in the history of political thought.

To avoid these pitfalls, one needs above all to read *The Prince* carefully. First, Machiavelli often uses sensational tag lines when trying to get noticed; thus he proclaims *it is much safer to be feared than loved*, but then he qualifies his position throughout the rest of the chapter. The entire argument needs to be noted and the tag line situated within it before rushing to a conclusion about Machiavelli's position. Second, if one wants to truly understand *The Prince*, one must be familiar with the rest of Machiavelli's writings, the most salient of which are represented in this edition's appendices. This is by no means an exhaustive list, and depending on what theme or context is being considered, Machiavelli's other writings or different selections from the works represented in the appendices will be more appropriate. The *Discourses on Livy* in particular are important, as they have a symbiotic relationship with *The Prince* that is grounded in Machiavelli's cyclical conception of history, and following the advice of only one of these texts is a recipe for limited success. Third, one must be aware, as much as is possible, of Machiavelli's context. Aside from the brief biography and historical comments provided here, this means understanding his relation to his fellow Florentines, his beloved ancients, and the various traditions in which he walked.

Florence during the Italian Renaissance

The world into which Niccolò Machiavelli was born on 3 May 1469 was a tumultuous one characterized by extremes. Learning and the arts flourished, new technologies such as the printing press and artillery were transforming the world in profound and exciting ways, and the power of the Catholic Church in Europe was showing signs of distress that would soon result in the Protestant Reformation.

Italy was especially chaotic. Unlike other European powers that were unified absolute monarchies and moving in the direction of becoming nation-states, Italy remained a collection of small republics, principalities, city-states, and the papacy. The main centres of power—Florence, Milan, and Venice in the north; Naples in the south; and Rome and the papal states sandwiched in between—constantly squabbled and fought with little permanent change to the political landscape.

Politically, Machiavelli's hometown of Florence lurched, often violently, from a façade of a republic controlled by the Medici, through a humiliating foreign invasion, into a religiously tinged populist wave of near fanaticism under the Dominican preacher Girolamo Savonarola (1452–98), to a secular republic, before relapsing into an unabashedly autocratic form of rule under Lorenzo de' Medici (the younger, 1492–1519), only to briefly resurrect itself as a republic which would be permanently extinguished shortly after Machiavelli's death. All of this within the span of less than thirty-five years, and all of it in the shadows of the glory that had been the Roman Republic.

Machiavelli's family had aristocratic roots but had lost all financial and political influence. His father, Bernardo Machiavelli (c. 1426/29–1500), was a lawyer but never accumulated much wealth, only a personal library which his son Niccolò devoured. Despite their financial constraints, however, his family was able to provide the young Machiavelli with a reasonable and well-rounded humanist education. He studied under two unknown tutors and a renowned Latin teacher, Paolo da Ronciglione, and was well acquainted with the ancient historians Livy, Polybius, and Tacitus, the biographer Plutarch, the Roman poet and philosopher Lucretius, Roman playwrights such as Plautus, to varying extents the philosophies of Plato, Aristotle, and Xenophon, as well as the proud humanist writers of Italy, including Petrarch (1304–74) and Dante (c. 1265–1321). However, as far as the leading families of Florence were concerned, Machiavelli was essentially born a commoner, a birthright that would plague him and hinder his aspirations throughout his life.

Due to his low social status, little else is known of Machiavelli until he entered public life in 1498. From the start, Machiavelli's successes and failures were intertwined with the status of the Medici, the powerful banking family that ruled Florence under the guise of a republic for most of the fifteenth century. Under the Medici, Florence had the institutions of a republic, but the elections for government offices were continually fixed to ensure that only Medici supporters and allies were awarded positions. Cosimo de' Medici (1389–1464) was the first of the Medici to effectively rule Florence, followed by his grandson, Lorenzo the Magnificent (1449–92). Lorenzo managed to keep Florence secure through a carefully executed policy of playing the interests of the various Italian powers off one another. This policy bought peace in the short term but gradually weakened all the Italian political entities through repeatedly engaging them in wars that were aimed only at maintaining the political status quo on the Italian peninsula, as opposed to a unification of Italy. These wars drained the Italian powers militarily and economically. Venice, Milan, and Florence, in particular, were wealthy mercantile centres, and the rich prefer to fight with their money as opposed to their blood or the blood of their children, especially in wars that accomplish little; as a result, these (and all Italian) cities grew increasingly reliant on mercenaries and their celebrity generals for hire, the *condottieri*.

Therefore, when Lorenzo the Magnificent died on 8 April 1492, his son Piero (1472–1503) inherited a Florence that was cash-strapped and unable to defend itself. The vulnerabilities of the various Italian powers, not just Florence, were exposed for all of Europe to see when the French, under Charles VIII (r. 1483–98), invaded in 1494. The French invasion was characteristic of earlier Italian wars, in that it involved one city asking an ally for help in achieving a military objective that was otherwise unobtainable. In this case, Ludovico Sforza (il Moro), duke of Milan (1452–1508), encouraged Charles to pursue his hereditary claim on Naples in order to allow Sforza to secure his own position in Milan. Ludovico was regent to his nephew, Gian Galeazzo Sforza (1469–94), the rightful ruler of Milan, and was both reluctant to relinquish power to his nephew and convinced that his nephew's supporters were bringing Naples to

their cause. Ludovico hoped the French invasion would eliminate this threat to his position; however, he failed to understand
the ineffectiveness of the Italian armies and to foresee the swift
and easy success of the French. Overnight the situation changed
from Italians fighting low-stakes, farcical wars that maintained
a balance of power among the various kingdoms and republics
to Italians fighting off foreign invasions, often with the help of
other foreigners, in bloody high-stakes battles for their indepen-
dence and lives. As far as the rest of Europe was concerned, the
Italian peninsula was simply a trophy which France, Spain, and
the Holy Roman emperor were all interested in claiming, or at
the very least in keeping from their rivals.

It was in the context of this first French aggression by Charles
VIII that Machiavelli came to public life. Piero de' Medici,
lacking the leadership skills and political acumen of his famous
father, panicked at the approach of the French army and hast-
ily negotiated a peace with Charles that was little more than an
unconditional surrender. Florence was humiliated. Enraged, the
Florentines ousted the Medici from power, exiled Piero, and
formed a new government with Piero Soderini (1450–1522)
made *gonfalonier*, standard bearer or head of government, for life.
Florence was now a republic not only in name but in fact. The
fall of the Medici opened the door to lower-class citizens such
as Machiavelli to hold office and participate in public life. He
was elected as head of the Second Chancery of the Republic of
Florence and quickly became the Secretary to the Ten of Liberty
and Peace in 1498. With his formidable powers of observation,
penetrating insights, and ability to succinctly and discreetly com-
municate his assessments of political figures and situations to his
superiors, Machiavelli immediately proved himself a skilled civil
servant and diplomat.

In the fifteen years he served the Republic of Florence,
Machiavelli was sent on numerous diplomatic missions throughout Italy as well as to the courts of France and the Holy Roman
emperor, and he met many of the political figures he would later
write about. Despite his skill, however, his birthright and irrever-
ent personality prevented him from being fully accepted by the
aristocratic families that remained influential within the republic. Still, his career would have undoubtedly continued had it not
been for circumstances beyond his control.

Just as the overthrow of the Medici enabled Machiavelli to
enter Florentine politics, their reinstatement would force him out
of that arena. The French returned in 1508: this time Louis XII

(r. 1498–1515) and Spanish forces had been invited into Italy by Pope Julius II (r. 1503–13) as part of the League of Cambrai to help him curtail Venice's expanding influence. However, once the Venetians had their ambitions quashed and were no longer a threat to the papacy, Julius II turned on France, fearing its growing presence, and in 1510 formed the Holy League to rid Italy of the French. The Holy League grew to include the papal forces, Venice, England, Spain, and the Holy Roman emperor. Machiavelli read the situation well and encouraged Soderini to join the anti-French forces, but the gonfalonier for life refused, choosing to honour an existing treaty with France. The Holy League proved victorious, and after the French withdrew in 1512, Julius II punished the Republic of Florence for not supporting him. The republic was overthrown, Soderini was exiled, and the Medici were reinstated with the help of Spanish troops.

Once again, Machiavelli's fate was tied to the Medici; between his low birthright and his close ties to Soderini, he was distrusted by the Medici and was dismissed from his government posts. Matters worsened quickly when Machiavelli was implicated in an anti-Medici conspiracy. He was arrested and repeatedly subjected to the *strappado*, a form of torture in which the victim is raised high into the air by a rope attached to a bond that secures the wrists behind the back and let to fall, stopping just short of the ground. The combination of the victim's weight, position, and gravity often caused dislocated shoulders and other painful injuries. Machiavelli never confessed throughout these interrogations, and with only minimal evidence against him (his name appeared on a list found in the possession of a conspirator) he was released under a general amnesty to celebrate Cardinal Giovanni di Lorenzo de' Medici's ascension to the throne of St. Peter as Pope Leo X (r. 1513–21). With papal backing, the Medici in Florence had nothing to fear from alleged minor players like Machiavelli— but all had not been forgiven. A crueller fate than the strappado, Machiavelli was barred from the Palazzo Vecchio and the political life of Florence and was exiled to live in relative poverty on his family's estate just outside of Florence.

Marginalized, unemployed, and denied the opportunity to engage in his greatest passion, Machiavelli began writing *The Prince* sometime between his release from prison on 10 March 1513 and his famous letter to his friend Francesco Vettori (1474–1540), dated 10 December 1513 (see Appendix I2), in which he references working on the project. Currently, the most detailed and persuasive argument regarding the book's completion is provided by Connell, who maintains that Machiavelli completed *The Prince* in 1514 and made minor revisions to it throughout the first half of 1515, with it being presented to Lorenzo de' Medici between the latter half of May and the beginning of July of that year. Machiavelli's exile would also allow him to frequent the Orti Oricellari, the ornate gardens where the wealthy and politically connected Bernardo Rucellai (1448–1514) hosted gatherings of philosophers, historians, literati, and humanists, and provide him with the opportunity to write the *Discourses on Livy*, the *Florentine Histories*, *The Art of War*, numerous poems including *The Golden Ass* and the *Tercets on Fortune*, his plays *Mandragola* and *Clizia*, as well as the novella *Belfagor: The Devil Who Married*.

Machiavelli would spend the next decade trying to have his voice heard by the Medici in the hope that they would restore him to the realm of Florentine politics. He would have varied successes along the way, most notably the commission to write the *Florentine Histories* as well as being appointed to oversee the fortifications of Florence in 1526. His other successes, such as his plays *Mandragola* and *Clizia*, were unrelated to the Medici. However, the limited inroads he made with the Medici made him untrustworthy to those in power when the Medici were overthrown and expelled in 1527. Machiavelli died shortly thereafter, on 21 June, still excluded from Florentine politics. During his exile he wrote to teach others what circumstances would not let him do himself, a duty he describes in the preface to the second book of the *Discourses on Livy*, and unbeknownst to him, his activities while in exile would catapult him onto the world stage posthumously. Had he remained employed by the various regimes that ruled Florence, he would have been but a footnote to history, a brilliant civil servant whose ideas likely would have never fully materialized due to the short-sightedness and incompetence of his superiors. However, forced to write—to gain employment, to be heard, to fight off the boredom of his exile—he secured himself a place in history that outshines that of all his political and intellectual contemporaries. The Borgias and the Medici may have been glorified on television, but *The Prince* has been read by generation after generation for over half a millennium.

Key Concepts in Machiavelli's Thought

Fortune and Virtù

Fortune is a concept that permeates almost every piece of writing Machiavelli produced. In its most basic form, Fortune represents whatever the prince cannot control. Machiavelli's most famous treatment of Fortune occurs in chapter 25 of *The Prince*, where he acknowledges that many hold the view that the world is one in which all things are ruled by Fortune and God, but he rejects this in favour of the position that Fortune governs roughly half of the prince's actions and leaves the rest to the prince. God is left out of the discussion. His rationale and only defence of this claim is that such a position does not entirely negate free will.

Machiavelli portrays Fortune in two ways in this chapter, comparing her to a raging river whose force can be anticipated and redirected, but not opposed, and to a woman who can be overpowered by a young and audacious prince. Machiavelli's final pronouncement on Fortune in *The Prince*, an innocent comment slipped in between these two very optimistic images, is that Fortune changes and the successful prince will be the one who can anticipate this change and adjust his behaviour accordingly; those princes that do not change with Fortune are doomed to failure. But the message remains thoroughly positive, change appears possible, and Machiavelli advises the prince to be impetuous because in the long run this course of action seems to work best.

The only weapon the prince has against Fortune is his *virtù*, a term which Machiavelli never defines and which has little in common with the traditional Christian conception of virtue. Complicating matters, Machiavelli often uses other terms to express the specific sense of *virtù* that he wants to convey in a passage, but those terms are never wholly synonymous with *virtù* and possess their own connotations as well. Despite these difficulties, the term clearly refers to personal traits of the would-be ruler and includes strength and fierceness, forethought and prudence, cunning, audacity, a sense of vision and a desire to show off (to be seen executing grand schemes), the ability to appear conventionally moral but to possess the willingness and stomach to discard conventional moral norms when necessary, and, above all, the ability to adapt to changing circumstances.

On the other hand, Machiavelli presents a more nuanced rationale and increasingly pessimistic view of the prince's relationship with Fortune throughout his other writings. In the *Discourses on*

Livy 2.29 (see Appendix A), Machiavelli maintains that all great rulers are nothing without Fortune, for at the very least they owe to her the opportunity to display their *virtù*. Further, in the *Tercets on Fortune* (see Appendix B) Machiavelli offers a third portrayal of Fortune, elevating her from a mere woman, as in *The Prince*, to a goddess. This promotion comes with an increase in power, as Machiavelli describes her as omnipotent and ascribes to her a decided wickedness that makes her an enemy of the prince. Machiavelli places a unique spin on the mythology of the Roman goddess, turning her from a benevolent deity into a malevolent one. For instance, he describes her palace as being filled with a variety of wheels, spinning at different speeds and in different directions and subject to sudden changes in speed and bearing. These wheels are driven by Laziness and Necessity, the forces that spur political bodies to order or disorder. On the rim of each wheel are the lives of people, some rising in their fortunes while others are in decline after their place on the wheel has reached its zenith or changed tack unexpectedly. Fortune oversees them all, delighting in making individual persons rise and fall at her will. The successful prince must anticipate not only the turning of the wheel he rides but also the motion of the other wheels, for when the turn of his wheel becomes unfavourable, his only recourse is to jump to another wheel. Certainly this is a grimmer depiction of the plight of the prince—he is reduced from the aggressive man who seizes what he wants (let us be clear: the imagery in chapter 25 is that of a sexual assault) to being a monkey dancing to Fortune's ever-changing tune. A humbling thought to be sure, but nowhere nearly as depressing as the treatment of Fortune in Machiavelli's unfinished poem *The Golden Ass* (see Appendix E). In this work, Fortune appears as the goddess Circe and is again described as omnipotent, and Machiavelli makes it clear there is neither escape from her nor victory over her.

Fortune wins in the end—always. Hardly the uplifting message that Machiavelli wanted to put into a book he hoped would result in employment with Florence's new masters, still less the advice that would encourage a prince, Medici or not, to unite the Italian powers and rid the Italian peninsula of foreign armies. But the advice is consistent with Machiavelli's views on Fortune in *The Prince*. He knew his audience, so he places the best spin he can on the relationship between the prince and Fortune: if the prince makes preparations and acts aggressively, more often than not he will find that things go his way. Yet as Machiavelli well knows, the political world being in a state of constant flux means that any success can only be temporary. *Virtù* will provide a winning streak—but only for so long. Even Rome fell.

History and Human Nature

The efficacy of the advice contained in *The Prince* is founded on two assumptions: first, that the study of history is pedagogically useful to rulers, and second, that human nature is generally constant across all cultural and historical contexts. In chapter 6 of *The Prince*, Machiavelli makes it clear that history is a good teacher when he invokes the image of the prudent archer, who aims higher than his target, not so that he can reach the height at which he aims, but that the extra height will allow him to hit or come closer to his original mark. Likewise, the prudent prince will seek to imitate the great leaders of ancient times; if he is of equal *virtù* he can hope to be equally as great, and if he is of lesser *virtù*, aided by their example he can still hope to approach their greatness. The reason history can be instructive, Machiavelli argues, is that human nature is a constant. Circumstances may change, but the average person's response to praise and insult, the lure of wealth and threat of scarcity, appeals to patriotism, imminent danger, and so on remains basically the same. Machiavelli makes two dramatic claims about human nature in chapter 17: the first is that people are fickle and insincere in their support; the second is that *men forget more quickly the death of a father than the loss of their patrimony*. Great tag lines to be sure, but when taken in context, they amount to little more than the claim that people are primarily self-interested beings. In chapter 9, Machiavelli advises the prince to make sure his subjects always need him, because once they recognize his staying in power is in their interest, he can always rely on their support. As for the difference between the reaction to the loss of a father as opposed to one's wealth, Machiavelli knew—from painful personal experience—that it was human nature to always hope for a reinstatement of wealth and position but also to accept when a loss was truly irreversible (Celenza 93). For Machiavelli the average person was self-interested, relatively short-sighted, and capable of virtue and hope, but only to a limited extent and only under certain circumstances.

Machiavelli also held a conception of history as cyclical, a view he appropriated without acknowledgement from the Greek historian Polybius. The notion of a cyclical history is barely mentioned in *The Prince*, with the only passage that suggests anything close to it appearing in chapter 3, where he praises the wisdom of the Romans for being quick to go to war, claiming "they enjoyed the benefit of their ingenuity (*virtù*) and prudence, for time brings with it all things and can bring with it good as well as bad and bad as well as good" (p. 62). Yet the concept looms large in Machiavelli's thought—Machiavelli explicitly lays out his cyclical conception of history in the *Discourses on Livy* 3.1 and the *Florentine Histories* 5.1 (see Appendix F), illustrates it in the *Tercets on Fortune* and *The Golden Ass*, and makes a bold statement that an understanding of it is key to political success in book 1 of *The Art of War* (see Appendix G). Given how prevalent the idea is and what it amounts to, *The Prince* must be read against this backdrop.

When Machiavelli maintains that history is cyclical, he does not mean that events will repeat themselves in an exact pattern. He simply means that societies will generally go through a process of initial chaos and disorder, their founding, in which violence is prevalent and necessary, and then if successful they will grow through a period of maturity characterized by order and rule of law, before beginning to decay. As the *virtù* of the founding prince will die with him and is unlikely to be present to the same extent in his progeny, Machiavelli encourages the wise prince who desires a state that will endure to transform his principality into a republic, characterized not by the leadership of one individual but by social institutions that mimic the effects of the founder's *virtù*. In short, once his state is as secure and well ordered as possible (and his mortality is making itself felt), the prudent prince will put aside his copy of *The Prince* and start reading the *Discourses on Livy*, a book about republics, constitutions, and the rule of law.

This cycle between order and disorder can be reset through a variety of means—constitutional provisions such as the office of dictator, the *virtù* of individual rulers, and the intervention of Fortune—but if the corruption becomes too widespread or insufficient remedies have been prepared in advance, the only resort is the rise of a prince-like figure to rejuvenate the state by extraordinary and violent means. The alternative is that the state will become weakened to the point that it falls prey to a stronger state. In principle, Machiavelli argues in *Discourses on Livy* 1.2, a political body could run through these cycles indefinitely, forever forestalling its death; but the chance of such sustained *virtù* is so implausible that Machiavelli concedes that sooner or later a state will fail to rejuvenate itself and fall victim to another state's expansion.

Morality

Machiavelli is often credited with ushering in the era of modern political science, the study of politics through a methodology that bracketed moral norms, as opposed to classical political thought which saw politics and ethics as intimately intertwined and inseparable. This portrayal of Machiavelli is not as obvious as its advocates maintain, regardless of whether one looks at *The Prince* or the *Discourses on Livy*. Machiavelli certainly breaks with classical and Christian authors in his treatment of politics as largely prudential in nature, but he never treats politics as completely devoid of norms. In *The Prince*, the *Discourses on Livy*, and the *Life of Castruccio Castracani* (see Appendix H), Machiavelli makes it clear that norms are involved in politics; it is just that they are not always the same norms that the classical and Christian authors hold. Some of these norms allow for political societies to be ranked against one another; longevity is the historical yardstick by which all political societies are judged: the longer a state lasts, in one sense, the greater it is (it was obviously well ordered). Others, such as avoiding outright wickedness (*The Prince*, chapter 8), are necessary for a ruler to attain glory, which is the goal of all truly great rulers.

Whether It Is Better to Be Loved Than to Be Feared

Trying to be heard above the roar of others who also sought the Medicis' favour, Machiavelli wrote as a provocateur. His treatment of whether it is better to be loved or feared in chapter 17 appears shocking; after all, he does tell the would-be prince that it is better to be feared than loved. This is where many a commentator stops, latches onto the tag line Machiavelli uses to provoke, and assumes the rest of his argument. A close reading of the chapter, however, quickly reveals that there is much more to Machiavelli's advice. In the first place, he is clear that the most desirable position for a prince is to be simultaneously loved and feared. Unfortunately, Machiavelli laments, this is rarely possible even for the most skilled prince. Forced to settle for a second-best solution, the prince should opt for being feared over being loved. However, fear is not what it may appear to be, as Machiavelli's rationale makes clear. Fear is not terror: it is merely a respect of the prince's ferocity combined with an understanding of the fact that the people's best interests are tied to that of the prince. This is why Machiavelli is so quick to add a caveat to his advice: be feared, but never become hated. Princes who misconstrue fear as terror become hated, and there is no defence against being hated. Machiavelli then proceeds to warn of and counsel against the most common vices of rulers that lead to their becoming hated: sexual misconduct with one's subjects, abuse of punitive powers, and stealing from them. By the end of the chapter, Machiavelli has merely dressed up a piece of common sense in scandalous clothing: fear—the ability of the prince to intimidate his rivals and the fear of the people at the potential loss that comes with a change of regime—is preferable because it provides the prince with control over people's loyalties, whereas love leaves loyalty beyond the prince's control. Fear, however, does not mean wanton cruelty or abuse of power.

Generosity

In chapter 16 Machiavelli advises the prince against the virtue of generosity as it is traditionally practised. Once one has read past the controversy of Machiavelli's tag line, *generosity, when used so that you may be thought of as a generous person, will harm you*, his analysis of generosity makes it clear that Machiavelli does believe in generosity; it is simply not the same conception of generosity that Christian writers hold. For a prince to be generous in the traditional sense of the word, Machiavelli observes, he must give away his resources. This is a self-defeating virtue, because soon he will have nothing left to give away, at which point his inability to bestow benefits on others will become a source of offence to those who are accustomed to receiving these benefits or a humiliation for the prince, as he will be thought poor, weak, and effeminate. If he seeks to avoid these consequences and tries to maintain this generosity, the prince will be forced to impose on his subjects either through increased taxation or outright thievery, which will make him hated. So generosity is a losing proposition no matter how one looks at it. Machiavelli's counsel is to transform generosity by placing strict limitations on what can be given away. The spoils of war, because they do not come at the expense of the prince or his citizens, can and should be given away; otherwise, the prince should seek to be generous to his people by not being liberal with his resources. True, he will offend some who expect benefits from him; but the many who are spared onerous taxation and would not have benefited from these favours will come to recognize the prince's ability to live within his means as the virtue of true generosity. The support of the people, whose numbers far exceed those who typically benefit from a prince's generosity, will prevent the few who are disappointed at the prince's refusal to provide them with lavish gifts from acting against him. Thus Machiavelli does not decry generosity per se but rather rejects the traditional conception of this virtue and advocates for an alternative conception of it that he thinks is more sustainable and effective.

Keeping and Breaking Promises

In a similar manner, Machiavelli argues in chapter 18 that the prince should not always keep his word. At first glance this is immoral advice, but a closer look at Machiavelli's argument reveals that his advice is merely that one should not honour one's promises if, and only if, keeping the promise would hurt one's interests and the reason for making the promise is no longer relevant. These in themselves are significant restrictions that make his advice a far cry from advocating breaking faith whimsically: there must be a relevant set of reasons before one can renege on a promise. Machiavelli offers a justification for such behaviour that changes the nature of the advice, too: one can and should break faith when these conditions are met, because others will do the same. In short, the prince who plays by the rules in all situations is at a disadvantage against others who will break the rules. Thus, Machiavelli's counsel is to break with conventional moral standards *only* when one is forced to do so by the necessity imposed on them by circumstances.

Religion

Machiavelli's overall irreverence and provocative tag lines are undoubtedly largely responsible for the outrage his book caused, but his brutal critique of Christianity in both *The Prince* and the *Discourses on Livy* made him a target for the accusation of not only preaching immorality but impiety as well. In chapter 11, Machiavelli treads carefully, praising ecclesiastical principalities for not having to be ruled because God maintains them, and claims that he will not discuss them for this reason. Of course, Machiavelli immediately proceeds to discuss the political actions of various popes, whom he treats on par with secular princes. Worth noting is that despite the success of Alexander VI (r. 1492–1503) in strengthening the Church, Machiavelli ranks Julius II (r. 1503–13) as being more worthy of praise, for his efforts and successes at strengthening the Church were for the sake of the Church itself, as opposed to Alexander VI, who used the Church to further his family's wealth and influence. Given that Machiavelli treated the pope as just another prince with an army, it is no wonder that the Catholic Church took a dim view of *The Prince*.

That religion and arms go hand in hand is reiterated in chapter 6 and in *Discourses on Livy* 3.30, when Machiavelli briefly discusses the Dominican preacher and republican advocate Girolamo Savonarola (1452–98), who whipped Florence into a religious frenzy in the wake of Charles VIII's invasion, claiming it was divine punishment for the sins of the Florentines. Savonarola pushed ideals of repentance intermingled with republicanism and achieved great influence in Florence, culminating in the bonfire of the vanities. This event involved the public burning of a person's prized possessions for all to witness to demonstrate that the person was turning their attention from worldly goods toward God. As Savonarola's influence expanded he came into conflict with Pope Alexander VI, who unsuccessfully tried to silence him and buy him off with the offer of becoming a cardinal. Unable to bring Savonarola to heel, Alexander VI had him arrested for heresy, tortured until he confessed, and then publicly executed in gruesome fashion: he and two of his most loyal supporters were hanged, their bodies burned, and their ashes discarded into the River Arno. Machiavelli compares the success and fate of Savonarola to those of another legendary religious leader, Moses, who not only had to free his people from the military powerhouse that was Egypt but also had to use force to quell dissent among his people and cull their numbers, killing "countless men" (*Discourses on Livy* 3.30) to eliminate those who, out of envy, opposed his plans for the Israelites. Machiavelli draws a simple but shocking conclusion: armed prophets succeed, while unarmed prophets are doomed to failure.

Machiavelli does not despise religion per se, only the slothful interpretation of Christianity that was prevalent in his day. In fact, Machiavelli encourages the prince to uphold whatever religious practices his people have, as lack of respect for religion is a clear sign of corruption within a state. Yet he clearly holds the Christianity of his day in contempt for its effect on people and Italy. In chapter 12 Machiavelli partially implicates the clergy for initiating the use of mercenaries in Italy, and in *Discourses on Livy* 1.12 he sets Italian patriotism against the Church when he holds the Church responsible for keeping Italy weak and fractured by continually thwarting the aspirations of any Italian family that made significant political gains, preventing unification.

Machiavelli extends this critique of Christianity to show that it has a negative effect on all men, making them effeminate and more concerned with the next life than this one, and he laments how Christianity esteems the contemplative man over the man of action. In *Discourses on Livy* 2.2 he points to the ferocity of ritual in Roman religion and the timidity of Christian ritual to underscore the lack of fear and awe that Christianity inspires, a position he repeats in book 2 of *The Art of War*. It is Machiavelli's hope that Christianity can be rejuvenated in a vigorous fashion and become a more positive social force within the Italian cities of his day.

Mercenaries and Armies

Machiavelli criticizes mercenaries as being both ineffective and costly in chapter 12, and he blames their use for the deplorable state of affairs in which the Italians found themselves. Mercenaries, like any profession, are of varying quality. Unfortunately, the mercenaries typically employed in Renaissance Italy were largely undisciplined thugs with little training and no sense of professionalism. This is evident in how quick they were to abandon their employers if their pay was late or a better offer came along, and also in their preference for siege warfare, which was relatively risk free and a source of prolonged employment for mercenaries but devastating to civilian populations.[1] The fact that they lacked consistent leadership, often serving under whatever condottieri a city hired, added to their ineffectiveness. Machiavelli summarizes the situation succinctly in the *Florentine Histories* 5.1, where he laments that these wars were mockeries because they were of no consequence: no one was killed, no cities were sacked, and no princedoms were destroyed.

In chapter 13, Machiavelli's analysis of military matters extends to auxiliary troops, the regular army of an ally which one borrows, and he is even-handed in his appraisal of them. He acknowledges their superiority to mercenaries in that they have received proper military training, are united under the leadership of a general, and are bound by loyalty to both their military commander and their ruler. However, this combination of a more effective fighting force alongside a loyalty that is not to the prince, but to an ally, makes relying on these troops very dangerous according to Machiavelli, for they will serve the prince's interests only so long as he is on

---

1 For an in-depth discussion of the effects of siege warfare on civilian populations in the Renaissance, see Hale, *War and Society*.

good terms with their ruler. Auxiliary troops will abandon the prince or, worse, turn on him at the word of their ruler, and because they are a fiercer fighting force than mere mercenaries, the prince who relies on auxiliary troops instead of his own army essentially invites a well-disciplined foreign army into his territory.

The only military option which is effective and secure, and which the prince can safely rely upon, is a militia comprised of his own citizens. The general call for a militia was not unprecedented and had been made by Florentine humanists such as Francesco Petrarch, Coluccio Salutati (1331–1406), and Leonardo Bruni (1370–1444) throughout the fourteenth century, but Machiavelli added his own insights to the general argument and dressed it up with his characteristic flare. A militia can receive proper military training as a unified force, would only have to be paid when called upon to fight (and would be more forgiving of a delay or absence of payment), and would fight with a loyalty and zeal that no enemy could match, for they would be fighting for their homeland—their families, lands, and cities—not merely a salary.

When it comes to the prince's role in military affairs, Machiavelli paints a dramatic picture of a warrior-prince who actively engages in strategy and battle, not someone who directs his forces from the safety of a fortress or a bunker. In chapter 14 Machiavelli insists that the prince make war his sole occupation, in thought by studying military history and analyzing why great leaders of the past succeeded or failed in their various endeavours, and in deed by hunting so that the prince remain physically fit and capable of wielding a weapon, as well as learning the nuances of geography and terrain for strategic purposes in his own territory and beyond. The warrior-prince is invoked in *The Prince* because the text was written for chaotic times; the tone is markedly different in the republican-themed *Discourses on Livy*, where there is more of a distinction between military and political leadership, as well as in book 1 of *The Art of War*, where Machiavelli is adamant that successful rule requires a knowledge of how to conduct war, but also of how to rule in times of peace.

Machiavelli's Relation to the Ancients and to His Contemporaries

When reading Machiavelli, one must always remember that he was writing in a context that saw the convergence of multiple literary, philosophical, and political traditions, and that was itself rapidly evolving. To ignore these phenomena is to distort Machiavelli's contributions, for despite his claims in the preface to book 1 of the *Discourses on Livy* that he is offering something new, as much as Machiavelli breaks with these traditions and authors, he also echoes many of their forms and ideas.

Machiavelli uses, rejects, and twists the works of the ancients to fit his various purposes. Throughout all his works he clearly assumes a metaphysics consistent with, if not inherited from, the Roman philosopher and poet Lucretius, whom he studied before entering public life.[1] In the *Discourses on Livy* and the *Florentine Histories* he employs the cyclical account of history found in the Greek historian Polybius, and he quotes the Roman historian Tacitus. Cicero's *De officiis* is also used without acknowledgement throughout *The Prince*, albeit in a more complicated manner. Most significantly, the doctrine of the centaur, including the strength of the lion and the cunning of the fox, is clearly taken from *De officiis* (Book 1, sec. 34 and 41), but Cicero's preference for pursuing ends through dialogue and virtue is rejected in *The Prince*, which, written for dangerous and corrupt times, elevates the use of violence and dissimilation to necessities, even if only temporary ones. Likewise, Machiavelli's controversial argument against generosity also has its roots in *De officiis* (Book 1, sec. 42, 52; Book 2, sec. 52), as does his argument that no true glory can be attained through criminal means (Book 1, sec. 62).[2]

The *speculum principum* genre, also known as the mirror-for-princes genre, is another example of how Machiavelli inhabits a tradition while seriously adjusting it to his own ends. These books, numerous enough throughout Europe that they constituted a genre, were dedicated to rulers and typically held up an archetype of the Christian prince as a mirror for a ruler to look into and emulate, so that the archetype could be said to be his reflection. The advice generally advocated the pursuit of Christian virtues as the only means to true glory as a leader. While Machiavelli maintains in chapter 18 that the prince should appear to hold all the Christian virtues, he breaks with the mirror-for-princes genre in three ways: first, by opening new, non-Christian avenues to glory; second, by insisting that these other paths are necessary; and third, by scandalously proclaiming that the Christian path, if followed uncompromisingly, will lead to political ruin. Hence his biting judgement regarding Moses and Savonarola.

---

1 For discussions of the impact of Lucretius on Machiavelli's thought, see Brown; Rahe.

2 For a more complete list of links between *The Prince* and Cicero's *De officiis*, see Colish.

Medical and astrological terminology, which were prominent in his day (natural astrology was taught at universities), are also employed by Machiavelli throughout his works. Specifically, he utilizes the medical theory that persons possess certain "humours" which explain their personalities.[1] He also conducted a personal correspondence with astrologers.[2] However, Machiavelli's commitment to Renaissance models of medicine or to astrology is questionable—he certainly never advocates astrology to the prince, only that religious rituals be used to justify the prince's authority and decisions, help unite the populace, and motivate the troops. And his political advice regarding the model of the humours is to turn it on its head. Whereas Renaissance medicine sought to maintain a balance of the humours to achieve health, Machiavelli throughout *The Prince* and the *Discourses on Livy* praises conflict as a means of generating strength and excellence. Properly managed and channelled, conflict provides both the opportunity and the energy for greatness. Here again, Machiavelli is neither an astrologer nor a physician, but he uses their terminologies because his initial audiences were familiar with these terms and would understand what he meant by them. As these were the conceptual tools he had for expressing himself, they obviously affected his thought in various ways, but Machiavelli should no more be thought of as endorsing traditions because he used them than someone who accuses another of making a "Freudian slip" should be thought of as accepting any or all of Freud's theories.

Thus Machiavelli was not writing in a vacuum, nor did he constitute a radical break with the past across the board. Rather, he was interacting with a range of traditions, and he used and abused them strategically for his own ends. At times these traditions or authors are his support, even if he has to misrepresent them in order to claim their endorsement, while at other times he uses the terminology of the ancients or his own Florence simply because the terms are in vogue and he knows that his intended audience will understand them in a certain way. Reading too much into any of these uses in an effort to categorize Machiavelli or uncover hidden motives in his writing can lead to some interesting pieces of intellectual history, but it amounts to little more than armchair psychoanalysis.

---

1 A person's temperament was thought to result from the mixture of their particular combination of blood, phlegm, yellow bile, and black bile.
2 For a discussion that stresses Machiavelli's involvement with astrology and the theory of the humours, see Parel, *The Machiavellian Cosmos*.

Initial Reactions to *The Prince*[1]

The initial audience of *The Prince* was the Medici. Originally, the dedicatee was Giuliano de' Medici, but Connell argues persuasively that it became known to Machiavelli that Giuliano had been advised by his cousin Cardinal Giulio de' Medici not to employ him in any capacity, forcing Machiavelli to dedicate the book to Lorenzo de' Medici, often known as Lorenzo the Younger, instead (Connell 511–12). *The Prince* is concise, as the Medici were not scholars and had neither the patience nor the intellectual acumen to read a massive treatise of political theory. Machiavelli knew that he had to keep things short, practical, and engaging, while standing out from the numerous sycophants and courtiers who were vying for the Medici's attention and who were not encumbered by the handicaps of low birthright, association with the former government, and the taint of conspiracy. So Machiavelli proved daring in how he approached his subjects.

A problem that has plagued readers of *The Prince* from early on is the fact that Machiavelli wrote a second political treatise, the *Discourses on Livy*, which at first glance lies in direct opposition to *The Prince*. This view was reinforced by an anecdotal account of Machiavelli's reaction to Lorenzo de' Medici's lack of interest in the text. While the report was first noted in Italian by Riccardo Riccardi (1558–1612) many decades after it allegedly occurred, Reginald Pole (1500–58), visiting Florence from England, is said to have been told a similar tale of Machiavelli's reaction much earlier. Riccardi claims that after being ignored by Lorenzo de' Medici, who was more impressed by a gift of hunting dogs from someone else than by Machiavelli's work, Machiavelli proclaimed that if the Medici followed the methods in *The Prince*, "they would see that conspiracies resulted from them." Riccardi further claims, "It was as if he meant to say that his book would enact revenge for him" (Machiavelli, *Lettere* xiv). This account stresses that *The Prince* was written specifically with Lorenzo's temperament in mind.

Many readers of Machiavelli have dismissed this alleged reaction, but its existence has led others right up to the present day to view *The Prince* as an attempt to sabotage tyrants in general, and Lorenzo de' Medici in particular (see Dietz). This interpretation

---

1   For a more extensive list of the interpretations of *The Prince* within the Italian context, see Anglo; Giorgini; Richardson.

inspired a general attitude that *The Prince* was not to be taken seriously, variously described as a rushed and insincere résumé to the Medici, the product of an immature mind, or even a satire, and that it was somehow an aberration from the *Discourses on Livy*, a work that was deemed to represent Machiavelli's true political vision.

This interpretation is suspect for several reasons. First, Machiavelli was eager to find employment with the Medici in Florence, as evidenced by his repeated requests of politically connected individuals favourably disposed toward him to intervene on his behalf, as well as by his declaration in a letter to his long-standing friend Francesco Vettori, dated 10 December 1513 (see Appendix I2), that he would be willing to accept any task from the Medici, even rolling a stone, if it meant a return to political life. Second, one must keep in mind that Lorenzo was not the initial dedicatee of *The Prince*; rather, it was Giuliano de' Medici, and Giuliano was more mature and had a different temperament than Lorenzo. For an interpretation of *The Prince* as an act of sabotage to work, the text would have to possess an ability to corrupt any and all readers, a tall order even for a book as notorious as *The Prince*. Third, the same basic messages found in *The Prince* can also be found, with different presentation and emphasis, in the *Discourses on Livy*, and individual ideas that Machiavelli covers in *The Prince* appear throughout the rest of his corpus. In this sense, *The Prince* is not uncharacteristic of Machiavelli's other writings. Further, not only did the composition of the two works overlap (at least partially), but Machiavelli also references each work in the other, and upon reading both it is clear that there is a symbiotic relationship between the two texts grounded in his cyclical conception of history.

So how is Machiavelli's statement to be explained? The comment may very well have been uttered—neither Riccardi nor Pole heard the comment first hand, but they received it from Machiavelli's circle of intellectuals—although context and firsthand experience of Machiavelli's personality, which neither Riccardi nor Pole was privy to, can place a very different interpretation on Machiavelli's words. The *Discourses on Livy* is written as a guide to organizing a well-ordered state, with special attention given to political institutions and rule of law; it is a work of political science approaching the modern usage of the term. *The Prince*, however, is written as a guide to navigating the dangerous and violent world of founding a new state or rejuvenating a state that is no longer well ordered but has been weakened by significant internal corruption and is bordering on chaos. Despite the appearance of laws, *The Prince*, with its focus on the prince as an individual person needing to possess *virtù*, is more artistry than science. It has to be. Politics is an activity not unlike sports or playing a musical instrument: the theory can be learned, but if one does not possess the required relevant physical talents and opportunities to perform in venues where one will be noticed, no amount of theory will make one successful. In short, *The Prince* is addressed to the politician as artist, not as scientist. Seen in this light, Riccardi's story is plausibly a commentary by Machiavelli on the likelihood that Lorenzo, a man so devoid of insight as to completely dismiss Machiavelli's gift of political knowledge and wisdom, did not possess the ability to understand and apply the precepts of *The Prince*, and had he tried, he would have made such a terrible mess of things that the attempt would have led to his ruin.

Prior to its posthumous publication in 1532, *The Prince* circulated in manuscript form throughout Florence and in other Italian cities such as Rome and Venice. What is known of the immediate reception of *The Prince* comes from marginal notes found in some of these manuscripts as well as the publications of Machiavelli's contemporaries who made use of *The Prince* in their own works. Marginal notes, private "notes to oneself" by the owner of the manuscript, reveal little outrage at any of Machiavelli's arguments (Richardson 19–20). Public reaction, however, is more polarized, characterized by admiration for Machiavelli's brazen insight and a reluctance to be seen as endorsing such a controversial work.

Just as Machiavelli used and abused the ancients to help make his arguments, so too did many of his contemporaries seize upon *The Prince* in a variety of ways to advance their own arguments. The most famous of Machiavelli's contemporaries to comment on his writings was Francesco Guicciardini (1483–1540), a friend of Machiavelli, who actively wrote in response to both *The Prince* and the *Discourses on Livy*. While he agreed with Machiavelli's denunciation of idealism in politics as naivety, he rejected Machiavelli's approach to history, claiming that the past was an ineffective guide to present conduct because material conditions had changed significantly; he further argued against Machiavelli's conception of human nature as self-interested, insisting that people were naturally inclined toward virtue. Far from a pedantic squabble, Guicciardini's critique is a wholesale dismissal of the approach Machiavelli employs in all his major writings. Others, such as Agiostino Nifo (1473–1545), appropriated Machiavelli's arguments to further their own agendas. Nifo borrowed heavily from Machiavelli's arguments in *The Prince* and rearranged them in a shamefully self-serving manner so as to make them appear to support his own contribution to the mirror-for-princes genre, *De regnandi peritia*, published in 1523 (Anglo 42–84). Still others tried to paint Machiavelli in a favourable light. Traiano Boccalini (1556–1613), a renowned satirist, put forth a republican reading of *The Prince* and maintained that Machiavelli's text was cleverly designed to reveal the tyrannical elements of princely rule under the guise of offering helpful advice to princes. This view in particular became common and would be echoed by Jean-Jacques Rousseau (1712–78) in *The Social Contract* 3.6.

Despite the diverse range of reactions to *The Prince*, a common thread emerges: *The Prince* was increasingly read in isolation from Machiavelli's other works, and the notoriety of Machiavelli was becoming more prominent than the content of *The Prince* in the minds of those who read and commentated on it. For example, Benedetto Varchi (1503–65) makes claims about Machiavelli's poor reputation on account of the reaction to circulated manuscripts of *The Prince*, which may have been factual, but then proceeds to make historically inaccurate claims vilifying his personality, such as the false claim that Machiavelli died of disappointment when the government position he had hoped to obtain in the restored republic of 1527 was awarded to Donato Giannotti (1492–1573). In fact, Giannotti received this position three months after Machiavelli's death (Giorgini 628–29). The scandal that Machiavelli had become was made official, so to speak, in 1559 when Pope Paul IV (r. 1555–59) ensured Machiavelli's worldly immortality and the place of *The Prince* in history when he added the book to the Catholic Church's *Index Librorum Prohibitorum*, an imprimatur of infamy that also proclaimed how daring and innovative Machiavelli's little book was.

Less than two decades later, Innocent Gentillet (1535–88) envisaged a link between the spread of Machiavelli's works in France, the Italian influence in the French court through Catherine de' Medici (1519–89, wife of Henry II, king of France, r. 1547–59), and the horrific St. Bartholomew's Day massacre of 1572 in which thousands of Huguenots were murdered in a wave of state-sponsored Catholic mob violence throughout France. Gentillet's belief in this connection prompted him to write his *Anti-Machiavel*, published in 1576, criticizing Machiavelli as lacking sufficient experience or an appropriate understanding of history to offer a credible political philosophy, condemning him as a mere advocate of immorality and impiety, and calling for his writings to be banned in France. Gentillet's critique was the first substantial treatment of Machiavelli outside of Italy, so it had the advantage of presenting Machiavelli to an audience largely incapable of judging Gentillet's account. So extensive and damning was Gentillet's assessment in the eyes of the public that it effectively reduced Machiavelli to a caricature of villainy that in due course became part of European popular culture. Hence the stereotype of the murderous Machiavel in English theatre, where writers such as Shakespeare and Marlowe used this stock character as a template for heinous villains, which the public would identify as Machiavellian but which bore little resemblance to the Florentine civil servant or his ideas. In a similar manner, modern psychology uses the term Machiavellianism to denote a personality trait of skillful manipulation and a willful disregard for conventional moral norms that is part of the "dark triad" of narcissism, psychopathy, and Machiavellianism. This term invokes the caricature that is commonly taken for Machiavelli but evinces only a cursory familiarity with and a shallow understanding of his writings.

More Recent Interpretations of Machiavelli and *The Prince*[1]

As the influence of the moral condemnation of the Catholic Church has waned, Machiavelli's reputation has been reformed and a variety of more positive interpretations of him have emerged. During the Risorgimento period, for example, Machiavelli was seen as a patriot who dreamed of Italian unification and inspired and challenged future generations to make his dream a reality. More recently, Benedetto Croce (1866–1952) interpreted Machiavelli as the founder of modern political science as a discipline autonomous of moral considerations.

Numerous leftist intellectuals have also been drawn to Machiavelli. In his *Prison Notebooks*, Antonio Gramsci (1891–1937) saw Machiavelli as a revolutionary, a proto-communist who fought against the failing feudal political structures and in the process of doing so unwittingly articulated the archetype of the communist party. For Gramsci the prince is nothing more than an anthropomorphizing of the proletariat's will.

Agreeing with many of Gramsci's points, Louis Althusser (1918–90), in his *Machiavelli and Us*, developed Machiavelli's thought in new ways that he considered crucial to the future of

---

1 For a more extensive list of the varied interpretations of Machiavelli that had proliferated by the mid-twentieth century, see Berlin.

Marxism. Althusser saw in Machiavelli a subversive materialism that opened the door to new opportunities for political revolution. Whereas Marx's historical materialism was governed by laws that made political revolutions both necessary and inevitable, Althusser interpreted Machiavelli's materialism as part of a neglected tradition in the West, one that is characterized by contingency. This reading of Machiavelli becomes key to the development of Althusser's theory of aleatory materialism. Revolutions are not inevitable and their success is not guaranteed, so progress occurs only through political actors doing things within the conjuncture, the unique set of circumstances in which they find themselves.

Also focusing on the contingency of the moment, this time as it relates to the power of the citizenry, Antonio Negri (1933–2023), in his *Insurgencies: Constituent Power and the Modern State*, explores his theory of constituent power through Machiavelli's insistence that the ultimate foundation of the prince's power lies in the support of the people; it is only with the support of the masses that the prince is secure, and it is the masses that make a change of regime possible. Negri focuses on the fact that this constituent power becomes evident only in moments of crisis, which means that real power and real change come through constituent power being exercised in revolutionary fashion to forge a new political reality when constitutions have failed.

The interpretation of Machiavelli among non-Marxists is more varied. In "The Originality of Machiavelli," Isaiah Berlin (1909–97) interpreted Machiavelli as a proto-liberal pluralist who was perhaps the first political thinker to realize, even if he never frames the issue explicitly, that the world is filled with incommensurate values among which people must ultimately choose. Quentin Skinner (b. 1940) and the Cambridge school maintain that a responsible interpretation of Machiavelli must be rooted in the historical circumstances in which Machiavelli was writing. In this spirit, Maurizio Viroli (b. 1952) reads *The Prince* as a text designed to summon a redeemer of Machiavelli's day to unify Italy, rejuvenate it, and return it to some semblance of its former good order and glory. Leo Strauss (1899–1973) stresses the need to ground interpretations solidly in the texts Machiavelli left behind. On this basis, he concludes in his *Thoughts on Machiavelli* that Machiavelli is a teacher of evil, a view echoed by Sheldon S. Wolin (1922–2015) in his *Politics and Vision: Continuity and Innovations in Western Political Thought*, where Wolin characterizes the Florentine's approach to politics as turning "an economy of violence" into a science.

Claude Lefort's (1924–2010) approach to Machiavelli offers an explanation for the range of diverse interpretations of the Florentine's work. He rejects the approach of the Cambridge school and the Straussians and maintains in his *Machiavelli in the Making* that Machiavelli is more to us than he was to his contemporaries, because they were limited in their reading of him by their proximity to him and their greater knowledge of his intentions. Our distance, Lefort argues, allows for a greater range of interpretations and creates more room for us to be part of the work. In this way, our reading of Machiavelli says more about ourselves—our political and ideological commitments, our concerns and fears—than it does about Machiavelli. Lefort essentially poses the postmodern question of whether an author's intentions are authoritative, or even relevant, to reading a work, and his answer is not merely a resounding "no" but an insistence that dethroning the authoritativeness of Machiavelli the author and embracing the distance, filled with varied interpretations, creates a more meaningful interpretation and keeps *The Prince* relevant. And, to a point, Lefort is absolutely correct. A neutral reading is only a mirage; readers always engage the text with a filter composed of their own intellectual commitments, and this colours their interpretation.

Clearly a meaningful reading of Machiavelli must transcend his historical context; otherwise, how could his work be relevant to us? Machiavelli wholeheartedly endorses this position too, as his entire use of history in both *The Prince* and the *Discourses on Livy* rests on his account of human nature as unchanging. Circumstances may change, but how persons react to them remains largely constant. However, there are limitations to a responsible, if not plausible, interpretation, and this is where it is equally clear that the Cambridge school and the Straussians also have merit. Focusing on *The Prince* to the exclusion of Machiavelli's other works obviously provides an incomplete picture of some of his most important concepts, such as Fortune and his understanding of history as cyclical, while not appreciating his intellectual, historical, and political context leads to a skewed view of his position in history and mistaken ideas about what he was trying to do. *The Prince* is a sincere, well-planned, and integral part of Machiavelli's political vision, but it remains just a part. Reading *The Prince* exclusively, and in isolation from the *Discourses on Livy* in particular but also from Machiavelli's other writings, is to fundamentally misunderstand Machiavelli from the start.

Niccolò Machiavelli: A Brief Chronology

1469	Niccolò di Bernardo Machiavelli born on 3 May in Florence.
1492	Death of Lorenzo de' Medici ("Lorenzo the Magnificent"). Piero de' Medici assumes control of Florence.
1494	Rodrigo Borgia elected Pope Alexander VI. France, under Charles VIII, invades the Italian peninsula. Piero de' Medici negotiates a humiliating peace at the first sign of the French. Piero is exiled. Florence returns to republican rule, in part due to Savonarola's influence.
1495	The League of Venice is formed—consisting of Venice, Milan, Spain, the Holy Roman Empire, and later the papal states and Florence—and forces the French out of Italy.
1497	Machiavelli produces a transcription of Lucretius' *De rerum natura* (*On the Nature of the Universe*). The influence of Savonarola and his supporters reaches its height in the bonfire of the vanities.
1498	Machiavelli is elected to head the Second Chancery of the Republic of Florence and quickly becomes the Secretary to the Ten of Liberty and Peace. Savonarola is arrested, tortured to the point of confession, and executed for heresy.
1499	Louis XII of France (Charles VIII's successor) invades Italy, takes Milan.
1500	Machiavelli's first diplomatic mission to France. He meets Louis XII, king of France, and Georges d'Amboise, cardinal of Rouen.
1501	Marries Marietta Corsini.
1502–03	Is sent on several diplomatic missions in which he meets with Cesare Borgia at the height of Borgia's success but also is able to observe the collapse of the latter's power base in the wake of the illness and death of his father, Alexander VI, which coincided with his own convalescence.
1503	Pope Alexander VI dies. After Pope Pius III dies less than a month after his election as pope, Cardinal

	Giuliano della Rovere succeeds him as Pope Julius II.
1506	Machiavelli is sent on a diplomatic mission to the new pope. Organizes the Florentine militia. Writes the *Ghiribizzi* for Giovanni Battista Soderini, which touches on several ideas he will later develop in *The Prince* and in the *Tercets on Fortune*.
1507–08	Is sent on a diplomatic mission to Emperor Maximilian I. Trying to limit Venetian power, Pope Julius II forms the League of Cambrai in 1508, consisting of the papal forces, Louis XII of France, Ferdinand II of Aragon, Henry VII of England, and Maximilian I.
1510–11	Further diplomatic missions to France.
1510–12	The League of Cambrai collapses in 1510 when the pope becomes more concerned about French power in Italy. In order to push France out of the Italian territories, Julius II forms the Holy League in 1511, originally consisting of his forces and those of Venice, but expands to include those of England, Spain, and the Holy Roman emperor. Soderini, against Machiavelli's advice, refuses to join the Holy League.
1512	The French are defeated at the Battle of Ravenna and withdraw from Italy. As punishment for its refusal of support, Julius II reinstates the Medici in Florence with the help of Spanish troops. The Republic of Florence is overthrown, Soderini flees, and Machiavelli is forced out of office.
1513	Machiavelli is implicated in an anti-Medici conspiracy. He is arrested and tortured with the strappado but never confesses to anything and the evidence against him is minimal. Pope Julius II dies. Giovanni di Lorenzo de' Medici is elected Pope Leo X. With Medici power in Florence now secured by the influence of the papacy, Machiavelli is released under a general amnesty celebrating the new pope, but he is banned from the Palazzo Vecchio and essentially exiled to his family's meager estate in Sant' Andrea in Percussina. His writing career begins and he starts work on both *The Prince* and the *Discourses on Livy*.
1514–15	Completes *The Prince* in 1514, making revisions in early 1515. The presentation of *The Prince* to its dedicatee Lorenzo de' Medici occurs sometime between

	mid-May and the first few days of July 1515.
1515–16	Completes *The Art of War*.
1515–17	Begins attending the meetings of an intellectual circle led by Cosimo Rucellari in the Orti Oricellari.
1517	Begins his unfinished poem *The Golden Ass*.
1517–19	Completes the *Discourses on Livy*.
1518	Travels to Genoa to represent the interests of Florentine merchants.
1518–19	Completes *Mandragola*.
1520	Travels to Lucca to represent the interests of Florentine merchants. While there, writes *The Life of Castruccio Castracani* and *Discourses on Florentine Affairs*. He is commissioned to write the *Florentine Histories* by Cardinal Giulio de' Medici (who becomes Pope Clement VII in 1523).
1521	*The Art of War* is published, the only ostensibly political work to be published while Machiavelli is alive. Pope Leo X dies.
1522	The Orti Oricellari disbands when several of its members are implicated (some arrested and executed) in a conspiracy to assassinate Cardinal Giulio de' Medici. Machiavelli escapes the attention of the authorities.
1523	Giulio de' Medici is elected Pope Clement VII.
1525	Machiavelli's play *Clizia* is publicly performed. He receives work in Venice representing the interests of Florentine merchants.
1526	The *Florentine Histories* is presented to Pope Clement VII and is favourably received. Machiavelli is put in charge of overseeing the fortifications of Florence. The War of the League of Cognac begins, pitting the Holy Roman Emperor Charles V against the forces of Pope Clement VII, Milan, Venice, France, and eventually England.
1527	Rome is sacked by the forces of Emperor Charles V. The Medici are again forced out of Florence and the republic is briefly restored. Machiavelli is not trusted by the new government because of the inroads he has made with the Medici. Machiavelli dies on 21 June.
1531	The *Discourses on Livy* are published posthumously. The Republic of Florence is overthrown, and Alessandro de' Medici is made ruler by Charles V.

1532	*The Prince* and the *Florentine Histories* are published posthumously.
1559	*The Prince* and other works by Machiavelli are placed on the *Index Librorum Prohibitorum* by Pope Paul IV.
1560	The first Latin translation of *The Prince* is published.
1640	The first English translation of *The Prince* is published.

A Note on the Translations

The Prince is translated from the Italian "Edizione Nazionale delle Opere di Niccolò Machiavelli" by Manuela Scarci. The *Discourses on Livy* were translated from the Italian by Christian E. Detmold from *The Historical, Political, and Diplomatic Writings of Niccolo Machiavelli* (James R. Osgood and Company, 1882), modernized by Michel Pharand. The remaining appendices were translated from the Italian by Kirsty Jane Falconer—based primarily on the complete edition of Machiavelli's works printed in Geneva by Pietro Alberto, dated 1550 (although scholars agree that this is a false dating intended to circumvent the 1559 papal ban on Machiavelli's writings)—and cross-referenced with the 1971 Sansoni edition of the *Complete Works*, edited by Mario Martelli.

Select Historical Figures Relevant to Machiavelli's Life and The Prince

Achilles – (P^1 14 and 18) Mythical hero of the *Iliad*.

Agathocles – (*P* 8) 361–289 BCE. Tyrant of Syracuse.

Alexander (the Great) – (*P* 3, 4, 8, 14, 16, and 19; *DL* 1.20) 356–323 BCE. Built upon his father's military successes and conquered Persia. Aristotle was his tutor.

Alexander VI, Pope (Cardinal Rodrigo Borgia) – (*P* 3, 7, 8, and 18) 1431–1503. r. 1492–1503. Father of Cesare Borgia, used France and the papacy's resources to support Cesare's military ambitions throughout Italy. Fell ill suddenly, possibly from malaria or poisoning in a botched attempt to assassinate a rival, and died shortly thereafter.

Borgia, Cesare – (*P* 3, 7, 13, 17, and 20) 1475–1507. Illegitimate son of Pope Alexander VI. Sometimes referred to as Duke Valentino. Fell sick at the same time as his father but survived.

Caesar, Julius – (*P* 14 and 16; *DL* 1.10 and 24) 100–44 BCE. Roman statesman and general who plunged the Roman Republic into a brutal civil war, from which he emerged victoriously crowned as dictator for life. The concentration of power in his person, as opposed to political structures, signalled the end of the Roman Republic and laid the foundation for the Roman Empire.

Charles V – 1500–58. Holy Roman emperor (1519–56), also ruler of Spain (1516–56), the Netherlands, Aragon, Naples, Sicily, Sardinia, and many territories in the new world. Invited into Italy by Pope Clement VII in 1508 to fight the Venetians, but the pope turned on him in 1511 and formed the Holy League to rid Italy of his influence.

Charles VII – (*P* 13) 1403–61. r. 1422–61. King of France.

---

1 References in parentheses refer to the historical figure's appearance in specific chapters of *The Prince* (*P*) or the *Discourses on Livy* (*DL*).

Charles VIII – (*P* 3, 11, and 12) 1470–98. r. 1483–98. King of France. Invaded Italy in 1494 to exercise a hereditary claim on the kingdom of Naples. Encouraged to do so by Ludovico Sforza.

Chiron the Centaur – (*P* 18) Mythical creature (half-man, half-horse) said to have taught princes.

Cicero, Marcus Tullius – 106–43 BCE. Famous Roman politician, orator, and philosopher. Machiavelli makes use of Cicero's *De officiis* to further his own arguments in chapters 8, 16, 17, and 18 of *The Prince*.

Clement VII, Pope (Cardinal Giulio de' Medici) – 1479–1534. r. 1523–34. Commissioned Machiavelli to write the *Florentine Histories*. Formed the League of Cognac against Emperor Charles V and was humiliated when Charles's forces sacked Rome in 1527.

Colonna – (*P* 7 and 11) Influential Roman family that had long-standing hostilities against their rivals, the Orsini.

Cyrus II (the Great) – (*P* 6, 14, 16, and 26) c. 590/80–529 BCE. r. 559–529 BCE. Founder of the Persian Empire, which occupied much of central and southwest Asia.

Darius I – (*P* 7) 521–489 BCE. King of Persia.

Darius III – (*P* 4) c. 380–330 BCE. r. 336–330 BCE. The last king of Persia. Weakened by repeated losses to Alexander the Great.

David – (*P* 13; *DL* 1.19) Fought and killed Goliath, insisting on doing so with his own weapons, even if that meant failure. Would later become king of Israel.

Ferdinand of Aragon (Ferdinand the Catholic) – (*P* 12, 13, and 21) 1452–1516. r. 1479–1516. King of Spain, who drove the French out of Naples in 1504 and became king of Naples in 1505.

Forlì, Countess of (Caterina Sforza) – (*P* 3 and 20, *DL* 3.6) 1463–1509. Held her territories after the death of her husband, thwarting an uprising through deceit and betrayal, until she eventually lost to Cesare Borgia in 1500.

Gracchi (brothers Tiberius Sempronius Gracchus and Gaius Sempronius Gracchus) – (*P* 9; *DL* 1.4) Tiberius 163–133 BCE, Gaius 153–121 BCE. Tribunes of the plebs, each assassinated by opponents of their controversial efforts to redistribute land from the rich to the poor.

Hannibal – (*P* 17) 247–185 BCE. Carthaginian general who fought the Romans.

Hiero II of Syracuse – (*P* 13) 306–215 BCE. King of Syracuse. Killed all his mercenary soldiers when he realized they could not be kept or released without great danger to the Syracusans.

Julius II, Pope (Cardinal Giuliano della Rovere) – (*P* 2, 7, 11, 13, 16, and 25) 1443–1513. r. 1503–13. Enemy of the Borgia family. Once he became pope, he stripped Cesare Borgia of all power and territory and exiled him from the Italian peninsula.

Leo X, Pope (Giovanni de' Medici) – (*P* 11) 1475–1525. r. 1513–21. Granted the amnesty which freed Machiavelli from prison.

Louis XI – (*P* 8) 1423–83. r. 1461–83. King of France.

Louis XII – (*P* 3, 7, and 12) 1462–1515. r. 1498–1515. King of France. Invited by Pope Julius II to enter Italy in 1508 as part of the League of Cambrai to help curb Venetian ambitions, but became the object of the Holy League in 1511 when Venice had been subdued and the pope came to fear France's power in Italy.

Lucretius (Titus Lucretius Carus) – 99–55 BCE. Roman poet and philosopher, most famous for his poem *De rerum natura*, which espouses the atomism of Epicurus. Machiavelli translated and commented on the poem during his youthful studies of Latin, and its influence can be seen in passages of both the *Discourses on Livy* and *The Golden Ass*.

Maximilian I – (*P* 23) 1459–1519. r. 1493–1519. Holy Roman emperor. Repeatedly involved in the wars of Italy. Most significant for fighting against the Venetians as part of the League of Cambrai in 1508 and then fighting against the French as part of the Holy League in 1511.

Medici, Lorenzo de' (Lorenzo the Magnificent) – 1449–92. r. 1469–92. Head of the wealthy Medici banking family and de facto ruler of Florence, even though Florence purported to be a republic. His foreign policy maintained the status quo among the Italian powers, involving relatively bloodless but financially costly wars, and secured peace and prosperity in his day for Florence.

Medici, Lorenzo II de' – (*P* Dedicatory Letter) 1492–1519. r. 1516–19. Dedicatee of *The Prince*; had a reputation for being autocratic as well as uninterested in actually ruling.

Medici, Piero II de' – 1472–1503. r. 1492–94. Son of Lorenzo the Magnificent. Forced to flee Florence after negotiating a humiliating peace with Charles VIII in 1494.

Moses – (*P* 6 and 26) c. 1300 BCE. Old Testament figure who led the Israelites out of enslavement in Egypt (Exodus 5–14) and culled his own followers when they became too numerous and unruly to lead effectively (Exodus 32:25–31). An example of an armed prophet.

Nabis – (*P* 9 and 19) 207–192 BCE. Tyrant of Sparta. Tried rebuilding Sparta's military might, allied with Philip V of Macedon against the Romans, but switched to Rome's side when the war turned against the Macedonians. Afterwards Rome attacked Nabis and defeated him.

Orco, Remirro de – (*P* 7) 1452–1502. Spanish captain charged by Cesare Borgia with pacifying the Romagna region. Infamous for his excessive harshness and for being brutally liquidated by Borgia after the Romagna was brought under control, so as to protect Borgia's reputation and keep him from becoming hated.

Orsini – (*P* 7, 8, 11, and 13) Influential Roman family that had long-standing hostilities against their rivals, the Colonna. Paolo and Francesco Orsini conspired against Cesare Borgia at Senigallia in December 1502 but were outsmarted by Borgia, who had them executed in early 1503.

Petrarch, Francesco – (*P* 26) 1304–74. Famous Italian poet quoted by Machiavelli in his rousing and patriotic "Exhortation" at the end of *The Prince*.

Philip II of Macedonia (father of Alexander the Great) – (*P* 12 and 13; *DL* 1.20) 382–336 BCE. r. 359–336 BCE. King of Macedon. Rejuvenated Macedon, bringing it from the brink of extinction to the status of a world power.

Philip V of Macedon – (*P* 3 and 24) 237–179 BCE. r. 221–179 BCE. King of Macedon.

Polybius – c. 200–118 BCE. Greek historian from whom Machiavelli adopts a cyclical conception of history espoused in *Discourses on Livy* 3.1, *Florentine Histories* 5.1, as well as the *Tercets on Fortune* and chapter 5 of *The Golden Ass*.

Romulus – (*P* 6) Mythical founder of Rome. First king of Rome. Murdered his brother, Remus.

Rouen, Cardinal of (Georges d'Amboise) – (*P* 3 and 7) 1460–1510. Bishop of Rouen and minister to Louis XII.

Saul – (*P* 13) c. 1080–1012 BCE. r. c. 1050–1012 BCE. First king of Israel. Provided David with arms to fight Goliath, which David refused, insisting he could rely only on his own weapons.

Savonarola, Girolamo – (*P* 6) 1452–98. Dominican friar and charismatic preacher who advocated a form of republicanism and spiritual renewal. He and his supporters held the bonfire of the vanities and did much to morally reform Florence. When his activities ran afoul of Pope Alexander VI, he was excommunicated, arrested for heresy, tortured until he confessed, and then executed in a public spectacle in 1498.

Sforza, Ludovico (Ludovico il Moro) – (*P* 3) 1450–1508. r. 1494–1500. Encouraged Charles V to assert his hereditary claim on Naples in an attempt to stymie support for his nephew, Gian Galeazzo Sforza, who was a political obstacle to his continued rule of Milan.

Sixtus IV, Pope – (*P* 11) 1414–84. r. 1471–84. Engaged in the conflicts among various Italian powers, although none of these wars meaningfully changed the status quo. He endorsed the infamous Pazzi conspiracy of 1478 against the Medici, which saw an assassination attempt on Lorenzo the Magnificent during a mass, resulting in two years of war between the papacy and Florence.

Soderini, Piero di Tommaso – 1452–1522. Began his political career under the Medici in Florence and was made gonfalonier for life of the Republic of Florence in 1502. His refusal to listen to Machiavelli's advice to join the Holy League against France in 1511 led to the overthrow of the republic and his exile in 1512.

Tacitus – c. 56–118 CE. Roman historian. Machiavelli quotes him in the *Discourses on Livy* and paraphrases him without acknowledgement in chapter 13 of *The Prince*.

Theseus – (*P* 6 and 26) Legendary Greek hero and founder of Athens.

Vettori, Francesco – 1474–1539. Florentine statesman, diplomat, and historian who rose alongside his friend Machiavelli in the wake of the Medici expulsion of 1494. He had tensions with the Soderini regime and was instrumental in plotting the return of the Medici in 1512. His political connections and high birthright enabled his political career to continue and flourish despite the numerous regime changes in Florence.

Virgil (Publius Vergilius Maro) – (*P* 17) 70–19 BCE. Latin poet most famous for his *Aeneid*, which tells the story of Rome's founding.

Xenophon – (*P* 14; *DL* 2.2) c. 430–354 BCE. Student of Socrates. Historian, philosopher, and soldier. Machiavelli cites his work *On Tyranny* in *Discourses on Livy* 2.2.

Map of Renaissance Italy

DUCHY OF SAVOY

Milan

REPUBLIC OF VENICE

Venice

DUCHY OF MILAN

Ferrara

DUCHY OF FERRARA

REPUBLIC OF GENOA

Bologna

PAPAL STATES

Lucca

Forlì

DUCHY OF URBINO

REPUBLIC OF LUCCA

Florence

REPUBLIC OF FLORENCE

Urbino

Senigallia

Pisa

Siena

Perugia

ADRIATIC SEA

REPUBLIC OF SIENA

PAPAL STATES

CORSICA

REP. OF GENOA

Rome

NAPLES

SARDINIA

Naples

TYRRHENIAN SEA

N

W   E

S

SICILY

Map by Andrew Slivchack

THE PRINCE

CONTENTS

NICCOLÒ MACHIAVELLI

To the Magnificent Lorenzo de' Medici[1]

It is customary, in most instances, for those who seek the favour of a prince, to come before him with those things that they hold most dear or which they see give him the most pleasure; therefore, one often sees that princes are made presents of horses, arms, cloth of gold, precious stones and similar ornaments suited to their greatness. Wishing, therefore, to commend myself to Your Magnificence with some token of my devotion to you, I have not found among my belongings anything I prize so much or value so highly as the knowledge of the deeds of great men, which I learned through a long experience of modern affairs and constant reading of those in antiquity; having with great diligence and for a long time pondered and examined these deeds, and having now set them down in this little volume, I send them to Your Magnificence. And although I consider this work unworthy of coming before Your Magnificence, I trust, nevertheless, that your humanity will move you to accept it, since I could not give you a greater gift than the means to be able to understand, in a very short time, all that I learned in many years and with many hardships and many dangers to myself. I have neither adorned nor filled this work with long phrases or pompous or grandiloquent words, or with any other contrived or extrinsic ornamentation with which many customarily embellish and adorn their works; for I wished either that nothing bring it honour or that solely the variety of the material and the gravity of the subject make it pleasing. Nor do I wish it to be considered presumptuous for a man of low and inferior status to dare examine and regulate the rule of princes; for, just as those who paint landscapes place themselves down in the plain to consider the nature of mountains and the high places, and place themselves up high to consider the nature of low-lying places, similarly, to know well the nature of people one must be a prince, and to know well that of princes one must be of the people.

---

1 Lorenzo di Piero de' Medici the Younger (1492–1519), grandson of Lorenzo the Magnificent (1449–92) and son of the disgraced Piero de' Medici (1472–1503). Machiavelli originally intended to dedicate his work, which he referred to as *On Principalities*, to Giuliano de' Medici (1479–1516) but was forced to change his plans when it became known to him that Giuliano was under orders by Cardinal Giulio de' Medici (1478–1534) not to hire Machiavelli in any capacity.

Accept, therefore, Your Magnificence, this small gift in the spirit with which I send it. If you read and consider it diligently, you will discern in it my earnest desire that you achieve the greatness that Fortune and your other qualities promise you. And if Your Magnificence will turn your eyes at some time from the summit of your lofty position to these lowlands, you will realize how undeservedly I suffer a great and continuous malignity of Fortune.

CHAPTER 1

How Many Kinds of Principalities There Are and by What Means They Are Acquired

All states and all dominions that have ruled, and continue to rule, over men have been and continue to be either republics or principalities. Principalities are either hereditary, in which case the line of their prince has ruled for a long time, or they are new. The new ones are either altogether new, as was Milan for Francesco Sforza,[1] or they are members added to the hereditary state of the prince who acquires them, as is the Kingdom of Naples for the King of Spain.[2] Such dominions thus acquired are either accustomed to living under a prince or are used to living free and are acquired either with the arms of others or with one's own, either by Fortune or by merit (*virtù*).

CHAPTER 2

On Hereditary Principalities

I will omit discussing republics, because I have discussed them at length in the past.[3] I shall turn my attention only to the principality and I shall proceed by weaving together the threads mentioned above, and I shall discuss how these principalities are governed and maintained.

I say then that in hereditary states, accustomed to the rule of the blood line of their prince, there are far fewer difficulties in maintaining them than in new states, because it is sufficient for the prince only not to abandon the ancestral ways and, in addition, to temporize with unexpected events, so that, if such a prince is of ordinary industry, he will always preserve his state, unless an extraordinary and excessive force deprive him of it; and should he be deprived of it, at the slightest difficulty met by the usurper, he will reacquire it. We have in Italy, for example, the Duke of Ferrara[4] who withstood the attacks by the Venetians in 1484 and

---

1 Francesco Sforza (1401–66) became duke of Milan in 1450, ending Milan's brief period of republican rule.
2 Ferdinand the Catholic (1452–1516).
3 Machiavelli is referring to his *Discourses on Livy*.
4 Machiavelli's reference is to two dukes: Ercole I d'Este (1431–1501), who stayed in power through a war with Venice in 1482–84 (*continued*)

those by Pope Julius in 1510 for no other reason than his ancient rule in that dominion; since the natural prince[1] has fewer reasons and less need to give offence, it is inevitable that he be better loved; unless extraordinary vices make him hated,[2] it is reasonable that he be naturally well liked by his subjects. In the antiquity and duration of his rule the memories of and reasons for innovations are extinguished, because one change always dovetails into another.

CHAPTER 3

Of Mixed Principalities

But the difficulties lie in the new principality. And firstly, if it is not altogether new but is as an added member, so that the whole can be called almost mixed, its instability arises mainly from a natural difficulty that is intrinsic in all new principalities. That is that men willingly change their ruler thinking to improve their lot; this belief makes them take up arms against him. But they deceive themselves, for later they see by experience that conditions have become worse. This follows from another natural and ordinary necessity, which requires that a prince must always offend his new subjects, with men-at-arms and with countless other injuries which the new acquisition brings along with it. As a result, you have made enemies of all those you have harmed by occupying that principality and you are unable to keep as friends those who put you there, for you cannot satisfy them in the manner in which they had expected. You cannot use strong medicine against them, since you are obligated to them, for however strong one might be with his armies, in entering a province, one always needs the support of its inhabitants. For these reasons, Louis XII, King of France, quickly occupied Milan and just as quickly lost it;[3] and for that first time, Ludovico's[4] own forces alone were sufficient to

---

that did not go well for him; and Alfonso I d'Este (1476–1534), his son, who was able to quickly overcome Pope Julius II's (r. 1503–13) efforts to oust him in 1510 and later efforts by Pope Leo X (r. 1513–21).

1 A hereditary prince.

2 See chapters 15–19 for Machiavelli's treatment of these vices.

3 Louis XII (1462–1515) took control of Milan in 1499.

4 Ludovico Sforza (1452–1508), duke of Milan, also known as Ludovico il Moro, retook Milan in February of 1500 but lost it for a second time two months later.

take it away from him, because the very people who had opened the gates to him, finding themselves deceived by their own opinion and by the future benefits they had expected, could not tolerate the grievances brought about by the new prince. It is true that upon seizing them for the second time, the rebellious countries are lost with greater difficulty because the prince taking advantage of the rebellion is less cautious in strengthening his position by punishing the culprits, unmasking the suspects and reinforcing his weakest points. So that if the first time it was sufficient for France to lose Milan to one Duke Ludovico clamoring at its borders, for France to lose it later, a second time, it needed the whole world[1] against it and that its armies be annihilated or chased away. This was borne out of the above-mentioned reasons. Nevertheless, Milan was lost both the first and the second time. We have examined the universal reasons of the first time; what now remains to say are the reasons of the second time and to see what remedies Louis XII had and which remedies one could have, if he were in his same situation, in order to secure the conquest better than France did.

I say, therefore, that these conquered states, when added to the older conquering state, are either of the same province and the same language, or they are not. When they are, it is much easier to hold on to them, especially when they are not used to living in freedom. And in order to hold on to them securely it is sufficient to have killed the lineage of the prince who used to rule over them. As for the rest, if one keeps the same conditions and because the customs are not dissimilar, men live quietly, as we have seen in Brittany, Burgundy, Gascony and Normandy, which have been with France for a long time. And although there is some difference in the language, nevertheless, customs are similar, and people blend easily; and he who conquers them, if he wants to keep them, must take two precautions: one, that the blood of their old prince be extinguished; the other, that their laws and taxes not be altered, so that in a very short time it forms one body with the old principality.

But when one conquers states in a province different in language, in customs and in political organization, herein lie the difficulties and here one must have great fortune and possess great

---

1 The Holy League, consisting of Venice, Spain, England, and the Holy Roman emperor, and the papal forces of Julius II, compelled Louis XII of France (r. 1498–1515) to abandon Milan and leave the Italian peninsula in 1512.

industry in order to keep them. And one of the greatest and most efficient remedies would be that the conqueror live there. This would render the possession more secure and longer lasting, as the Turk did in Greece.[1] Despite all the other measures he implemented in order to keep that state, if he had not gone to live there, it would have been impossible to keep because when you are on site one can see the uprisings begin and you can quickly suppress them. If not on site, one hears about them when they have grown large and there is no longer any remedy possible. Furthermore, the province is not pillaged by your officials and the subjects are satisfied because able to seek recourse to the prince who is near; thus, they have more reason to love him if they want to be good and more reason to fear him if they want to be otherwise. If a foreigner wanted to attack that state, he would be more cautious. So much so that living there, the prince can lose it only with great difficulty.

A second excellent remedy is to set up colonies in one or two locations so that the new state is almost shackled with them, because one must either do this or station there plenty of men-at-arms and infantry. Establishing colonies is not costly and, with little or no money, one can set them up and maintain them, offending only those from whom one takes land and houses in order to give them to the new inhabitants. Those offended in this way represent a very small part of that state and they remain poor and dispersed and unable to harm the prince. As for everybody else, they remain on the one hand unaffected—and for this reason they ought to quiet down—and on the other hand fearful of making mistakes for the dread of being stripped of all their possessions like the others. I conclude that these new colonies are not costly, are more loyal, are less offensive, and the offended can do no harm since they are poor and dispersed, as was said above. For this must be noted: men are to be either coddled or extinguished, since they take revenge for small slights but not for grave ones, so that the offence one gives to a man must be such that one does not fear reprisal.[2] In keeping troops rather than establishing colonies, one spends much more, being obliged to use up all the income from that state in keeping guard over it, so that the acquisition turns into a loss. Furthermore, one gives a greater offence because one harms the entire state since the army travels around

---

1 After conquering Constantinople, Sultan Mehmet II (1432–81) made it
   the capital of the Ottoman Empire, which included more than Greece.
2 See *Discourses on Livy* 2.23.

changing lodgings. Everyone feels this hardship, and everyone becomes the prince's enemy; these are enemies who can harm him, beaten but in their own home. From all points of view, therefore, keeping guard in this manner is useless as much as establishing colonies is useful.

Also, he who is in a province dissimilar from his own, as described above, must become the leader and the defender of his neighbouring lesser powers and scheme to weaken the more powerful ones and ensure that a foreigner as powerful as himself not enter the region through some happenstance. Such a foreigner will always be brought in by the discontented either because they are too ambitious or too fearful, as already seen with the Aetolians who brought the Romans into Greece. In fact, the Romans entered every other province because they were brought in by the inhabitants of that province. The natural order of things is that, as soon as a powerful foreigner enters a province, all its less powerful inhabitants ally themselves with him, moved by the envy they hold for the one who has power over them; so that with respect to these lesser powers, it takes him little effort to win them over because they quickly, willingly and all together form a whole with the state he has acquired there. He needs only to ensure that they do not gain too much power or authority. With his forces and their support, he can easily put down those who are powerful in order to remain in all things arbiter of that province. He who does not comply with these rules will quickly lose everything he has conquered and, while he holds it, will have infinite difficulties and hardship.

The Romans, in the provinces they conquered, followed these rules well: they favoured the less powerful while not increasing their power, put down the powerful and did not allow powerful foreigners to gain influence, and established colonies. I want the province of Greece to suffice as an example. The Achaeans and the Aetolians were favoured; the Macedonian kingdom was put down; Antiochus was driven away. Nor did the merits of the Achaeans and the Aetolians induce the Romans to allow them to expand their territory; nor did Philip of Macedonia persuade them to be his friends without first putting him down; nor could the power of Antiochus convince them to allow him to hold any authority in that province. For the Romans did in these cases what all wise princes should do: not only did they take care of current problems but also of future ones, sparing no effort anticipating them in order to avoid them, because in foreseeing problems from a distance, one can easily remedy them. However, waiting for them to be upon you, the medicine is too late because the illness has become incurable. One can say about this what physicians say about consumption: that in the beginning it is easy to cure and difficult to recognize but, as time goes on, not having recognized nor treated it at the beginning, it becomes easy to recognize but difficult to cure. So it happens in affairs of state: recognizing from a distance the diseases that spread in a state—which is not a given except in a prudent ruler—they can be quickly cured. When they are not recognized, and they are left to grow to the point that everyone recognizes them, there is no remedy to be had. The Romans, then, by recognizing problems from afar, always found a remedy and never allowed them to develop further in order to avoid a war, because they knew that war cannot be avoided, but only deferred to the advantage of others. Therefore, they wanted to make war against Philip and Antiochus in Greece in order not to fight them in Italy; and they could have, at that time, avoided both the one and the other, but they did not want to. Nor did they ever like what is on the lips of the wise men of our times—to enjoy the benefits of time. Rather, they enjoyed the benefit of their ingenuity (*virtù*) and prudence, for time brings with it all things and can bring with it good as well as bad and bad as well as good.

But let us return to France and examine whether any of the things mentioned so far were done. And I will speak of Louis,[1] and not of Charles,[2] as the one whose progress could better be seen since he held territory in Italy for a longer period of time. You will see that he did the exact opposite of what should be done to securely hold a state different from his own. King Louis was brought into Italy by the ambition of the Venetians who wanted to gain, with his coming, half the state of Lombardy. I do not want to criticize that decision taken by the King because, wishing to gain a foothold in Italy and having no friends in this land (on the contrary, the conduct of King Charles having caused all doors to be shut to him), he was compelled to accept what friendships he could find. And the decision would have been well taken if he had not made any other mistake in his other maneuvers. After he had conquered Lombardy, the King quickly regained the reputation that Charles had lost him: Genoa surrendered; the Florentines became his friends; the Marquis of Mantua, the Duke of Ferrara, the Bentivoglio, the Countess of Forlì, the Lords of Faenza, Pesaro, Rimini, Camerino, and Piombino, and the people of Lucca, Pisa,

---

1   Louis XII.
2   Charles VIII (1470–98), Louis XII's predecessor.

and Siena all came to meet him in order to become his friends.[1] Only then could the Venetians realize the recklessness of the decision they had taken: in order to acquire a couple of pieces of land in Lombardy, they made the King the lord of two thirds of Italy.

Let one consider now with what little difficulty might the King have maintained his reputation in Italy if only he had observed the rules mentioned above and had kept safe and defended all those friends of his who (there being a good number of them both weak and fearful, some of the Church, some of the Venetians) were always forced to side with him; and through them, he could have easily secured himself against whomever remained powerful. But no sooner was he in Milan than he did the opposite, giving aid to Pope Alexander[2] so that he might occupy Romagna; nor did he notice that with this decision he made himself weak, casting aside his friends and those who had thrown themselves into his lap, and had made the Church great, by adding so much temporal power to its spiritual power that gives it already so much authority. And having made a first mistake, he was obliged to follow it up with others until, to put an end to Alexander's ambition and prevent him from becoming lord of Tuscany, he was forced to come to Italy.

It was not enough for him to have made the Church great and to have cast aside his friends; he wanted the Kingdom of Naples, and to have it, he divided it with the King of Spain;[3] and where he had been the supreme arbiter of Italy, he brought in an associate, so that the ambitious and malcontents of that province had someone else to whom to turn; and where he could have left a tributary King[4] to rule that kingdom, he drove him out in order to replace him with one who, in turn, could drive him, Louis, out. The desire to acquire is truly a very natural and ordinary thing; and when men can do so, they will be praised or, at least, not blamed; but when they cannot and want to do so at all costs, herein lie the blame and the error. If France, therefore, could have attacked Naples with its own forces, it should have done so; if it could not, it should not have divided up that kingdom; and if the division of

---

1   Marchese Francesco Gonzaga (1500–40) ruled Mantua, Ercole I d'Este ruled Ferrara, the Bentivoglio ruled Bologna, Countess Caterina Sforza (1463–1509) ruled Imola and Forlì, Astorre Manfredi (1485–1503) ruled Faenza, Pandolfo IV Maletesta (1475–1534) was lord of Rimini, and Giovanni Sforza (1466–1510) ruled Piombino. Lucca, Pisa, and Siena were all republics.
2   Alexander VI (1431–1503), father of Cesare Borgia.
3   Ferdinand the Catholic.
4   The existing king, Frederick of Naples (r. 1496–1501).

Lombardy with the Venetians deserves to be excused, since with it France gained a foothold in Italy, this other division deserves to be criticized, because it cannot be excused by that necessity.

Louis had thus made these five mistakes: he had eliminated the lesser powers; had increased the power of one already powerful in Italy; had brought into that province a very powerful foreigner; had not come to live there; had not established colonies. Yet, if he had lived, these errors might not have harmed him, had he not made a sixth: depriving the Venetians of their state.[1] For had he not made the Church great nor brought Spain into Italy, it would have been most reasonable and necessary to put them down; however, having taken those first two decisions, he should have never consented to their ruin; for, as long as they were powerful, they would have kept others back from any campaign in Lombardy, both because the Venetians would have never allowed this unless they themselves had become lords of Lombardy, and because the others would not have wanted to take it away from France to give it to them, the Venetians; and they would not have had the courage to attack them both. And if someone were to say: King Louis ceded Romagna to Alexander and the Kingdom of Naples to Spain in order to avoid a war, I reply with the reasons given above: that one should never let turmoil develop in order to avoid a war, because one never avoids it but instead defers it to his disadvantage. And if others were to allege the pledge that the King had given to the Pope, to undertake that campaign himself in return for the annulment of his marriage[2] and the Cardinal's hat for Rouen,[3] I reply with what I will say further on about the word given by princes and how it should be honoured.[4]

King Louis lost Lombardy, therefore, by not following any of the rules followed by others who have taken provinces and wished to retain them. Nor is this a miracle in any way, but very reasonable and ordinary. And I spoke about this at Nantes with the Cardinal of Rouen when Valentino—for this was what Cesare Borgia, son of Pope Alexander, was commonly called—occupied

---

1 The League of Cambrai, of which France was a member, defeated Venice in May 1509.

2 Louis XII desired an annulment of his marriage to Jeanne de Valois (1464–1505) so that he could marry his predecessor's widow, Anne of Brittany (1477–1514), as a means of keeping the Duchy of Brittany under French control.

3 Georges d'Amboise (1460–1510), the Archbishop of Rouen, was made a cardinal as part of this deal.

4 See chapter 18.

Romagna; for when the Cardinal of Rouen told me that Italians did not understand war, I replied to him that the French did not understand politics; for if they did, they would not have allowed the Church to come to such greatness. And we have seen from experience that the greatness of the Church and that of Spain in Italy has been caused by France, and France's ruin has been caused by them. From this one can derive a general rule that never or rarely fails: that anyone who is the cause of someone else's power comes to ruin himself, because that power is brought about either by clever ingenuity or by force, and both of these things are suspect to the one who has been made powerful.

CHAPTER 4

Why the Kingdom of Darius, Occupied by Alexander, Did Not Rebel Against His Successors After the Death of Alexander

Considering the difficulties one has in maintaining a newly acquired state, one might wonder how it happened that, although Alexander the Great had become lord of Asia in just a few years[1] and, soon after occupying it, had died, his successors, despite that fact that it would have been reasonable for that entire state to rebel, maintained it nevertheless and had no other difficulty in keeping it than that which arose among themselves due to their own ambition. I reply that all principalities of which we are aware are governed in two different ways: either by one prince and all the others as his servants who by his grace and permission help him as ministers govern the kingdom; or by one prince and barons who not by the grace of their lord hold that rank but by the antiquity of their bloodline; these barons have their own states and their own subjects who recognize them as masters and hold for them a natural affection. Those states that are governed by one prince and his servants hold their prince in greater authority because in all his province there is no one who is recognized as superior to him and if they obey anyone else, they do so as his minister and official and do not hold any particular affection for him.

Examples of these two types of government in our times are the Turkish Emperor and the King of France. The entire monarchy

---

1 Alexander III of Macedon (356–323 BCE), also known as Alexander the Great, expanded his rule throughout Asia between 334 and 327 BCE.

of the Turk is governed by one lord; the others are his servants. Dividing his kingdom into sanjaks, he sends various administrators there, changing and exchanging them as he likes. But the King of France is placed in the midst of a multitude of ancient lords of that state, recognized as such by their subjects and loved by them; they have their inherited privileges and the King cannot take them away without endangering himself. Whoever considers, therefore, the one or the other of these two states, will have difficulty acquiring the Turkish state, but once it has been conquered, great ease in keeping it. Inversely, he will find in some respects a greater ease in seizing the Kingdom of France but great difficulty in keeping it.

The reasons for the difficulties in acquiring the Turkish kingdom are that one cannot be invited by the princes of that kingdom nor hope to facilitate his campaign through the rebellion of those around the ruler. This is due to the reasons given above; since they are all slaves and obligated to him, it is more difficult to corrupt them and, if they were to be corrupted, one cannot hope them to be of very much use for they cannot bring a following for the reasons advanced above. Therefore, whoever attacks the Turkish kingdom must necessarily think that he will find it united and he is better off relying on his own forces than hoping for unrest caused by others in that state. But once conquered and defeated on the battlefield so that new armies cannot be raised, he need only fear the family of the prince. Once extinguished, he has no one else to fear since others have no credit with the people. And just as the victor before the victory could place no hope in them, after this he has nothing to fear from them.

The opposite occurs in kingdoms governed similarly to France, because you can enter it with ease winning over some barons, given that you can always find some malcontents and some who want a change. These barons, for the reasons already stated, can open the way to that state and facilitate your victory; then, if you wish to hold on to it, that victory brings with it endless difficulties both from those who supported you and from those that you have oppressed. Nor is it sufficient for you to have extinguished the bloodline of the prince because there are always lords who become the heads of new revolts; unable to either satisfy them or extinguish them, you will lose the state at any opportunity.

Now, if you will consider the nature of Darius's government,[1] you will find it similar to the Turkish kingdom; and therefore

---

1   Darius III (380–330 BCE) ruled Persia until Alexander defeated him. A cousin killed him after he fled in the wake of his loss to Alexander.

Alexander first had to defeat him completely and deprive him of any possibility to fight on the battlefield again; after this victory, with Darius dead, that state was secure for Alexander for the reasons discussed above; and his successors, had they been united, could have enjoyed it without much effort; nor did any disorder arise in that kingdom other than what they themselves caused. But states organized such as France are impossible to keep in such peace and tranquility. In the same manner there arose the frequent rebellions against the Romans in Spain, France and Greece, because of the many principalities that existed in those states. While the memory of those principalities lived on, the Romans were uncertain of their hold on them; but once that memory was erased, with the power and the long duration of their empire, they became secure in their hold on them. And even the Romans who came later, though fighting among themselves, could draw a following from those provinces according to the authority that each had been able to establish for himself; and those provinces, because the bloodline of their ancient rulers had been extinguished, recognized only the Romans. Having taken into account all these things, therefore, no one will marvel at the ease with which Alexander held on to the state of Asia and at the difficulties that others experienced in keeping what they had acquired, such as Pyrrhus[1] and many others; this is not a result of lesser or greater merit (*virtù*) of the victor but rather of the differences in the situations.

CHAPTER 5

How Cities or Principalities Should Be Governed That Lived Under
Their Own Laws Before They Were Occupied

When those states that are acquired as I have described are used to living under their own laws and in freedom, if one wants to hold on to them, there are three methods: the first, destroy them; the second, go there in person to live; the third, allow them to live under their own laws, exacting a tribute from them and creating therein a government of the few that will keep the state friendly to you. For such a government, having been created by that prince,

---

1 Pyrrhus (319–272 BCE), king of Epirus, took Sicily from the Romans but was unable to hold onto it. He was renowned for being a military genius, although his victories were often very costly.

knows that it cannot be without his friendship and his power, and it must do everything possible to support that state; and a city used to living free is held more easily by means of its own citizens than with any other method, if one wants to preserve it.

As examples, there are the Spartans and the Romans: the Spartans held Athens[1] and Thebes[2] by creating therein a government of the few, yet they lost both again. The Romans, in order to hold Capua, Carthage, and Numantia, destroyed them and did not lose them; on the other hand, they wished to hold Greece much as the Spartans had done, making it free and leaving it under its own laws, and they did not succeed, so that they were compelled to destroy many cities of that province in order to hold on to it. For in truth there is no sure way of keeping them other than destroying them. And whoever becomes the lord of a city used to living in freedom and does not destroy it, may expect in turn to be destroyed by it; for such a city can always find a motive for rebellion in the name of liberty and its own ancient political order, which are never forgotten neither because of the passing of time nor because of benefits received; and whatever one does or provides for, the inhabitants, unless they are disunited and dispersed, will never forget neither that name nor those orders; and immediately, at every opportunity, they will return to them, just as Pisa did after one hundred years of being held in servitude by the Florentines.[3] But when cities and provinces are used to living under one prince, provided that the bloodline of the prince is extinguished, since on the one hand they are used to obeying, and on the other they no longer have the old prince, they will not be able to agree on choosing a new prince among themselves and they do not know how to live in freedom; for this reason, they are slower to take up arms and a prince can, with greater ease, win them over and firmly establish himself with them. But in republics there is greater vitality, greater hatred, greater desire for revenge; the memory of their ancient liberty does not and cannot let them rest, so that the most secure path is either to destroy them or to go live there.

---

1   In the wake of the Peloponnesian War that saw Athens defeated by Sparta, the Spartans subjected Athens to the rule of the Thirty Tyrants in 404 BCE, only to have them overthrown the following year.
2   Sparta set up an oligarchy to rule Thebes in 382 BCE, which was overthrown in 378 BCE.
3   Florence held Pisa from 1405 until 1494, when it used Charles VIII's invasion as an opportunity to regain its freedom.

CHAPTER 6

On New Principalities That Are Acquired by One's Own Arms and Skill (*virtù*)

No one should marvel if, in speaking of principalities that are totally new both as to their prince and state, I bring up the loftiest examples; since men almost always walk on paths beaten by others and proceed in their actions by imitation, unable however to keep completely to the paths made by others or match the ingenuity (*virtù*) of those they imitate, a prudent man must always enter those paths taken by great men and imitate those who have been most excellent, so that if one's own ingenuity (*virtù*) does not reach theirs, it will have at least a whiff of it. He should do as prudent archers do who, deeming the place they intend to hit too far and knowing the range (*virtù*) of their bow, set their aim much higher than the intended place, not in order to reach with their arrow such a height, but rather to be able to reach, with the help of such a high aim, the designated target.

I say, therefore, that in new principalities, where there is a new prince, one finds more or less difficulty, in maintaining them, according to the greater or lesser skill (*virtù*) of the one who acquires them. And because this event of becoming a prince from a private citizen presupposes either skill (*virtù*) or Fortune, it seems that both the one and the other of these two things should mitigate in part many difficulties; nevertheless, he who has relied less upon Fortune, has lasted longer. Greater ease is generated by the fact that the prince, having no other state, is compelled to live there in person.

But to come to those who, by means of their own skill (*virtù*) and not by Fortune, have become princes, I say that the most excellent are Moses, Cyrus, Romulus, Theseus,[1] and the like. And although one should not discuss Moses because he was a mere executor of things ordered by God, nevertheless he must be admired for that grace that made him worthy of speaking with God. But let us consider Cyrus and the others who have acquired or founded kingdoms; you will find them all admirable and, if their actions or single measures are considered, they will not appear different from those of Moses, who had so great a teacher. And examining their actions and their lives, one can see that they

---

1 Moses, Cyrus, Romulus, and Theseus are the founders of four great ancient states: Israel, Persia, Rome, and Athens, respectively.

had nothing else from Fortune but the opportunity, which then gave them the matter into which they were able to introduce whatever form they thought fit; and without that opportunity the prowess (*virtù*) of their mind would have been extinguished, and without that prowess (*virtù*) the opportunity would have come in vain.

It was therefore necessary for Moses to find the people of Israel in Egypt, enslaved and oppressed by the Egyptians, in order that they might be disposed to follow him to escape that servitude. And it was necessary for Romulus not to remain in Alba and to be abandoned at birth so that he might become King of Rome and founder of his country. It was necessary for Cyrus to find the Persians malcontent with the empire of the Medes, and the Medes soft and effeminate after a long period of peace. Theseus could not have demonstrated his skill (*virtù*) had he not found the Athenians scattered. These opportunities therefore made these men successful and their exceptional ingenuity (*virtù*) made that opportunity known, whereby their country was ennobled and became very prosperous.

Those, like these men, who become princes by equally skillful means (*vie virtuose*), acquire the principality with difficulty but they maintain it with ease, and the difficulties they have in acquiring the principality arise in part from the new political order and customs they are compelled to introduce in order to found their state and gain their security. And one should take into consideration that nothing is more difficult to deal with, nor more dubious to execute, nor more dangerous to manoeuvre than the initiative to introduce a new order of things, for he who introduces it has for enemies all those who do well under the old order, and only tepid defenders in all those who may do well under the new order. This tepidness arises in part from fear of their adversaries who have the laws on their side, in part from the incredulity of men who do not truly believe in new things unless they see a concrete demonstration of them. Therefore, it happens that whenever those who are enemies have the opportunity to attack, they do so with partisan zeal, and those others defend tepidly, so that together with them one is in grave danger.

It is necessary, however, if one wants to discuss this matter well, to examine whether these innovators stand by themselves or depend on others, that is if, in order to carry out their design, they need to beg or are able to use force. In the first case, they always end up badly and never accomplish anything; but when they rely on themselves alone and can use force, then they seldom find themselves in peril. Hence, all armed prophets were victorious, and the unarmed ones came to ruin; because, besides the things that have been said, people are fickle by nature, and while it is easy to convince them of something, it is difficult to hold them to that conviction; and, therefore, one must organize things in such a way that, when they no longer believe, one can make them believe by force. Moses, Cyrus, Theseus and Romulus would not have been able to make their peoples observe their constitutions for very long had they been unarmed; as in our times it befell Brother Girolamo Savonarola[1] who came to ruin with his new political orders when the people began no longer to believe in him; and he had no means of holding steadfast those who had believed, nor of making the disbelievers believe. Men such as these, therefore, have great problems in moving forward and all the dangers are scattered along their path and they must overcome them with their skill (*virtù*); but, once they have overcome them, and they begin to be held in veneration, having extinguished those who were envious of their qualities, they remain powerful, secure, honoured, happy.

To such lofty examples I want to add a lesser one, which will have some relation to the others and I want it to suffice for all other similar ones: this is Hiero of Syracuse.[2] From a private citizen, this man became prince of Syracuse; nor did he receive anything from Fortune other than the opportunity, for when the people of Syracuse were oppressed, they chose him as their captain; and from there he proved worthy of being made their prince. Even as a private citizen his ability (*virtù*) was such that it is written of him that "he lacked nothing to make him a ruler except a kingdom." He abolished the old militia and organized a new one, left old friendships behind and made new ones, and as soon as he had friendships and soldiers of his own, he was able to build any building he wished on such a foundation: so, he had great trouble in acquiring but little in maintaining.

---

1 Girolamo Savonarola (1452–98) whipped Florence into a republican-tinged religious furor in the wake of the Medici expulsion of 1494, claiming that the French invasion had been God's punishment for the Florentines' moral laxity. His success in moral and political matters lasted only until he became critical of Alexander VI, who, when he found that he could not bribe the Dominican to stop his preaching, had him arrested, tried for heresy, and executed.

2 Hiero II of Syracuse (c. 308–215 BCE).

CHAPTER 7

On New Principalities That Are Acquired Through the Arms and Fortune of Others

Those private citizens who become princes through Fortune alone do so with little effort but maintain their standing with much effort, and they do not encounter any difficulty on their path, because they fly there, with all the difficulties arising once they are in place. And such men are those who are granted a state either for money or by favour of him who grants it, as it happened to many in Greece in the cities of Ionia and of the Hellespont, where they were made princes by Darius[1] so that they might hold on to those cities for his own security and glory; such were also those emperors who from private citizens attained the imperial crown by bribing their soldiers. These men rely solely on the will and fortune of him who has granted them the state, two things that are very unpredictable and unstable, and they do not know how to maintain their rank and are unable to do so. They do not know how because, if one is not a man of great genius and talent (*virtù*), it is not reasonable to expect that he, having always lived as a private citizen, would know how to be in command; they are unable to because they do not have forces that are friendly and faithful. Further, the states that spring up at once, like all other things in nature that are born and grow quickly, cannot have roots and general grounding such that the first bad weather does not destroy them; unless they, who have become princes so suddenly, as has been said, are men of such ability (*virtù*) that they immediately know how to preserve what Fortune has placed in their lap, and they lay afterwards the foundations that others have laid before they became princes.

In connection with the two ways of becoming a prince just mentioned, by ability (*virtù*) or by Fortune, I want to give two examples that have taken place in our time within living memory: and these are Francesco Sforza and Cesare Borgia. Francesco, through the appropriate means and his own great ingenuity (*virtù*), from a private citizen became Duke of Milan, and what he had acquired with a thousand woes, he maintained with little effort. On the other hand, Cesare Borgia, commonly called Duke Valentino, acquired his state through his father's fortune and lost it in the same manner, even though he used every means and did

---

1 Darius I (521–486 BCE), king of Persia.

all those things that a prudent and capable (*virtuoso*) man ought to do in order to put down deep roots in those states that the arms and fortune of others had granted him. For, as stated above, anyone who does not lay the foundations beforehand, could, with great resourcefulness (*virtù*), lay them afterwards, although this would be accomplished at the cost of inconvenience to the architect and danger to the building.

Therefore, if one considers the steps taken by the Duke, one will see that he had laid for himself great foundations for his future power, which I do not deem superfluous to examine because I myself would not know what better precepts to give to a new prince other than the example of his actions; and if the measures he took were of no profit to him, it was not his fault because this arose from an extraordinary and extreme malignity of Fortune. Alexander VI, in wanting to make his son, the Duke, great, had many difficulties both present and future. Firstly, he could not see a way of making him a lord of any state that was not already in possession of the Church; and had he considered taking what belonged to the Church, he knew that the Duke of Milan and the Venetians would not allow it because Faenza and Rimini were already under the protection of the Venetians. Furthermore, he saw that the armies of Italy, and in particular those that could have been of use to him, were in the hands of those who had reason to fear the greatness of the Pope and therefore he could not trust them, since they were all in the hands of the Orsini, the Colonna, and their allies.[1] It was therefore necessary to disrupt the order of things and throw into disarray the states of Italy in order to seize the rule of some of them. This was easy for him because he found the Venetians who, motivated by other reasons, had decided to bring the French back into Italy, which not only did he not oppose but made easier by the annulment of the first marriage of King Louis.[2]

The King, therefore, came into Italy with the help of the Venetians and the consent of Alexander; no sooner was he in Milan than the Pope had obtained from him troops for his campaign in Romagna, which was granted to him because of the reputation of the King. Having therefore acquired Romagna and beaten the Colonna, the Duke wanted to hold on to it and

---

1 The Orsini and the Colonna were the most prominent noble families in Rome and were engaged in a long-standing struggle to control both Rome and the papacy.
2 Louis XII's marriage to Jeanne de Valois. See chapter 3.

advance further, but two things prevented him from doing so: one, his own troops, whom he did not think were loyal; the other, the will of France. That is, the troops of the Orsini, of which he had made use, might fail him and not only prevent him from acquiring more but take away what he had acquired; and the King might do the same to him. The Orsini had already given evidence of this when, after the capture of Faenza, he attacked Bologna and saw the reluctant engagement of the Orsini troops in that attack; as for the King, he learned what was in his heart when he attacked Tuscany after the capture of the Duchy of Urbino: the King made him desist from that campaign. Hence the Duke decided to rely no longer on the armies and fortune of others. And the first thing he did was to weaken the factions of the Orsini and the Colonna in Rome; he won over all their followers who were noblemen, making them his own noblemen by giving them great sums of money, and honoured them by bestowing upon them, according to their capabilities, military and political appointments, so that in a matter of a few months, their affection for their faction died out in their hearts and turned all to the Duke. After this, he waited for the opportunity to defeat the Orsini faction, having already dispersed the Colonna family; when a good opportunity came his way, he made even better use of it. When the Orsini realized, belatedly, that the greatness of the Duke and of the Church meant their own ruin, they convened a meeting at Magione in Perugian territory. This gave rise to the rebellion of Urbino, uprisings in Romagna, and endless dangers for the Duke, who overcame them all with the help of the French. Having regained his reputation, trusting neither the French nor other external forces, so as not to have to put them to the test, he turned to deceit; and he knew how to dissimulate his intent so well that the Orsini, through Lord Paulo, reconciled with him; the Duke did not spare any act of kindness to reassure Paulo, giving him money, clothes and horses, so that the simplicity of the Orsini brought them to Senigallia and into his hands.[1] Rid of these leaders and having turned their supporters

---

1 Cesare Borgia (1475–1507) outsmarted conspirators at Senigallia on 25 December 1501 by lulling the leaders of the conspiracy into a false sense of security and then seizing them by force. He strangled Vitellozzo Vitelli (1458–1502) and Oliverotto of Fermo (1475–1502) shortly afterwards and executed Paolo and Francesco Orsini three-and-a-half weeks later. Machiavelli was in close proximity to these events as he was on a diplomatic mission to Borgia's camp when they unfolded. He received a full account of the thwarted conspiracy from Cesare Borgia himself and produced a detailed account of what Borgia told him in his *Description*

into his friends, the Duke had thus laid very good foundations for his power, since he had taken possession of all of Romagna along with the duchy of Urbino. Above all, he thought he had gained for himself the friendship of Romagna and all its people, since they had had a taste of their wellbeing under his rule. And since this part is remarkable and worthy of being imitated by others, I do not want to leave it out. When the Duke took over Romagna and found that it had been ruled by impotent lords who had rather despoiled their subjects more than governed them, and who had given them reason for disunity rather than unity, so that the entire province was full of thievery, quarrels and all sorts of other misdeeds, he deemed it necessary to give it good governance in order to make it peaceful and obedient to his monarchical authority. Therefore, he put in charge Messer Remirro de Orco,[1] a cruel and decisive man, to whom he gave absolute power. This man, in little time, forced the province into peace and unity, gaining in the process a great reputation for himself. Later the Duke thought that such excessive authority was not necessary and feared that it might become hateful, so he set up a civil court in the middle of the province, with a very distinguished president, wherein each city had its own advocate. And since he knew that the past rigorous measures had generated a certain hatred against himself, in order to purge the minds of the people and win them completely over to himself, he wanted to show that, if any cruelty had been committed, it had not originated from him, but from the harsh nature of his minister. Having seized the opportunity to do this, one morning, in Cesena, he had Remirro exhibited in the piazza in two pieces, with a wooden block and a bloody axe next to him. The ferocity of that spectacle left those people satisfied and amazed at the same time.

But let us return to where we left off. I say that, finding himself very powerful and in part secure against immediate dangers since he had armed himself the way he wanted to and since he had in large measure dismissed those forces that were close to him but that could have nevertheless harmed him, the Duke still had to reckon with the King of France if he wanted to continue his conquest, because he knew that the King, who had realized his error too late, would not allow him to continue. For this reason, he began to seek out new friendships and to temporize with France

---

of the Methods Used by Duke Valentino when Killing Vitellozzo Vitelli, Oliverotto da Fermo, and Others.

1 Remirro de Orco (d. 1502) was Cesare Borgia's most trusted and competent lieutenant in both military and political matters.

during the campaign the French undertook against the Spaniards who were besieging Gaeta. His intention was to secure himself against them, and he would have quickly succeeded if Alexander had lived.

And these were his decisions regarding immediate matters. As for the future, first of all he had to fear that the new successor to the papal throne might not be his friend and might try to take away from him what Alexander had given him. He thought of securing himself against this possibility in four ways: first, by extinguishing all families related to those lords he had despoiled in order to deprive the Pope of that opportunity; second, by winning over all the noblemen in Rome, as I have already mentioned, in order to be able to keep the Pope in check through them; third, by drawing to his side the College of Cardinals as much as possible; fourth, by acquiring so much power before the Pope died as to be able to withstand a first attack all by himself. Of these four things, at the death of Alexander, he had accomplished three, and the fourth almost nearly accomplished, because of the despoiled lords he killed as many as he could capture, and very few managed to stay alive; he had won over to his side the Roman noblemen; and he controlled a very large portion of the College of Cardinals; and as for new acquisitions, he had planned to become lord of Tuscany, and he already had in his possession Perugia and Piombino and had taken Pisa under his protection. And as soon as he no longer needed to fear France (in fact, he no longer had to, since the French had already lost the Kingdom of Naples at the hands of the Spaniards, so that for both the one and the other it was necessary to buy his friendship), he would have pounced on Pisa; and Lucca and Siena would have no other option than to surrender, in part out of spite for the Florentines, in part out of fear; the Florentines would have had no remedy for this. Had he succeeded (and he would have in the same year that Alexander died), he would have acquired so many forces and such a reputation that he would have been able to stand alone and no longer depend on the fortune and forces of others, but rather on his own power and ingenuity (*virtù*).

But Alexander died five years after his son had first drawn his sword, leaving him with only the state of Romagna secured and all others up in the air, between two very powerful enemy armies, and leaving him mortally ill.[1] There was in the Duke so much

---

1 Reminiscent of Castruccio Castracani's dying lament. See *The Life of Castruccio Castracani of Lucca.*

ferocity and so much sagacity (*virtù*), and he understood so well how men had to be won over or lost, and so sound were the foundations he had laid down in so short a time that, had he not had those armies so close up against him or had he been healthy, he would have overcome every difficulty. And that his foundations were good is seen by the fact that Romagna waited for him for more than a month; in Rome, albeit half alive, he was safe; and although the Baglioni, the Vitelli, and the Orsini came to Rome, they found none willing to join them against him; if he could not make Pope someone he wanted, he was at least able to make sure it was not someone he did not want. But had he been healthy at the time of Alexander's death, everything would have been simple; and he himself told me, on the day Julius was elected Pope,[1] that he had thought of what might happen upon his father's death and that he had found a remedy for everything, except that he had never thought that, at the time of his father's death, he himself would be on the verge of dying.

Therefore, having summarized all the Duke's actions, I would not know what to reproach him with; on the contrary, I think I can propose him, as I have indeed done, as a model worthy of imitation to all those who have risen to power through fortune and with the arms of others; because he, possessing great courage and noble intentions, could not have conducted himself differently, and his plans were thwarted solely by the brevity of Alexander's life and by his own illness. He, then, who deems it necessary in his new principality to protect himself against his enemies, to gain friends for himself, to win either by force or by fraud, to make himself loved and feared by the people, to be followed and respected by soldiers, to eliminate those who can or must harm you, to replace old political orders with new ones, to be severe yet appreciated, magnanimous and generous, to do away with disloyal armies and to create new ones, to maintain the friendship of kings and princes in such a way that they will assist you with gratitude or offend you with caution—such a person cannot find more recent examples than this man's deeds.

One can only criticize him in making Julius Pope, which was a bad choice; because, as has been said, unable to get a Pope of his choice elected, he could have prevented anyone from being Pope; and he should have never allowed to ascend to the papacy

---

1   Machiavelli was part of a Florentine legation to Rome during the conclave that resulted in Cardinal Giuliano della Rovere (1443–1513) being elected Pope Julius II.

any cardinal whom he might have offended or who, upon becoming Pope, might have reason to fear him. Among those he had offended were San Pietro ad Vincula,[1] Colonna,[2] San Giorgio,[3] Ascanio;[4] any of the others, upon becoming Pope, would have had reason to fear him, except for Rouen[5] and the Spaniards; the latter because they were related to him and were in his debt, the former because of his power, since he was connected to the Kingdom of France. The Duke, therefore, above all else, should have made Pope a Spaniard; failing that, he should have accepted Rouen and not San Pietro ad Vincula. And anyone who believes that new benefits make great men forget old injuries deceives himself.[6]

The Duke, then, erred in this choice and it was the cause of his ultimate downfall.

CHAPTER 8

On Those Who Have Acquired a Principality Through Wickedness

But because there are two more ways one can from a private citizen become a prince, which cannot entirely be attributed either to Fortune or to ability (*virtù*), I believe I should not omit them, although one of them could be dealt with at greater length where republics are discussed. These are: when one ascends to a principality by wicked or nefarious means, or when a private citizen becomes prince of his native city through the favour of his fellow citizens.[7] And in discussing the first way, it will be illustrated by two examples—one ancient, the other modern—without entering into the merits of the issue, since I consider it sufficient, for anyone forced to do so, to imitate them.

Agathocles the Sicilian,[8] not only from an ordinary citizen but from a lowly and abject position, became King of Syracuse. This man, a potter's son, always led, at every stage of his existence, a

---

1 Machiavelli refers to Cardinal Giuliano della Rovere (who would become Pope Julius II) by the name of his church, San Pietro ad Vincula.
2 Cardinal Giovanni Colonna (d. 1508).
3 Cardinal Raffaello Riaro (1460–1521) is referred to by the name of his church, San Giorgio.
4 Cardinal Asciano Sforza (1455–1501).
5 Cardinal Georges d'Amboise, archbishop of Rouen. See chapter 3.
6 See *Discourses on Livy* 3.4.
7 See chapter 9.
8 361–289 BCE.

wicked life; nonetheless, he accompanied his wicked actions with such vigour (*virtù*) of mind and body that, when he joined the military, he rose through the ranks to become the praetor of Syracuse. Having been established in that rank and having decided to become prince and to hold with violence and no obligation to others that power that had been granted to him by consent, he reached an agreement with Hamilcar the Carthaginian, who at the time was on a military campaign in Sicily. One morning he assembled the people and the Senate of Syracuse, as if he were about to deliberate on things concerning the republic, and at a prearranged signal, he had his soldiers kill all the senators and the wealthiest men of the people; once they were dead, he seized and held power in that city without any opposition from his fellow citizens. And although he was defeated twice by the Carthaginians and in the end besieged, not only did he defend his city, but, leaving behind part of his men to defend the city in the siege, with the rest he attacked Africa, and in a short time he freed Syracuse from the siege and brought the Carthaginians to dire straits; they were obliged to make peace with him and be content with the possession of Africa and leave Sicily to Agathocles.

Anyone, therefore, who examines the actions and genius (*virtù*) of this man, will see nothing or little that can be attributed to Fortune; since, as was said before, not with the support of others but by rising through the ranks of the military, which he earned with a thousand hardships and dangers, did he come to power in the principality, which he later maintained by many brave and risky resolutions. Nevertheless, it cannot be called ability (*virtù*) to kill one's fellow citizens, to betray friends, to be without faith, without mercy, without religion; by these means one can acquire power but not glory.[1] For, if one were to consider Agathocles's genius (*virtù*) for getting in and out of danger and the greatness of his spirit in enduring and overcoming adversities, one can see no reason why he should be judged inferior to any other most excellent captain; nonetheless, his ferocious cruelty and inhumanity, along with countless wicked deeds, do not permit us to celebrate him among the most excellent of men. One cannot, therefore, attribute to fortune or ability (*virtù*) what he achieved without the one and the other.

In our days, during the reign of Alexander VI, Oliverotto of Fermo,[2] who many years earlier had been left as a child without

---

1 See *Discourses on Livy* 3.40.
2 Oliverotto Euffreducci, killed by Cesare Borgia in the wake of the conspiracy at Senigallia in 1502.

a father, was brought up by a maternal uncle by the name of Giovanni Fogliani. In the early days of his youth, he was sent to serve as a soldier under Paulo Vitelli, so that, once he had mastered that discipline, he might attain some excellent rank in the military. Then, when Paulo died,[1] he served under Vitellozzo, his brother, and in a very short time, because he was ingenious and vigorous in body and mind, he became the commander of his troops. But since it seemed to him servile to be with others, he thought of occupying Fermo for himself with the support of Vitellozzo and the aid of some citizens of Fermo, who held more dear the enslavement of their city than its liberty. He wrote to Giovanni Fogliani that, having been away from home for many years, he wanted to come to see him and his city and inspect parts of his properties; and since he had toiled for no other reason than to acquire honour, so that his fellow citizens might see that he had not squandered his time away, he wanted to come in an honourable fashion, escorted by one hundred horsemen from among his friends and servants; and he begged his uncle to be so good as to order that the people of Fermo receive him honourably, all of which would bring not only honour to him, but to Giovanni himself, since he had raised him.

Giovanni, therefore, did not fail in any duty due to his nephew; he had him received honourably by the people of Fermo and lodged him in his house, where Oliverotto spent a few days arranging what was needed for his forthcoming wickedness. Then, he invited Giovanni Fogliani and all the foremost citizens of Fermo to a magnificent banquet. When the meal and all other entertainment customary to such banquets were over, Oliverotto deliberately began to discuss certain serious matters, speaking of the greatness of Pope Alexander and his son, Cesare, and of their undertakings. After Giovanni and others responded to his remarks, all of a sudden, he got up saying that those were matters to be discussed in a more secluded place, and he retired to another room, followed by Giovanni and the others. No sooner were they seated than from hiding places in that room emerged soldiers who killed Giovanni and all the others. After the murders, Oliverotto mounted a horse and rode through the streets from one end of the city to the other, and laid siege to the members of the supreme magistracy in the palace, so that out of fear they were forced to

---

1 Paulo Vitelli (1465–99) was a mercenary captain in the employ of Florence. He was executed in 1499 by the Florentines, who believed that he had betrayed them in their war with Pisa.

obey him and constitute a government of which he made himself prince; and having killed all those who, unhappy with him, could have harmed him, he consolidated his power with new civil and military orders, so that in the space of one year that he held the principality, he was not only secure in the city of Fermo but had also become feared by all its neighbours. His defeat would have been as difficult as that of Agathocles had he not let himself be tricked by Cesare Borgia, when at Senigallia, as was said above, the Duke captured the Orsini and the Vitelli; there, he, too, was captured, a year after he committed the parricide and, together with Vitellozzo, who had been his teacher in ingenuity (*virtù*) and wickedness, he was strangled.[1]

Some might wonder how Agathocles and others like him, after countless betrayals and cruelties, could live for such a long time secure in their cities and defend themselves from external enemies, and never be conspired against by their own citizens, while many others were unable to maintain their state by means of cruelties, even in peaceful times, not to mention in the uncertain times of war. I believe this originates from the fact that cruelties can be well used or badly used. Well used are those cruelties (if one is allowed to speak well of evil) that are committed all together at once, out of necessity to protect oneself, and are not continued but instead converted into as many benefits for one's subjects as one can. Badly used are those cruelties that, although few at the outset, grow with time rather than diminish. Those who follow the first method can remedy their condition with God and with men, as Agathocles did; the others cannot possibly remain in power. Therefore, it should be noted that, in seizing a state, the occupier must examine and plan all offences that are necessary to commit, and he must do them all at once so as not to have to repeat them every day and, by not repeating them, reassure men and win them over by bestowing benefits upon them. Anyone who behaves differently, either because of indecision or because of the wrong decision, is always obliged to keep a knife in his hand; nor can he ever rely on his subjects and they cannot trust him because of their fresh and repeated injuries; in fact, injuries are to be inflicted all together at once, so that, tasted for a shorter period of time, they offend less;[2] and benefits must be bestowed a bit at a time, so that they might be savoured better. Above all, a prince

---

1 See chapter 7.
2 See *Discourses on Livy* 1.45.

must live with his subjects in such a way that no unforeseen circumstance may make him alter his course, whether he is pursuing good or evil; for when necessities arise under adverse conditions, there is no time to resort to evil, and if you do good, it will not be useful to you, because it will be judged as forced and no merit will be attributed to you.

CHAPTER 9

On the Civil Principality

But coming to the other case, when a private citizen, not through wickedness or any other intolerable violence, but with the favour of his fellow citizens becomes prince of his native land (this can be called a civil principality, whose acquisition relies neither on fortune alone nor on skill [*virtù*] alone, but rather on a combination of cunning and luck), I say that one ascends to this principality either with the favour of the people or with that of the nobility, for these two different humours are found in every city, and they originate from the fact that the people do not wish to be commanded or oppressed by the nobility, and the nobles wish to command and oppress the people; and these two contrasting appetites give rise to three effects: either principality, or liberty[1] or licence. The principality is brought about either by the people or by the nobles, depending on whether one or the other has opportunity to do so; for when the nobles see that they cannot oppose the people, they begin to extol the merits of one of them and make him prince in order to be able, under his shadow, to satisfy their appetites; and the common people, as well, when they see that they cannot oppose the nobles, exalt the praises of one of them and make him prince in order to be protected by his authority.

Anyone who comes to the principality with the help of the nobles holds on to power with more difficulty than the one who gets there with the aid of the people, because he finds himself a prince among many who feel or appear to be his equals, and for this reason he cannot either command them nor handle them as he would wish. But he who comes to the principality with the favour of the people, finds himself alone and has around him no one, or very few, who might not be willing to obey. Further to this, one cannot honestly satisfy the nobles without injuring others, but

---

1 By this term, Machiavelli means a republican form of government.

one can satisfy the people, because their objective is far more honest, the former wanting to oppress, the latter wanting not to be oppressed. And further to this, a prince cannot ever secure himself if the people are his enemies because they are so many, while he can secure himself against the nobles because they are so few. The worst that a prince can expect from a hostile people is to be abandoned by them; but with a hostile nobility, not only does he have to fear to be abandoned but also that they rise against him; for, being more farsighted and cunning, the nobles take measures in a timely fashion that will save them, and they try to ingratiate themselves with the one whom they hope will win. Furthermore, the prince must necessarily live with the same common people, but not necessarily with the same nobles, for he can make them and break them every day, and take away or give back their reputation at will.

And in order to better clarify this part, I say that there are two types of nobles and that they should be considered chiefly in two ways: either they govern themselves in such a way as to bind themselves completely to your fortune or they do not. Those who do, and are not rapacious, are to be honoured and loved; those who do not should be considered in two ways. Either they behave in this manner out of cowardice and a natural lack of courage; in that case, you should use them, especially those who dispense good advice because in prosperity they bring you honour, in adversity you need not fear them. But when they do not bind themselves to your fortune out of malice or ambition, this is a sign that they think more of themselves than of you; and the prince must be wary of such men and fear them as if they were open enemies, because in adverse times they will always help in his ruin. Therefore, one who becomes a prince with the favour of the people must work to keep it, which is easy for him, since they ask nothing other than not being oppressed. However, one who, against the will of the people, becomes prince with the support of the nobles, must first of all try to win over the people, which should be easy for him if he takes them under his protection. And because men, when they receive good from those from whom they had expected evil, feel more indebted to their benefactor, the people will become more well disposed toward him than if he had risen to the principality with their favour. And the prince can win over the common people in many ways, for which, because they change with the circumstances, no sure rule can be given, and therefore I will omit them here. I shall conclude by saying that a prince must have the friendship of the people, or in adversity he will have no remedy. Nabis,[1] Prince of the Spartans, withstood the siege of all of Greece and one of Rome's most victorious armies, and he defended his city and his state against them; and when danger was near he needed only to rid himself of a few of his subjects; but if the people had been his enemy, this would not have been enough. And let no one challenge my opinion with that trite proverb, "He who builds on the people, builds on mud," because that is true when a private citizen lays his foundations on them and allows himself to believe that the people will come to his rescue when he is oppressed by his enemies or by the magistrates; in this case, he could find himself deceived, like the Gracchi in Rome[2] and in Florence Messer Giorgio Scali.[3] But when the prince who builds his foundations on the people is one who is able to command and is a man of courage, does not lose heart in adversities and does not neglect other preparations, and through his courage and political organization can inspire the people, he will never find himself deceived by them, and he will find that he has laid sound foundations.

Principalities of this type are usually at risk when they are on the verge of ascending from a civil to an absolute system of government, for these princes either rule by themselves or by means of magistrates. In the latter case, their position is weaker and more dangerous since it rests entirely on the will of those citizens who are appointed to those posts who, in times of adversity especially, can very easily take their state away from them, either by rising against them or by not obeying their orders. And the prince, in times of danger, has no time to assume absolute authority because the citizens and the subjects who are used to receiving their orders from the magistrates are not willing, in such predicaments, to follow his; in uncertain times he will always find a shortage of men he can trust, for such a prince cannot rely on what he sees in times of peace, when citizens need the state and therefore everyone comes running, everyone makes promises, and each one wants to die for

---

1   Nabis (c. 240–192 BCE). See *Discourses on Livy* 1.10 and 40, where he is characterized as a tyrant, and 3.6 for an account of his assassination.

2   The Gracchi brothers were tribunes of the plebs. They advocated for agrarian reforms that would have benefitted the lower classes but were assassinated by the nobles, Tiberius Sempronius Gracchus (b. 161 BCE) in 133 BCE and Gaius Sempronius Gracchus (b. 153 BCE) in 121 BCE. See *Discourses on Livy* 1.37.

3   Giorgio Scali was one of the leaders of the Ciompi regime in Florence. The Florentines executed him in 1382 after he became hated by the people for his arrogance. See *Florentine Histories* 3.18 and 20.

him, since death is so far; but in times of adversity, when the state needs its citizens, then few are to be found. And this experience is all the more dangerous because one can only go through it but once; and, therefore, a wise prince must think of a way by which his citizens will always and in every circumstance need him and the state, and then they will always be loyal to him.

CHAPTER 10

How the Strength of Every Principality Should Be Measured

In analyzing the qualities of these principalities, one must discuss another consideration, that is, whether a prince has so much power that, if necessary, he can stand by himself, or whether he always needs the protection of others; and in order to clarify this point, I say that I judge capable of standing by themselves those princes who, out of an abundance of either men or money, can put together a suitable army and engage in battle whoever should attack them; likewise, I judge those who always need others to be those princes who cannot take the field against the enemy but are instead forced to take refuge behind the walls and defend them. The first case has already been discussed, and we shall say later what is necessary. Nothing can be said of the second case other than to exhort these princes to fortify and provision their city, and to disregard the surrounding countryside. And anyone who has fortified his own city and, as it concerns the other aspects of government, has handled his subjects in the way explained above (and explained below), will be attacked with great caution, because men are always adverse to undertakings where they see difficulties, nor can it seem easy to attack someone who has his city well garrisoned and who is not hated by his people.

The cities of Germany[1] are completely free, have little surrounding territory and obey the emperor, when they wish, and fear neither him nor any other nearby power because they are fortified in such a way that everyone thinks that their capture would be tedious and difficult, for they all have suitable moats and walls, sufficient artillery, store in public warehouses enough to drink and eat and burn for a year. Besides this, in order to keep the lower classes fed without depleting public funds, they always have the possibility of giving them work for a year in those trades that

---

1 See *Discourses on Livy* 1.55 and 2.19.

are the backbone and the lifeblood of that city and of the undertakings from which the people earn a living. Moreover, they hold military exercises in high esteem and toward this end they have many regulations for maintaining them.

A prince, therefore, who has a strong city and who does not make himself hated by the people cannot be attacked; and even if this were to occur, anyone attacking him would depart in shame, because the affairs of the world are so changeable that it is impossible for anyone to maintain a siege for a year with his troops idle. And if someone answered, "If the people have their possessions outside the walls and see them burn, they will lose patience and the long siege and their own self-interest will make them forget their prince," I reply that a prudent and courageous prince will always overcome all such difficulties, at times by giving hope to his subjects that the evil will not last long, at times with the fear of the enemy's cruelties, at times by cleverly eliminating those men who seem to him too bold. In addition, the enemy will in all likelihood burn and destroy the surrounding territory upon arrival, at a time when men's hearts are still full of fervor and readily willing to defend their city; and, thus, the prince should hesitate so much the less, because after a few days, when hearts have cooled, the damage has been done and the evils incurred; there is no remedy. And now the people rally around their prince even more, for it would appear that he is obligated to them, since their homes have been burned down and their possessions destroyed in his defence. And the nature of men is such that they feel the obligation as much for the benefits they bestow as for those they receive. Therefore, if everything is taken into consideration, it will not be difficult for a prudent prince to keep his citizens' hearts steadfast both at the beginning and at the end of a siege, provided there are resources for sustenance and defence.

CHAPTER 11

On Ecclesiastical Principalities

There remain now only the ecclesiastical principalities to discuss; concerning these, all the difficulties occur before they are acquired, since they are acquired either by skill (*virtù*) or by Fortune and are maintained without either the one or the other, for they are sustained by the ancient institutions of religion, which have become so powerful and are of such a kind as to keep their princes in power no matter how they act. These princes alone have states and do not defend them, subjects and do not govern them; and the states, though left undefended, are not taken away from them, and the subjects, though left ungoverned, do not care, and they do not think about rebelling against them, nor are they able to do so. These principalities alone, then, are secure and happy; but since they are upheld by higher causes that the human mind is unable to reach, I shall not discuss them; for, being exalted and maintained by God, it would be the behaviour of a presumptuous and reckless man to discuss them.

Nevertheless, if someone were to ask me how it happened that the Church, in temporal matters, has attained such greatness, the fact remains that, up to the time of Alexander,[1] the Italian potentates—and not merely those defined as such, but every baron and lord, no matter how small—considered her temporal power of little importance, and now a King of France trembles before it and it has been able to throw him out of Italy and ruin the Venetians;[2] although all this is well known, it does not seem superfluous to me to recall a good part of it to memory.

Before Charles, King of France, came down to Italy,[3] this province was under the rule of the Pope, the Venetians, the King of Naples, the Duke of Milan, and the Florentines. These potentates had two main concerns: the first, that a foreigner not enter Italy with his armies; the other, that no one of them increase his territory. Those who caused the main concern were the Pope and the Venetians. And keeping the Venetians in check required the unity of all others, as in the defence of Ferrara; and to keep the Pope in check they made use of the Roman barons, who, divided into two factions, the Orsini and the Colonna, always had reason to squabble; standing with their weapons in hand under the Pope's eyes, they kept the papacy weak and unstable. And although from time to time a courageous Pope emerged, like Pope Sixtus,[4] neither Fortune nor political ability could ever free him from these encumbrances. And the brevity of their lives was the cause; for in the ten years, on average, that a Pope lived, he could barely put down one of the factions; and if, for instance, one Pope had almost extinguished the Colonna, another would emerge, an enemy of the Orsini, who would resurrect the Colonna and yet be

1 Alexander VI.
2 Under Julius II.
3 Charles VIII's invasion of 1494.
4 Pope Sixtus IV (r. 1471–84).

unable to destroy the Orsini for lack of time. This was the motive for which the temporal powers of the Pope were considered of minor importance.

Then came Alexander VI, and he, more than any other pontiff who ever lived, showed how much, with money and troops, a Pope could achieve. With Duke Valentino as his instrument and the invasion of the French as his opportunity, he accomplished all those things I discussed above in narrating the actions of the Duke. And although his intent was not to make the Church great, but rather the Duke, nonetheless what he did contributed to the greatness of the Church, which, after his death, once the Duke was destroyed, became the heir of his labours.

Then came Pope Julius[1] and he found the Church great, in possession of Romagna, having extinguished the Roman barons and, thanks to the blows inflicted by Alexander, having quashed their factions; and he also found the way open to accumulate money by a method never used before Alexander.[2] Julius not only continued these practices but also intensified them, and he set out to conquer Bologna, defeat the Venetians and drive the French out of Italy; and he succeeded in all these undertakings, and is worthy of even greater praise since he did everything to increase the power of the Church and not any one private individual. He also kept the factions of the Orsini and the Colonna in the same conditions in which he found them. And although among them were some leaders able to unleash unrest, all the same there were two things which have held them in place: one, the greatness of the Church, which confounds them; the other, not having any cardinals of their own, who are the cause of turmoil among them; nor will these factions ever be at peace as long as they have cardinals, for cardinals foster factions, both in Rome and outside of it, and those barons are obliged to defend them; thus, from the ambition of the prelates arise discord and disorder among the barons.

Therefore, His Holiness Leo X[3] found this pontificate very powerful; and it is to be hoped that, if others made it great by force of arms, he, by his goodness and countless other virtues (*virtù*), will make it still greater and venerable.

---

1 Julius II.
2 The sale of indulgences.
3 Giovanni de' Medici (1475–1521) was elected Pope Leo X on 11 March 1513.

CHAPTER 12

How Many Kinds of Troops There Are and On Mercenary Soldiers

Having examined in detail every kind of principality which I set out to discuss in the beginning and having considered to some extent the causes of their success or failure, and having demonstrated the ways in which many tried to acquire and maintain them, it remains for me now to discuss in general terms the offence and defence that can occur in each of the previously mentioned principalities.

We have said above that a prince must have sound foundations, otherwise he must necessarily come to ruin. And the most important foundations that all states can have—the new as well as the old or mixed—are good laws and good armies; and since there cannot be good laws where there are no good armies, and where there are good armies there are, of necessity, good laws, I will omit discussing the laws and will speak of the armies.

I say, then, that the armies with which a prince defends his state are either his own or mercenaries, either auxiliary or mixed. The mercenary and the auxiliary armies are useless and dangerous; and if a prince maintains his state by relying on mercenary troops, he will never be stable or secure, because they are disunited, ambitious, undisciplined, disloyal, brave among friends, cowardly among enemies; they have no fear of God and no faith with men; and your downfall is postponed as long as the attack is postponed; and in peace you are despoiled by them, in war by your enemies. The reason for this is that they have no other love nor any other reason that keeps them in the battlefield than a meager pay, which is not sufficient to make them want to die for you. They are happy to be your soldiers when you are not waging war, but as soon as war comes, they either desert or leave you. I should not find it difficult to convince anyone of this, since the present ruin of Italy is caused by nothing other than the fact that, for many years, she has relied on mercenary forces. These forces, at times, did make some gains for some and seemed brave in combat among themselves, but as soon as the foreign invader came, they showed themselves for what they were, so that Charles, King of France, was able to conquer Italy with chalk in hand.[1] And the man who used to say

---

1 A reference to how French quartermasters marked residences as lodgings for their troops with a piece of chalk during Charles VIII's invasion of Italy.

that our sins were the cause of the foreign invasions spoke the truth,[1] but they were not the sins he believed, rather the ones I just mentioned; and because they were sins committed by princes, the princes were the ones to pay the penalty for them.

I want to demonstrate further the inappropriateness of these armies. Mercenary captains are either excellent men or they are not; and if they are, you cannot trust them, because they will always aspire to their own greatness, either by oppressing you, their master, or by oppressing others against your wishes; but if the captain is not skillful (*virtuoso*), he will usually ruin you. And if someone were to argue that anyone bearing arms will do the same thing, be they mercenary or not, I would reply that armies have to be employed either by a prince or by a republic; the prince must go himself and assume the office of captain; the republic must appoint its own citizens; and when they send one who turns out to be incapable, they must replace him; and if he is capable, they must keep him in check with laws so that he does not overstep his limits. And we see by experience that only armed princes and armed republics make huge advances, and mercenary armies do nothing but harm; and it is more difficult for a republic armed with its own armies to be subdued to obedience by one of its citizens than a republic armed with mercenary armies. Rome and Sparta stood for many centuries armed and free; the Swiss are armed to the teeth and are completely free. Among the examples of ancient mercenary armies there are the Carthaginians, who, at the end of the first war with the Romans, risked being almost overcome by their mercenary soldiers, although the Carthaginians had their own citizens as captains.[2] After the death of Epaminondas, Philip of Macedonia was made captain of their troops by the Thebans, and after the victory he took away their freedom.[3] The Milanese, after the death of Duke Filippo,[4]

---

1 Savonarola preached that the French invasion of 1494 was divine punishment for the moral laxity of the Italian people.
2 The Mercenary War (241–237 BCE) which took place after the First Punic War.
3 Philip II of Macedon (382–336 BCE) had been instructed by the Theban general Epaminondas, who died in 362 BCE. Philip was asked to lead Thebes in the Third Sacred War in 353 BCE; he later turned on the Thebans and subjugated them by force in 338 BCE.
4 Duke Filippo Maria Visconti of Milan (1392–1447). The duke left no legitimate heirs, so the Milanese created the Ambrosian Republic as a response to the absence of a legitimate ruler with legal claim on their city.

recruited Francesco Sforza against the Venetians; after he defeated the enemy at Caravaggio, he joined them to oppress the Milanese, his masters. Sforza, his father, employed by Queen Giovanna of Naples, left her suddenly disarmed, so that, in order not to lose her kingdom, she was forced to throw herself into the lap of the King of Aragon. And if the Venetians and the Florentines have in the past expanded their territories with such armies, and their captains did not make themselves princes over them, but instead defended them, I reply that in this case the Florentines have been favoured by luck; for, among their gifted (*virtuosi*) captains they could have feared, some did not win, some were met with opposition, others turned their ambition elsewhere. The one who did not win was John Hawckwood,[1] whose loyalty, since he did not win, could not be tested; but everyone will admit that, had he won, the Florentines would have been at his mercy; Sforza always had the Bracceschi against him, so that they kept watch over each other;[2] Francesco turned his ambition to Lombardy, Braccio against the Church and the Kingdom of Naples.

But let us come to what occurred a short while back. The Florentines made Paulo Vitelli their captain, a most prudent man who rose from private life to a very great renown; had he taken Pisa, no one can deny that the Florentines would have had to stand by him, for, had he become a soldier in the service of their enemies, they would have had no remedy, and if they had kept him on, they would have been compelled to obey him.[3] As for the Venetians, if we consider their progress, we see that they acted securely and gloriously as long as they waged war themselves, which was before they started their campaigns on land; with their noblemen and their common people armed, they performed most skillfully and courageously (*virtuosissimamente*),[4] but when they began to fight on land, they abandoned this winning practice (*virtù*) and followed the customs of waging wars in Italy; and at

1 John Hawckwood (c. 1320–94) was an English mercenary captain who was employed by Florence in the 1390s. The campaigns he led were not offensive in nature.
2 Sforza was employed by Florence from 1400 to 1411. The Bracceschi, mercenaries commanded by Sforza's rival Andrea Fortebracci (1368–1424), were also employed by Florence near the end of Sforza's tenure in Florence.
3 The Florentines viewed Vitelli's failure to conquer Pisa as intentional and executed him. See chapter 8.
4 Between the ninth and thirteenth centuries, Venice had developed a significant sphere of influence based on naval power.

the beginning of their expansion on the mainland, since they did not have much territory and they enjoyed a great reputation, they had little to fear from their captains; but as they gained more territory, which was under Carmagnola,[1] they had evidence of this mistake; for seeing that he was a very gifted (*virtuosissimo*) captain, as soon as they defeated the Duke of Milan under his leadership and realizing, on the other hand, that he had cooled toward the war, they concluded that they could not win with him, because he did not have the drive for it, nor could they dismiss him for fear of losing what they had already acquired; in order to secure themselves against him, they were obliged to kill him. Later they had as their captains Bartolomeo da Bergamo, Roberto da San Severino, the Count of Pitigliano and the like, with whom they had to fear defeat rather than victory, as occurred later at Vailà, where, in a single day, they lost what they had acquired with great difficulty in eight hundred years;[2] for, from these armies, come only slow, tardy, and late acquisitions, and losses that are sudden and mind-boggling. And since these examples have brought me to Italy, which has been governed for many years by mercenary armies, I should like to discuss them, going back further in time, so that, when their origins and developments are seen, they can be eliminated. You must understand, then, how in recent times,[3] when the Empire began being driven out of Italy and the Pope began to acquire a greater reputation in temporal affairs, Italy divided into more states, because many of the large cities took up arms against their nobles who before, supported by the Emperor, had kept them oppressed; and the Church supported these cities in order to increase its own temporal power; in many other cities, their own citizens became princes. Therefore, since Italy had almost fallen into the hands of the Church and a few republics, and since the former were priests and the latter were citizens with no knowledge of armies, they began to hire foreigners. And the first who gave renown to this type of armies was Alberigo of Conio, from Romagna.[4] From his school came, among others, Bracco and Sforza, who in their day were the arbiters of Italy.

---

1   Francesco Bussone, also known as Il Carmagnola (c. 1385–1432).
2   Bartolomeo Calleoni of Bergamo (c. 1400–75), Roberto da Sanseverino (1418–87), count of Caiazzo, and Niccolò Orsini (1442–1510), count of Pitigliano, all proved to be inept and inadequate in their service to Venice, resulting in considerable damage to Venice's standing as a power.
3   The thirteenth and fourteenth centuries.
4   Alberigo da Barbiano (1348–1409), Count of Conio, is purported to have established the first Italian mercenary outfit.

After them came all the others who have had control of these armies up to our times. And the result of their military prowess (*virtù*) is that Italy has been overrun by Charles, plundered by Louis, violated by Ferdinand, and vilified by the Swiss. Their approach was, in the first place, to increase the reputation of their own forces by decreasing that of the infantry; they did this because, being men not at the head of a state and subsisting on the proceeds of their profession, a few foot soldiers would not give them a reputation and many they could not afford to feed; for this reason, they resorted to the cavalry, for, with a moderate number of horsemen, they were well rewarded and honoured. It had come to the point that, in an army of twenty thousand soldiers, there were hardly two thousand foot soldiers. In addition, they had used every ploy to spare themselves and their soldiers exertion and fear, not killing each other in the fray but instead taking prisoners without asking ransom; they would not attack cities at night, and those in the cities would not attack the tents of the besiegers; they made neither stockade nor trenches around the camp; they did not campaign in winter; all these things were allowed in their military organization and concocted by them in order to avoid, as was said, hardships and dangers: so that these men have led Italy into slavery and dishonour.

CHAPTER 13

On Auxiliary, Mixed, and One's Own Soldiers

Auxiliary armies, which are the other kind of useless armies, are those that arrive when you call on a powerful man to come help and defend you with his army, as was done by Pope Julius recently, who, having seen in the campaign of Ferrara the sorry performance of his mercenary troops, turned to auxiliary troops and came to an agreement with Ferdinand, King of Spain, that he help him with his men and his armies. These armies may be good and useful in themselves, but for anyone who calls on them they are almost always harmful, because if they lose, you remain defeated, and if they win, you remain their prisoner. And although ancient histories are full of such examples, nevertheless I do not wish to leave this recent example of Julius II, whose decision could not have been less ill-considered, for, in wanting to take Ferrara, he threw himself completely into the hands of a foreigner; but his good fortune gave rise to a third thing, so that he did not have to reap the fruit of his poor choice. In fact, when his auxiliary troops were routed at Ravenna, the Swiss rose up and drove back the victors, to the surprise of the Pope and others, so that he did not end up either a prisoner of the enemies, since they had fled, or of his auxiliaries, since he had won with other troops and not theirs.[1] And the Florentines, who were completely unarmed, brought in ten thousand French soldiers to take Pisa; for this decision they incurred more danger than in any other time of their struggles.[2] The Emperor of Constantinople,[3] in order to oppose his neighbours, brought ten thousand Turkish soldiers into Greece, who, when the war was over, refused to leave, which was the beginning of Greek servitude under the infidel.

Anyone, then, who wants not to win, should avail himself of these armies, for they are much more dangerous than mercenary troops; because with them ruin is ready-made: they are completely united, completely ready to obey others. But mercenary armies, once they are victorious, need some time and favourable circumstances before they harm you, for they are not united and have been chosen and paid by you; with them, a third party whom you may make their leader cannot immediately assert so much authority that he can harm you. In other words, with mercenaries the greatest danger is laziness, with auxiliaries it is valour and commitment (*virtù*). Therefore, a wise prince has always avoided these armies and turned to his own and would rather be defeated with his men than win with others, judging no true victory the one acquired by means of foreign armies.

I shall never hesitate to cite Cesare Borgia and his deeds as an example. The Duke entered Romagna with auxiliary forces, leading an army exclusively of Frenchmen, and with them he conquered Imola and Forlì; but later, not deeming these forces reliable, he resorted to mercenary troops, judging them to be less dangerous, and he hired the Orsini and the Vitelli; then, in dealing with them, he found them suspect, disloyal, and dangerous, and eliminated them and turned to his own; and one can easily see the difference between one and the other of these armies if one considers the difference in the reputation of the Duke when he had only the French with him, and when he had the Orsini and

---

1 The auxiliary troops Julius II relied on were routed on 11 April 1512 by the French, who were in turn forced to retreat by the Swiss a month later.
2 1498–1500.
3 Emperor John Cantacuzene (1292–1383).

the Vitelli, and when he was left with his own soldiers, relying on himself alone; we find that his reputation always increased, nor was he esteemed so highly as when everyone saw that he was, fully and absolutely, master of his own army.

I did not want to depart from citing recent Italian examples; nevertheless, I do not want to omit Hiero of Syracuse, since he is one of those I mentioned earlier.[1] This man, as I said, having been made captain of their armies by the Syracusans, understood immediately that mercenary forces were not useful because comprised of condottieri similar to our Italian ones; and since he thought he could neither keep them nor dismiss them, he had them cut up in pieces and henceforth waged war with his own troops and not with foreign ones.

I should also like to recall to memory an example from the Old Testament illustrating this point. When David offered to Saul to go and fight against Goliath, the Philistine challenger, Saul, in order to give him courage, armed him with his own weapons and armour; as soon as he put them on, David rejected them, saying that with them he could not fight at his best, and therefore wanted to face the enemy with his sling and his knife. In the end, the arms of others fall off your back or weigh you down or restrict you.[2]

Charles VII,[3] father of King Louis XI, having liberated France from the English by means of his good fortune and his skill (*virtù*), understood the necessity of arming himself with his own soldiers and established an ordinance in his kingdom concerning cavalry and infantry. Later his son Louis abolished the ordinance for the infantry and began to employ the Swiss; this mistake, followed by others,[4] is—as is now evident—the cause of the many dangers faced by that kingdom. By increasing the reputation of the Swiss, he devalued his own troops, for he abolished the infantry and obliged his cavalry to depend on the soldiers of others; now used to fighting alongside the Swiss, the French do not think they can win without them. Because of this, the French do not fare well against the Swiss and without Swiss help they do not fare well altogether. Thus, the armies of France have been mixed, made

---

1 See chapter 6.
2 See 1 Samuel 17:38–40 and 50–51. Machiavelli's depiction of the passage differs slightly from the biblical text, but the discrepancy distorts neither the biblical event in any significant way nor the lesson Machiavelli draws from it.
3 Charles VII (1403–61) assumed the throne in 1422 and eventually repelled the English, bringing to an end the Hundred Years' War in 1453.
4 Louis XI's (r. 1461–83) successors, Charles VIII and Louis XII.

up in part by mercenaries, in part by their own soldiers; taken all together, they are much better than a mercenary army alone or an auxiliary army alone, but much inferior to one's own troops. Let this example suffice, because the Kingdom of France would be invincible if the ordinance of Charles had been augmented or preserved; but the little prudence that is in men gives rise to things that may taste good at the beginning, but often we do not notice the poison that is just beneath, as I said above about consumptive fevers. Therefore, anyone who does not recognize the evils in a principality the moment they arise is not really wise; and this ability is given to few people. If we were to consider the beginning of the downfall of the Roman Empire, we would find it in their hiring the Goths as mercenaries,[1] because from that beginning the strength of the Roman Empire began to wane, and all that strength (*virtù*) that drained from it was given to the Goths.

I conclude, therefore, that without armies of its own, no principality is safe; on the contrary, it is completely at the mercy of Fortune, since there is no ability of any kind (*virtù*) that can defend it in times of adversity; and it was always the opinion and judgement of wise men that "nothing is as weak and unstable as the reputation for power not founded on one's own strength";[2] and one's own armies are those composed of subjects or citizens or dependents; all others are either mercenary or auxiliary. And the manner of organizing one's own troops is easily found if one examines the methods followed by the four I mentioned above[3] and if one understands how Philip, father of Alexander the Great, and many republics and princes have armed and organized themselves; on such examples I place my complete trust.

---

1   In the fourth century.
2   Tacitus, *Annals* XIII.19. Machiavelli takes a minor liberty with the passage.
3   Depending on how one reads this passage, Machiavelli is referring either to Cesare Borgia, Hiero of Syracuse, Charles VII, and David mentioned in this chapter, or to Moses, Cyrus, Theseus, and Romulus, whom he discussed in chapter 6.

CHAPTER 14

On a Prince's Duty Regarding the Military

A prince, therefore, must have no other objective, no other thought, nor must he take any other thing as his profession outside of war, its organization and discipline, for that is the only profession that befits he who rules, and it is of such value (*virtù*) that not only does it maintain those who were born princes, but also many times makes men rise from private life to that rank. On the other hand, one can see that when princes have preoccupied themselves more with luxuries than with arms, they have lost their state; and the first cause for losing it is neglecting this art, and the cause for acquiring it is being an expert in this art. Francesco Sforza, because he was armed, from a private citizen became Duke of Milan; his sons, in order to avoid the discomforts of arms, from dukes became private citizens.[1] For among the other evil consequences which this causes, being unarmed makes you contemptible, which is one of those infamies against which a prince should safeguard, as will be said below.[2] For there is absolutely no comparison between an armed man and an unarmed man, and it is not reasonable that an armed man obey an unarmed man willingly, and that the unarmed man should feel secure among armed servants; since there is contempt in the latter and suspicion in the former, and it is impossible for them to work well together. Therefore, a prince who does not understand military matters, besides the other disadvantages this causes, cannot be respected by his soldiers and cannot put his trust in them. He must, therefore, never get distracted from the thought of the practice of war, and in peacetime must train himself more than in times of war, which he can do in two ways: one with deeds, and one with his mind. As for deeds, besides keeping his men well organized and well trained, he must always be hunting[3] and, through that activity, accustom the body to hardships; at the

---

1 Machiavelli speaks loosely here, with "sons" referring most likely to Ludovico (il Moro) Sforza, and his brother Cardinal Asciano Sforza, who were taken prisoner by the French in 1500. First in line to succeed Francesco was his eldest son, Galeazzo Maria, who was assassinated in 1476; second in line was Galeazzo Maria's son, Gian Galeazzo, who was too infirm to rule. Ludovico ruled as regent in his stead.
2 See chapter 19.
3 See *Discourses on Livy* 3.39.

same time, he should learn to recognize the nature of his land and know how mountains slope, how valleys open up, how plains stretch out, and recognize the nature of rivers and marshes—all this he should do with the greatest of care. This knowledge is useful in two ways: first, you get to learn about your own country and you can better understand how to defend it; second, through the knowledge and experience of your land, you can easily understand other new sites that might be necessary to explore, because the mountains, valleys, plains, rivers, and marshes that are found in Tuscany, for example, have a certain similarity to those in other provinces, so that the knowledge of the land of one province easily allows one to become familiar with the others; and the prince who lacks this expertise lacks the most important qualification that a captain must have, because this teaches him how to attack the enemy, secure lodgings, lead armies, plan battles, and lay siege to a city to his advantage.

Among other praises given by writers to Philopoemen, Prince of the Achaeans,[1] is that in peacetime he would think of nothing else but how to wage war, and when he was out in the country with friends, he would often stop and reason with them: "If the enemy were on the hill and we were here with our cavalry, who would have the advantage? How could we attack them without breaking formation? If we wanted to retreat, how would we do it? And if they were to retreat, how would we follow them?" And, as they went about, he would present them with all the scenarios that an army might face, listen to their opinion, express his, corroborating it with his reasons, so that, because of these ongoing considerations, when leading his armies, no unexpected event could arise for which he did not have a remedy.

As for exercising his mind, the prince must read histories and in them study the deeds of excellent men, observe their course of action in wars, examine the causes of their victories and defeats, in order to avoid the latter and imitate the former; above all, he must do as some excellent man has done before him, who himself set out to imitate someone who had been praised and honoured before him, keeping his deeds and actions ever present, as it is said that Alexander the Great did with Achilles, Caesar with Alexander, Scipio with Cyrus; and anyone who reads the life of Scipio written by Xenophon,[2] then realizes how much glory that imitation brought to the life of Scipio, and how much, in chastity,

---

1 252–184 BCE.
2 Xenophon's *Cyropaedia*.

affability, humanity and generosity Scipio conformed to the qualities that Xenophon describes in Cyrus.

These are the ways that a wise prince must follow, and never be idle in peacetime; he must, with industry, capitalize on them in order to make use of them in times of adversity, so that when Fortune changes, she will find him prepared to resist.

CHAPTER 15

On Those Things for Which Men, and Particularly Princes, Are Praised or Blamed

There now remains to see what rules and conduct a prince must adopt in dealing with his subjects and friends. And since I know that many have written about this, I fear that, by writing about it again, I will be thought presumptuous, because, especially in discussing this subject, I will depart from the precepts given by others; but since my intention is to write something useful for anyone who understands it, I thought it more suitable to pursue the effectual truth of the matter rather than the imagination of it. And many have imagined for themselves republics and principalities that have never been seen or known to exist in reality;[1] for, the distance between how one lives and how one ought to live is such that, if anyone leaves behind what is done for what ought to be done, he learns the way to self-destruction rather than to self-preservation; because a man who wants to profess goodness and be good in all cases will inevitably come to ruin among many who are not good. Therefore, it is necessary for a prince, who wants to maintain his power, to learn how not to be good, and then use this ability according to necessity.

Leaving aside, then, things that have been imagined regarding a prince and speaking of those that are true, I say that all men, when spoken of, and especially princes, because they are placed at a higher level, have characteristics attributed to them that either bring them blame or praise. And this is why one is considered generous, another miserly (to use a Tuscan term, since "avaricious" in our tongue is still he who desires to acquire by thievery, while we call "miserly" he who abstains too much from using his own wealth); one is considered a giver, the other rapacious; one cruel,

---

1 Idealistic treatises such as Plato's *Republic* or instances of the *speculum principum* (mirror for princes) genre.

the other compassionate; one treacherous, the other loyal; one effeminate and cowardly, the other proud and courageous; one humane, the other arrogant; one lascivious, the other chaste; one sincere, the other cunning; one hard, the other lenient; one serious, the other superficial; one religious, the other unbelieving, and the like. And I know that everyone will admit that it would be a very praiseworthy thing if a prince had, of all the above characteristics, those that are deemed good; but since it is neither possible to have them all nor observe them entirely, given that human conditions do not permit it, it is necessary for the prince to be so prudent as to know how to avoid the infamy of those characteristics that would lose him the state, and to protect himself from those that would not lose it, if this is possible; but, if he cannot, he can give in to these latter ones with less caution. Moreover, he should not worry about incurring the infamy of those vices without which he would have difficulties maintaining his state, because, once all is carefully taken into consideration, one will find that something that appears to be a virtue pursued, would lead to his ruin; while some other thing that appears to be a vice, if pursued, results in his security and his wellbeing.

CHAPTER 16

On Generosity and Miserliness

Beginning, then, with the first two characteristics mentioned above, I say that it would be good to be considered generous; nevertheless, generosity, when used so that you may be thought of as a generous person, will harm you; because if it is used virtuously (*virtuosamente*) and as it should be, it will not be recognized, and you will not escape the infamy brought about by its opposite; therefore, if a prince wants to keep the reputation of being generous among men, it is necessary for him not to neglect any kind of extravagant grandeur, to the point that, in doing so, such a prince will dissipate all his wealth, and in the end, if he wants to maintain that reputation, he will need to burden the people with additional excessive taxes and take all possible measures necessary to raise money. This will begin to make him hateful to his subjects and, as he becomes poor, little esteemed by everyone; because of his generosity, having offended many and benefitted few, he will feel vulnerable at the first minor setback and will be at risk at the first sign of danger; when he recognizes this, he will want to pull back, and he will immediately incur the infamy of being miserly. A prince, therefore, unable to use this virtue (*virtù*) of generosity without damage to himself and in a manner for which he is known must, if he is wise, not care about being called a miser, because with time he will eventually be deemed ever more generous, given that, as a result of his miserliness, his income is sufficient for him, he can defend himself against those who wage war against him, and he can undertake enterprises without burdening his people. Therefore, he is generous with all those from whom he does not take anything, who are countless, and miserly with all those to whom he gives nothing, who are few.

In recent times we have seen great things only from those who were deemed miserly, for the others were destroyed. Pope Julius II, as soon as he had taken advantage of his reputation for generosity to gain the papacy, never thought of keeping it up, in order to be able to wage war. The King of France[1] waged many wars without imposing extra taxes on his people, because the extra expenses were met by his long-standing parsimony. And the present King of Spain,[2] had he been considered generous, would not have started nor won so many campaigns. Therefore, in order not to be obliged to rob his subjects, to be able to defend himself, not to become poor and contemptible, not to be compelled to become rapacious, a prince must consider it of little importance if he is called a miser, because that is one of those vices that keep him in power. And if one were to say, "Caesar, by means of his generosity, came to rule over the empire, and many others, because they were generous and were recognized as such, rose to very high stations," I reply: "Either you are already a prince, or you are on your way to becoming one; in the first case, this generosity is harmful; in the second, it is very necessary to be thought of as generous. And Caesar was one of those who wanted to attain the principality of Rome; but if, after attaining it, he had lived,[3] and he had not curbed his expenses, he would have destroyed the empire." And if someone were to object, "There have been many princes who, with their armies, have accomplished great deeds and they were thought of as very generous," I reply: "Either the prince spends his own money and that of his subjects or that belonging to someone else; in the first case, he must be frugal; in the second, he should not neglect any occasion to be generous; to the prince who

---

1 Louis XII.
2 Ferdinand the Catholic.
3 Julius Caesar was assassinated by Roman senators in 44 BCE.

goes out with his armies, lives on looting, pillaging and ransoms, disposes of what belongs to others, such generosity is necessary, or his soldiers would not follow him; and you can be more generous with what does not belong to you or to your subjects, as was Cyrus, Caesar and Alexander, because spending what belongs to others in no way hurts your reputation, rather, it adds to it; only spending what is your own harms you." And there is nothing that is more self-consuming than generosity; you lose the capacity to use it as you are using it, and you become either poor and contemptible, or, in order to escape poverty, you become rapacious and hateful. And among the things against which a prince should guard, the first is being contemptible and hated, and generosity leads to one and the other. Therefore, there is more wisdom in keeping the name of miser, which produces infamy without hate, than, only because you want to be called generous, to be forced to incur the name of rapacious, which produces infamy as well as hate.

CHAPTER 17

On Cruelty and Mercy and Whether It Is Better to Be Loved Than
to Be Feared or the Contrary

Proceeding now to the other qualities I mentioned above, I say that every prince must desire to be considered merciful and not cruel; nevertheless, he should be careful not use that mercy badly; Cesare Borgia was considered cruel, but his cruelty restored order in Romagna, united it and restored peace and loyalty. If one considers this well, one will see that he was much more merciful than the Florentine people, who, to avoid being called cruel, let Pistoia be destroyed.[1] Therefore, a prince must not care about incurring the infamy of being cruel when he keeps his subjects united and loyal, for, with very few examples of cruelty, he will be more merciful than those who, out of excessive mercy, let disorders continue, from which originate murders and thievery, because these usually harm an entire community, and those executions that come from the prince harm one particular individual. And among

---

1 The Florentine republic in which Machiavelli had served did not resolve or suppress civil conflict, which raged in Pistoia, a town under Florence's control. Machiavelli was dispatched on several occasions to Pistoia by the Florentine government and knew the situation well.

all princes, it is impossible for the new prince to avoid being called cruel because the new states are full of dangers; and Virgil, through Dido, states: "The harsh reality and the newness of my rule compel me to act in such a manner and to guard all borders of my land."[1] Nevertheless, a new prince must be cautious in believing and in acting, nor should he create his own fears, and he should proceed in a manner that is tempered by prudence and humanity, so that too much trust does not make him incautious and too much mistrust does not make him intolerable.

This gives rise to an argument: whether it is better to be loved than to be feared, or the contrary. The answer is that one would want to be both the one and the other; but because it is difficult to lump them together, it is much safer to be feared than loved, when one of the two must be relinquished. For one can generally say this about men: that they are ungrateful, fickle, impostors, they avoid dangers and are greedy for gain; and while you are good to them, they are all yours, and they offer you their blood, their property, their life, and their children, as I said above,[2] and when your need for them is remote but when it moves closer, they turn away. And that prince who relied on their word alone, finding himself exposed, without other preparations, comes to ruin; because friendships which are attained at a price, and not through greatness or nobility of spirit, are bought but they are not owned, and at the proper moment cannot be redeemed; and men are less hesitant in harming one who makes himself loved than one who makes himself feared; for love is based on a bond of obligation, which, since men are wicked, is broken at every opportunity that serves their self-interest; but fear is held by the dread of punishment, which never leaves you.

Nevertheless, the prince should make himself feared in such a way that, if he does not acquire love, he will avoid hatred, because being feared and not being hated can go well together; and he will always accomplish this if he abstains from the property of his citizens and his subjects and from their women;[3] and even if he should need to spill someone's blood, he should do it when there is proper justification and manifest cause; but above all he must abstain from the property of others because men forget more quickly the death of a father than the loss of their patrimony. Furthermore, the reasons for seizing their property are never

---

1 Virgil, *Aeneid* 1.563–64.
2 See chapter 9.
3 See *Discourses on Livy* 3.26.

lacking, and he who begins to live by thievery, finds reasons for appropriating what belongs to others; on the other hand, reasons to spill blood are rarer and disappear more quickly.

But when the prince is with his armies and in control of a multitude of soldiers, then he need not worry at all about being called cruel, because without that reputation no one ever held an army together and was ready for any feat. Among the admirable actions of Hannibal, we count this one: that, having led a very large army, made up of men of countless origins, to fight in foreign lands, no dissension ever arose either among them or against the prince, during his bad fortune as well as his good fortune. This could not have originated from anything other than his inhuman cruelty, which, together with his many abilities (*virtù*), made him respected and feared in the eyes of his soldiers; without that cruelty, his other abilities (*virtù*) would not have been sufficient to produce that effect; writers, having considered this superficially, on the one hand admire this achievement of his, while on the other condemn the principal cause of it. And that it is true that his other abilities (*virtù*) would not have sufficed, one can consider Scipio, a most exceptional man not only in his time but also in the entire memory of things that have been done, whose armies rebelled against him in Spain; this rebellion arose from nothing else but his excessive mercy, which had given his soldiers more liberty than was suitable to military discipline. For this he was rebuked in the Senate by Fabius Maximus who called him the corrupter of the Roman militia.[1] The Locrians, having been ruined by one of Scipio's officers,[2] were never avenged by him, nor did he reprimand that officer for the insolent behavior; all of which originated from his tolerant nature, so that, when someone in the Senate wanted to excuse him, he said that there were many men who knew better how not to err than to correct errors. Such a nature would have in time tarnished Scipio's fame and glory, had he continued with it in his command; however, living under the control of the Senate, this harmful trait of his was not only suppressed but also glorified.[3]

---

1 Quintus Fabius Maximus Cunctator (275–203 BCE) was a renowned Roman politician and military leader.
2 Locris was a Greek city in Calabria. Scipio neither punished his officers for their crimes in recapturing the city (which had a long-standing relationship with Rome) from Hannibal's forces nor did anything to prevent further misconduct by his troops, forcing the Locrians to take their grievances directly to the Senate.
3 See *Discourses on Livy* 3.21.

I conclude, therefore, going back to the issue of being feared and loved, that, since men love at their own pleasure and fear at the pleasure of the prince; a wise prince must rely on what is his, not on what belongs to others; he must strive only to avoid being hated, as was said.

CHAPTER 18

How Princes Should Keep Faith

Everyone understands how praiseworthy it is for a prince to keep faith and live with honesty and not with guile; nevertheless, we see from experience in our time that those princes who have done great things have shown little consideration for faith and have known how to trick the minds of men with guile, and in the end they have outdone those who laid their foundations on honesty.

You must know, then, that there are two ways of fighting: one by law, the other by force; the first is peculiar to men, the second to beasts; and since the first is often not sufficient, one needs to resort to the second; therefore, a prince must know well how to make use of both beast and man. This point was taught covertly to the princes by ancient writers, who write that Achilles and many others of those ancient princes were given to Chiron the centaur to be raised, so that he might look after them with his discipline. This, having one who is half-beast and half-man as a teacher, means nothing other than that a prince must know how to make use of the nature of one and the other, and that one without the other cannot last.

Therefore, since a prince must know how to make good use of the beast, he must choose, from among the beasts, the fox and the lion, for the lion cannot defend itself against traps and the fox cannot defend itself against wolves.[1] Therefore, it is necessary to be a fox to recognize the traps, and a lion to frighten the wolves; those who rely only on the ways of the lion do not understand. Therefore, a prudent ruler cannot and should not keep faith when observing it would end up harming him and when the reasons for

---

1 While the images of the fox and the lion were popular in the literature Machiavelli would have been familiar with, the specific use Machiavelli makes of them are in all likelihood taken from Cicero's *De officiis* 1.34 and 1.41. Machiavelli employs the same imagery Cicero uses but rejects the conclusions Cicero offers about the traits these animals represent.

which he promised it no longer exist; and if men were all good, this precept would not be good; but since they are wicked and would not keep faith with you, you likewise need not keep faith with them. Nor did a prince ever lack legitimate reasons to disguise his non-observance. One could give countless modern examples of this and show how many peace treaties, how many promises have been rendered null and void by the faithlessness of princes; and he who has made better use of the fox, has achieved the best results; but it is necessary to know how to mask well this nature and to be a great pretender and deceiver; and men are so naïve and so dependent upon the necessities of the present moment that he who deceives will always find someone who will let himself be deceived. Among recent examples, I should not like to omit one: Alexander VI never did anything, never thought of anything other than deceiving men, and he always found material that allowed him to do it, and there was never a man who had a greater ability to persuade, who with mightier oaths would affirm something, yet observe it less; nevertheless, his deceits always succeeded according to his wishes, because he knew well this aspect of the world.

A prince, then, does not need to have all the qualities listed above, but he absolutely must appear to have them; better still, I dare say this, that if he has them and abides by them always, they are harmful, and if he appears to have them, they are useful; for instance, to appear merciful, loyal, humane, sincere, religious, and also to be so, but with your mind so disposed that, should the need arise not to be so, you are able and know how to change and be the opposite. Let this be understood: that a prince, and especially a new prince, cannot abide by all those principles for which men are deemed good, for he is often compelled, in order to hold on to his state, to act against faith, against charity, against humanity, against religion; and, therefore, he must have a mind willing to turn to where the winds of Fortune and the changing circumstances lead him to be, and, as I said above, he must not deviate from the good if he can, but must know how to enter into evil if compelled.

A prince, therefore, must take great care not to let anything slip from his lips that is not full of the qualities mentioned above, and upon seeing and hearing him, he must seem all mercy, all faith, all sincerity, all religion; and nothing is more necessary than appearing to have this last quality; and men in general judge more by their eyes than by their hands, for everyone can see, few can feel; everyone sees what you appear to be, few feel what you are, and those few do not dare challenge the opinion of the many that have the majesty of the state to defend them; and in the actions of all men, and especially of princes, where there is no tribunal in which to appeal, one judges by the results.

Let a prince, then, win and maintain his state, and his means will always be judged honourable and praised by everyone, because the common people are taken by appearances and the outcome of a thing, and the world consists only of common people and the few have no room when the many have ground to stand on. A certain prince of the present time, who is best left unnamed, preaches nothing but peace and faith, and he is a great enemy of both one and the other; and had he abided by both the one and the other, they would have lost him his reputation and his state many times.[1]

CHAPTER 19

On Avoiding Contempt and Hatred

Since, of the qualities I mentioned above, I have already spoken of the most important ones,[2] I would like to discuss the others briefly under this general rule: that the prince, as was explained in part above,[3] ought to think about how to avoid those things that make him hated and contemptible; and whenever he will avoid this, he will have performed his duties, and he need not fear any danger if he incurs other infamies. What makes him hated is above all, as I said,[4] his being rapacious and a usurper of the property and women of his subjects: he must abstain from these; and whenever the multitude of men are not deprived of property or honour, they live happily, and one is left to contend only with the ambition of a few, which can be easily curbed in many ways. The prince becomes contemptible when he is changeable, superficial, effeminate, cowardly, indecisive; the prince must guard against these as if from a reef, and he must strive that greatness, courage, seriousness and strength be recognized in all his actions, and as for the private disputes of his subjects, he should insist that his judgements be irrevocable, and he should carry himself so as to elicit the opinion

---

1 Ferdinand the Catholic. See chapter 21.
2 See chapter 15.
3 See chapters 15–17.
4 See chapter 17.

that no one should think of deceiving or cheating him. The prince who creates such an opinion of himself is held in high esteem; and it is difficult to plot against someone who is highly esteemed; it is difficult to attack him, provided it is well known that he is an excellent man and revered by his people. For a prince must have two fears: one internal, concerning his subjects, one external, concerning foreign powers; he defends himself from the latter by means of good armies and good friends, and if he has good armies, he will always have good friends; and internal conditions will always remain stable when external ones are stable, that is, if they have not already been disturbed by a conspiracy; and even if external affairs were to change, provided he has organized matters and has acted as I said, as long as he does not lose heart, he will always resist every attack, as I said Nabis the Spartan did.[1] As for his subjects, when external affairs are stable, one should fear that they may conspire in secret; a prince can easily secure himself against this if he avoids being hated and despised and if the people are satisfied with him, which is necessary to accomplish, as was said extensively before. And one of the most potent remedies a prince has against conspiracies is not being hated by his people because, he who conspires always believes that the death of the prince will satisfy the people; but if he believes that he will offend the people, he will not have the courage to make such a decision, because the difficulties that face the conspirators are infinite; and from experience we see that there have been many conspiracies, but few have succeeded, because he who conspires cannot be alone; on the other hand, he can only take as his companions those he believes to be malcontent; and as soon as you reveal your intentions to a malcontent, you give him material to make himself content, because he can clearly hope for every advantage for himself, so much so that, seeing a sure gain on the one hand, and seeing it doubtful and full of dangers on the other, he must either be a very rare friend or an altogether implacable enemy of the prince, for him to keep faith with you. And in order to deal with the matter briefly, I say that on the side of the conspirator there is nothing but fear, jealousy, and the dread of punishment that terrify him, but on the side of the prince there is the majesty of the principality, the laws, the protection of friends and of the state that defend him; so much so that, if we add the goodwill of the people to all

---

1 See chapter 9. Nabis withstood all direct attacks against him but was betrayed and assassinated by a conspiracy planned by the Aetolian League in 192 BCE. See *Discourses on Livy* 3.6.

this, it is impossible that anyone could be so bold as to conspire against the prince; for, while a conspirator must ordinarily fear the unsuccessful outcome before the execution of his plot, in this case he has reason to be afraid even later, in the aftermath of his crime, since he has the people as his enemy, and he cannot hope to find refuge anywhere. Countless examples could be given on this subject, but I should be satisfied with one which occurred in our fathers' time. Messer Annibale Bentivoglio, Prince of Bologna and grandfather of the present Messer Annibale, was killed by the Canneschi family, who plotted against him; he was survived only by Messer Giovanni, then still an infant; but immediately after the murder, the people rose up and killed all the Canneschi. This originated from the goodwill of the people that the house of Bentivoglio enjoyed at that time in Bologna, which was so great that, since there was no one left from that house to rule the state after the death of Annibale, and since the citizens of Bologna had learned that there was in Florence a descendent of the Bentivoglio who, up to then, had been thought to be the son of a blacksmith, they came to fetch him in Florence, and they gave him the rule of their city, which was governed by him until Messer Giovanni came of an age suitable to rule.[1] I conclude, therefore, that a prince must consider conspiracies of little importance if the people are well disposed toward him; but if they are his enemy and they hate him, he must fear everything and everyone.

And well-ordered states and wise princes have diligently considered how not to dissatisfy the nobles and how to satisfy the common people and keep them contented, because this is one of the most important duties of a prince. Among the well-ordered and well-governed kingdoms of our time there is that of France, and in it one finds countless good institutions on which depend the liberty and the security of the King; the first among these is the parlement and its authority.[2] Because he who established that kingdom,[3] knowing the ambition of the nobles and their insolence, judging it necessary to keep a bit in their mouth on one hand, and on the other knowing the hatred, born out of fear, of the common people for them, and wishing to reassure them, he did not want to leave this task specifically to the King, in order to remove from him the burden he might incur from the nobles if he favoured the

---

1 These events took place in 1445. See *Florentine Histories* 6.9–10.
2 The Parlement of Paris was the highest court in France and should not be confused with a legislative body.
3 Louis IX (1214–70) instituted the Parlement of Paris c. 1254.

people and from the people if he favoured the nobles. Therefore, he instituted as judge an arbiter to be the one who would chastise the nobles and favour the people, without burdening the King; this measure could not be better nor more prudent, nor is there a greater reason for the security of the King and the kingdom. From this one can derive another noteworthy consideration: that princes ought to leave the administration of burdensome things to others and keep those that elicit gratitude to themselves. Again, I conclude that a prince should have consideration for the nobles but should not make himself hated by the people.

Considering the life and death of some Roman emperors, it might perhaps appear to many that they represent examples contrary to this opinion of mine, for they find that some led admirable lives and showed great strength of character (*virtù*), yet nevertheless lost their empire or were killed by their people, who had plotted against them. Wishing, therefore, to respond to these objections, I shall discuss the qualities of some emperors, in order to demonstrate that the causes for their ruin are not different from those I have advanced; at the same time, I shall point out what is noteworthy in the exploits of those times for the benefit of those who read about them. It will be sufficient for me to choose all those who succeeded to the empire, from Marcus the philosopher to Maximinus: these were Marcus, Commodus his son, Pertinax, Julianus, Severus, Antoninus Caracalla his son, Macrinus, Heliogabalus, Alexander, and Maximinus.[1] It should first be noted that, while in other principalities one must contend only with the ambition of the nobles and the disobedience of the people, the Roman emperors had a third difficulty: they had to tolerate the cruelty and the rapaciousness of their soldiers. This was so fraught with difficulties that it led many to ruin; because it was difficult to satisfy both the people and the soldiers, since the people loved peace, and for this reason they loved moderate princes, while the soldiers loved warlike princes that were insolent, cruel and rapacious; and they wanted the prince to demonstrate these characteristics against peoples so as to earn a greater pay and give vent to their own rapaciousness and cruelty. As a result, those emperors, who by nature or by training had no great reputation such that would allow them to keep both, the people

---

1 Marcus Aurelius (121–80), Commodus (161–92), Pertinax (129–93), Didius Julianus (137–93), Septimus Severus (145–211), Antoninus Caracalla (188–217), Macrinus (165–218), Heliogabalus (203–22), Alexander Severus (209–35), and Maximinus (173–238).

and the soldiers, in check, came to ruin. Most of them, especially those who came to power as new men, once they became aware of the incompatibility of these two humours, confined themselves to satisfying the soldiers and thought little about injuring the people; this was necessary because princes, unable to avoid being hated by someone, must first of all strive not to be hated by the many; and, when they cannot accomplish this, they must endeavour with diligence and assiduity to avoid being hated by the more powerful groups. Those emperors who came to power as new men and who, therefore, were in need of extraordinary support, relied on the soldiers rather than on the people. Nonetheless, this was either advantageous to them or not, according to whether a prince was able to keep his reputation among them.

For the reasons discussed above, it happened that Marcus, Pertinax and Alexander, all came to a ruinous end, except for Marcus, since they all led a moderate life, were lovers of justice, enemies of cruelty, humane, and kind-hearted. Marcus alone lived and died very honourably, because he succeeded to the empire by hereditary right, and he did not owe it either to the soldiers or to the people; later, because of his many abilities (*virtù*), which made him venerable, he always kept both the one and the other group in check and was never hated or despised. But Pertinax was created emperor against the will of the soldiers who, since they were accustomed to living outrageously under Commodus's command, could not tolerate the honest life that Pertinax wanted to impose on them; therefore, having made himself hated and, since he was old, having added contempt to that hatred, he was overthrown at the beginning of his administration. And here it must be noted that hatred can be acquired both by means of good deeds and of wicked ones; therefore, as I said above,[1] a prince who wants to maintain his state is often compelled not to be good, because when the community you think you need, in order to hold on to power, is corrupt—be they the common people or the soldiers or the nobles—you must indulge its humour and satisfy it; and then good deeds are your enemies. But let us come to Alexander. He was of such goodness that, among the praiseworthy deeds attributed to him, there is this: in the fourteen years he held power in the empire, no one was ever executed by him without a trial; nonetheless, since he was considered effeminate and a man who let himself be controlled by his mother, he came to be despised; the army plotted against him and killed him.

---

1 See chapters 15 and 18.

Discussing now, by contrast, the characteristics of Commodus, Severus, Antoninus Caracalla, and Maximinus, you will find them extremely cruel and rapacious; in order to satisfy their soldiers, these men did not spare any type of damage that could be visited on the people; everyone, except for Severus, had an unfortunate end. For in Severus there was so much ingenuity (*virtù*) that, by keeping the soldiers friendly to him, he was always able to rule happily, even though the people were oppressed by him; because that ingenuity (*virtù*) of his made him so admirable in the eyes of the soldiers and the people that the latter were somehow left astonished and stupefied, and the former reverent and satisfied.

And since the actions of this man, as a new prince, were great, I should like to demonstrate briefly how well he played the part of the fox and the lion, whose nature, as I said above,[1] is necessary for the prince to imitate. Since he knew the indolence of emperor Julianus, he persuaded his army, under his command in Slavonia, that it was appropriate to go to Rome in order to avenge the death of Pertinax, who had been killed by the praetorian soldiers. With this ruse, without revealing his aspirations to the throne, he marched with his army on Rome, and he was in Italy already before they knew of his departure. As soon as he arrived in Rome, the Senate, out of fear, acclaimed him emperor and had Julianus killed. After this beginning, Severus was left with two difficulties if he wanted to rule over the whole state: the first, in Asia, where Niger, in command of the Asiatic armies, had himself acclaimed emperor; the other, in the West, where Albinus was, who also aspired to rule the empire. And because he deemed it dangerous to disclose himself as an enemy of both, he resolved to attack Niger and deceive Albinus; he wrote to Albinus saying that, since the Senate had elected him emperor, he wanted to share that honour with him, and he sent him the title of Caesar and, by decree of the Senate, made him co-emperor; all these things were accepted as true by Albinus. However, once Severus had defeated and killed Niger and brought peace to the East, in the Senate he accused Albinus, hardly grateful for the benefits received from him, of having treacherously attempted to kill him, and that he must punish his ingratitude; afterwards, he attacked him in France and deprived him of both the state and his life. Anyone, therefore, who will diligently examine the actions of this man, will find that he was a very ferocious lion and a very cunning fox, and that he was feared and revered by everyone and by

---

1 See chapter 18.

the armies, but he was not hated; and he will not be surprised if Severus, although a new man, was able to hold such power, since his great reputation always protected him from that hatred that the people could have harboured for him because of his thievery. But Antoninus, his son, was himself a man endowed with many excellent qualities, which made him admirable in the eyes of the people and appreciated by the soldiers, because he was a military man, extremely capable of enduring any kind of hardship, disdainful of any type of delicate food and all luxuries, which made him loved by the armies. Nevertheless, his ferociousness and his cruelty were such and so unprecedented—since, after countless individual murders, he had killed most of the people in Rome and all of them in Alexandria—that he came to be hated greatly all over the world. He began to be feared also by those around him, so that he was killed by a centurion who was a member of his army. Here it must be noted that deaths such as this, which result from the deliberation made by an obstinate man, are unavoidable for princes, because anyone who is not afraid of death can harm them; however, the prince may well fear them less, because these instances are very rare; he must only take care of not inflicting a grave injury to anyone around him who is in his service and who assists him in ruling the principality—which Antoninus did, since he had dishonoured and humiliated that centurion by killing one of his brothers, and threatened him every day, yet nonetheless kept the man as a bodyguard, which was a bold decision to make and liable to bring him to ruin, as in fact it did.

But let us come to Commodus, who might have held the empire with great ease, having inherited it by birthright, since he was the son of Marcus; it would have been enough for him to follow in his father's footsteps, and both the people and the soldiers would have been satisfied; but being of a cruel and bestial nature, in order to be able to unleash his rapaciousness on the people, he resorted to indulging the armies and allowing them any abuse. On the other hand, not caring about his dignity, by often descending into the arenas to fight with the gladiators and doing other despicable acts unworthy of his imperial majesty, he became contemptible in the eyes of the soldiers; and being hated on the one hand, and despised on the other, he was conspired against and killed.

There remains to describe the characteristics of Maximinus. He was a very warlike man; and since the armies were extremely disturbed by the spinelessness of Alexander, whom I discussed above, after Alexander's death, they elected him to the empire, which he did not hold for very long, since two things made him hateful and contemptible: the first, his very lowly birth, and his having herded sheep in Thrace, which was very well known everywhere and considered undignified in the eyes of everyone; the other, his reputation for being a very cruel man, which he earned when, at the beginning of his principality, having deferred going to Rome and taking possession of his imperial throne, he had perpetrated many cruelties through his prefects in Rome and in every other part of the empire. Therefore, the whole world was indignant at his lowly birth and despised the dread of his cruelty; first Africa rebelled, then the Senate with all the people of Rome, and Italy as a whole conspired against him; these were joined by his own army which, laying siege to Aquileia and, finding it difficult to take the city, exasperated by his cruelty, and fearing him less once they saw just how many enemies he had, killed him.

I do not wish to discuss either Heliogabalus, or Macrinus, or Julianus, who, for being thoroughly contemptible, were quickly eliminated, but I will come to the conclusion of this analysis; I say that the princes of our own time, in the course of their rule, feel far less the difficulty of satisfying their soldiers to an extraordinary degree because, although they have to give them some consideration, this is quickly done, since none of these princes has armies inextricably joined to the government and the administration of their provinces, as were the armies of the Roman Empire. Therefore, if it was necessary then to satisfy the soldiers more than the people, it was because the soldiers were more powerful than the people; now it is necessary, for all princes except for the Turk[1] and the Sultan,[2] to satisfy the people more than the soldiers, because the people are more powerful. I make an exception for the Turk, for he always maintains around him twelve thousand foot soldiers and fifteen thousand cavalrymen, on whom depend the security and the strength of his kingdom; and it is necessary that, subordinating all other considerations to this one, they were kept friendly to that ruler. Likewise, since the kingdom of the Sultan is completely in the hands of the soldiers, it is fitting that he, without consideration for the people, keep the soldiers friendly to him. And you must note that the Sultan's state is different from all other principalities, since it is similar to the Christian Pontificate, which cannot be called either a hereditary principality or a new principality, because the sons of the old prince are not its heirs

---

1   Selim I (1470–1520), sultan of the Ottoman Turks.
2   Al-Ashraf Qansuh al-Ghawri (1441–1516), sultan of the Mamluks in Egypt.

and its rulers, but he who is elected to that rank by those with the authority to do so; and since this is an ancient system, it cannot be called a new principality, because none of the difficulties are found in the new principality; and although the prince is new, the organization of the state is old and set up to receive him as if he were their hereditary ruler.

But let us return to our subject. I say, therefore, that anyone who considers the above analysis will see that either hatred or contempt is the reason for the downfall of the emperors mentioned earlier, and will also know how it came about that, although some of them acted in one way and some the opposite way, in both ways one of them had a happy end and the others an unhappy one; because it was useless and damaging for Pertinax and Alexander, who were new princes, to want to imitate Marcus, who came to the principality by hereditary right, it was similarly dangerous for Caracalla, Commodus and Maximinus to imitate Severus, because they did not have enough ingenuity (*virtù*) to follow in his footsteps. Therefore, a new prince in a new principality cannot imitate Marcus's actions, nor is it necessary to follow those of Severus; rather, he must take from Severus those parts that are necessary to him in order to lay the foundations of his state, and from Marcus those that are useful and glorious in order to maintain a state that is already established and stable.

CHAPTER 20

On Whether Fortresses and Many Other Things Used by Princes Every Day Are Useful or Useless

In order to have a secure hold on the state, some princes have disarmed their subjects, some have kept the conquered lands divided into factions; others have fomented enmities against themselves, some others have turned to winning over those who were suspect at the beginning of their rule; some have built fortresses, some have demolished and destroyed them. And although one cannot provide a final judgement on these things, unless one considers the particulars of those states where such deliberations must be taken, nonetheless I will speak in generalities as the subject allows.

It has never happened that a new prince disarmed his subjects; on the contrary, when he has found them unarmed, he has always armed them, because, once you arm them, those arms become yours, those whom you suspect become loyal to you, and those who were loyal remain so and from being mere subjects they become your partisans; and since not all your subjects can be armed, once you have given benefits to those you arm, the others can be dealt with more securely, and the former recognize that difference in treatment and become obliged to you, while the latter excuse you, judging it necessary that those who are in more danger and who have more obligations should be more rewarded. But when you disarm them, you begin to offend them and show that you have no trust in them, because you think of them either as cowards or as untrustworthy, and either one or the other of these opinions arouses hatred against you; and because you cannot remain disarmed, you are forced to turn to mercenary soldiers, who have the characteristics described above; even if they were good, they would not be sufficient to defend you against powerful enemies and distrusted subjects. Therefore, as I have said above,[1] a new prince in a new principality has always instituted an army; history is full of such examples. But when a prince acquires a new state that is added as a member to his old one, then it is necessary for him to disarm that state, except for those men who have been his partisans in acquiring it; and even these, with time and opportunity, should be rendered soft and effeminate; and things should be organized in such a way that all the arms in your state be given to your own men that live close to you in your old state.

Our forefathers and those who were esteemed wise used to say that it was necessary to hold Pistoia by factions and Pisa by fortresses; and for this reason, they fomented factions in some of their subject cities, in order to hold on to them more easily. This might have worked at the time when in Italy there was, to a certain extent, a balance of power,[2] but I do not think it can be given as a precept today, because I do not think that factions ever do any good; on the contrary, when the enemy approaches, it is inevitable that divided cities are quickly lost, because the weaker faction will ally itself with the external forces, and the other will be unable to resist.

And the Venetians, moved, as I believe, by the reasons described above, fomented the Guelph and Ghibelline factions in their subject cities,[3] and although they never allowed them to

1 See chapter 12.
2 The Peace of Lodi, the period of relative peace that spanned 1454–94 on the Italian peninsula, bought about largely by the foreign policy of Lorenzo the Magnificent.
3 During the time Machiavelli was writing, the Guelphs supported the French king and the Ghibellines supported the Holy Roman Emperor Maximilian I (r. 1508–19).

come to bloodshed, nevertheless they fomented these conflicts, so that, taken by their quarrels, those citizens would not unite against them. This, as was seen, afterwards did not turn out to their advantage because, having been routed at Vailà, immediately one of those factions took courage and seized from them the entire state of Lombardy. Methods such as these denote weakness in the prince, for in a strong principality such divisions will never be permitted, because they are useful only in peacetime when, by their means, it is easier to handle your subjects; but when war comes, such a policy shows its fallacy.

There is no doubt that princes become great when they overcome the difficulties and obstacles that confront them; and for this reason, Fortune, especially when she wishes to make a new prince great—since he is in greater need of acquiring a reputation than a hereditary prince is—creates enemies for him and makes them take action against him, so that he might have the opportunity to overcome them and climb higher on the ladder his enemies have handed him. Therefore, many judge that a wise prince must, whenever he has the opportunity, cunningly foment some enmity against himself, so that, having suppressed it, his greatness will increase.

Many princes, and especially those who are new, have found more loyalty and more usefulness in those men who at the beginning of their rule were held suspect than in those who at the beginning were trusted. Pandolfo Petrucci, Prince of Siena,[1] ruled his state more with the assistance of those he had considered suspect than with others. But one cannot speak of this matter in generalities, because it varies according to the case. I shall only say this: that those men, who at the beginning of a principality have been enemies, if they are of the kind that need support to maintain their position, can always be won over by the prince with the greatest ease; and they are the more compelled to serve him loyally the more they know how necessary it is for them to erase with their actions the sinister opinion he had of them previously.[2] Therefore, the prince always derives greater usefulness from them than from those who, serving him with too much security, neglect his affairs.

And since the subject requires it, I do not wish to leave out a reminder for princes, who have recently conquered a state by

---

1 Pandolfo Petrucci (1450–1512).
2 Regardless of whether this is an intentional reference to himself, this was the situation Machiavelli found himself in after the reinstatement of the Medici in Florence in 1512.

means of internal support from its citizens: that they should consider carefully the reason that might have moved those who supported him to support him; and if it is not because of a natural affection toward him but only because those supporters were not satisfied with that state, he will be able to keep them friendly to him only with hard work and great difficulties, because it is impossible that he will be able to satisfy them. And on examining well the reason for this, with those examples that can be drawn from ancient and modern history, we will see that it is far easier for him to win over as friends those men who were satisfied with the preceding state and were, therefore, his enemies, than those who, being unsatisfied with it, became his friends and supported his occupation of it.

In order to hold on more securely to their state, the custom among princes has been to build fortresses that become as a bridle and a bit for those who would dare rebel against them, and as a safe refuge for them from a sudden attack. I praise this method, because it has been used since ancient times; nonetheless, Messer Niccolò Vitelli,[1] in our own time, was seen to demolish two fortresses in Città di Castello in order to hold on to that state; Guido Ubaldo, Duke of Urbino, having returned to his rule after Cesare Borgia had driven him out,[2] completely destroyed all the fortresses in that state, and judged that, without them, it would be more difficult to lose it a second time; the Bentivoglio, upon returning to Bologna, adopted similar measures.[3] Fortresses, then, are useful or not, according to the times, and if they are beneficial to you in one way, in another they do you harm. And one could argue this point in this manner: that prince who fears his own people more than foreigners should build fortresses, but that prince who fears foreigners more than his own people should do without them. The castle in Milan, built by Francesco Sforza, has done and will do more damage to the Sforza family than any other disorder in that state. However, the best fortress there is consists of not being hated by the people, because, although you may have them, if the people harbour hate for you, fortresses do not save

---

1   Niccolò Vitelli (1414–86). Vitelli was forced to abandon his lands by Cardinal Giuliano della Rovere in 1474, but he retook them in 1482 and promptly destroyed the fortresses.
2   Guidobaldo da Montefeltro (1472–1508) was driven out of Urbino in 1502 and returned in 1503.
3   The Bentivoglio had been forced out of Bologna by the forces of Julius II in 1506. They returned in 1511 and destroyed a fortress Julius II had built in their absence.

you, for the people will never want for foreigners to assist them once they have taken up arms against you. In our own day, we do not see that they have been of profit to any prince, except for the Countess of Forlì, when Count Girolamo, her husband, was killed, because by means of a fortress she was able to escape the attack from her people, wait for the assistance of Milan, and regain the state; and times were such then that foreigners could not assist her people; but later they were of little avail to her, as well, when Cesare Borgia attacked her and the people, her enemy, joined with the foreigner.[1] Therefore, both then and earlier, it would have been safer for her not to have been hated by the people than to have had fortresses. Having made all these considerations, I shall praise both he who builds fortresses and he who does not, but I shall blame anyone who, putting his trust in fortresses, cares little about being hated by the people.

CHAPTER 21

How a Prince Should Act to Acquire Esteem

Nothing makes a prince more esteemed than great undertakings and proving himself in rare and exemplary deeds. We have, in our own time, Ferdinand of Aragon, the present King of Spain. He can almost be called a new prince, because from being a weak King he has become, through fame and glory, the first King of Christendom. And if you consider his deeds, you will find them all very great and some extraordinary. At the beginning of his reign, he attacked Granada,[2] and on that campaign he laid the foundations of his state: first of all, he carried out that campaign undisturbed and without fear of interference, for with it he kept the minds of the barons of Castille occupied; they, concentrating on that war, did not think of making innovations; in the meantime, he acquired reputation and power over them without their realizing it; he was able to sustain his armies with the money of the Church and the people, and with that long war was able to lay foundations for his own army, which has since brought him honour. Besides this, in order to be able to undertake ever greater

1 See *Discourses on Livy* 3.6 and *Florentine Histories* 8.34. The two instances of Caterina Sforza's reliance on the fortress occurred in 1488 and December 1499 through January 1500.
2 A Muslim region in southern Spain, subjugated by Ferdinand in 1492.

enterprises, always making use of religion, he resorted to a pious cruelty, chasing away and ridding his kingdom of the Marranos;[1] nor could there be a more wretched and rarer example than this. Under the same cloak of religion, he attacked Africa, undertook the campaign in Italy,[2] has recently attacked France;[3] and in this manner he has always carried out and hatched great things, which have always kept the minds of his subjects in suspense and in awe of him, and engrossed in their outcome. And these actions of his originated one from another, so that between them there was never any time for men to work calmly against him.

It is also very useful for a prince to give some rare examples of his exceptional capabilities in governing the internal affairs of his state, such as the ones that are told about Messer Bernabò of Milan;[4] when the occasion arises that someone in public life performs an extraordinary act, be it good or evil, one should reward or punish him in a way that will be discussed at length. Above all, a prince must strive, in every action, to give to himself the reputation of a great man and an outstanding mind.

A prince also wins esteem when he is a true friend or a true enemy, that is, when without any hesitation, he comes forward to support one prince against another; this decision is always more useful than remaining neutral, because, if two of your neighbouring powers come to blows, either they are of the kind that, if one of them wins, you have reason to fear the victor, or they are not; in either of these two cases, it is always more useful to declare your allegiance and wage open war; because, in the first case, if you do not declare yourself, you will always fall prey to the victor, to the pleasure and the satisfaction of the vanquished, and you will have no reason nor anything to defend you or give you refuge; because whoever wins does not want suspect friends who may not help him in times of adversity; and whoever loses does not give you refuge because you did not want, arms in hand, to share his lot with him. Antiochus went to Greece, summoned there by the Aetolians,[5] to drive out the Romans; Antiochus sent envoys to the

---

1 "Marranos" was a slur referring to Jews and Muslims who chose to flee Spain to avoid forcible conversion to Christianity.
2 The conquest of the Kingdom of Naples in 1503.
3 Ferdinand was part of the Holy League formed by Julius II in 1510 to drive the French out of Italy. Ferdinand joined later and engaged the French in 1512.
4 Bernabò Visconti (1323–85), duke of Milan, well known for his effective use of cruelties.
5 See chapter 3.

Achaeans, who were friends of the Romans, to convince them to remain neutral; on the other hand, the Romans tried to persuade them to take up arms on their behalf. The matter came for deliberation before the council of the Achaeans, where Antiochus's envoy sought to convince them to remain neutral, to which the Roman envoy replied: "As for what these people tell you, not to get involved in the war, nothing is more contrary to your interests: without earning gratitude, without dignity, you will be the prize of the victor."[1] And it will always happen that he who is not your friend will demand your neutrality, while he who is your friend will require that you declare yourself by taking up arms; and indecisive princes, in order to avoid imminent dangers, follow the way of neutrality most of the time and are ruined by it most of the time. But when a prince courageously declares himself in support of one side, if the one with whom you ally yourself wins, although he might be powerful, and you are left at his mercy, he has an obligation to you and a bond of friendship is established, and men are never so dishonest as to oppress you with so great an example of ingratitude. Furthermore, victories are never so definitive that the victor can show no consideration, especially as it pertains to appearing just; but if the one with whom you ally yourself loses, he gives you refuge and he helps you while he can, and you become companions in a cause that may rise again.

In the second case, when those who fight are of the kind that you have nothing to fear from the victor, it is even more prudent for you to join a side, because you cause the downfall of a prince with the help of someone who, if he were wise, should be saving him; and should he win, he is left at your mercy, and it is impossible that he will not win with your assistance. It is to be noted here that a prince must be careful not to join a more powerful prince than himself in order to attack others, unless necessity compels him, as was said above, because, if you win, you are his prisoner, and princes must avoid as much as possible being left at the mercy of others. The Venetians joined forces with France against the Duke of Milan,[2] while they could have avoided such an alliance, which resulted in their ruin. But when an alliance cannot be avoided, as happened to the Florentines when the Pope and Spain went with their armies to attack Lombardy,[3] then the

---

1 Quoted with liberties from Livy, *History of Rome* 35.49.
2 The Venetians and France attacked Ludovico (il Moro) Sforza, duke of Milan, in 1499.
3 In 1512.

prince should join in, for the reasons given above. Nor should any state think that it can always make safe decisions; on the contrary, it should think that all decisions are dubious, because this is found in the order of things: one cannot ever try to avoid one difficulty without incurring another; but prudence consists in knowing the nature of the difficulties and in choosing the lesser of the two evils.

A prince must also show himself to be a lover of talent (*virtù*), giving hospitality to men of genius (*uomini virtuosi*) and honouring those who excel in their field. Moreover, he has to encourage his citizens to follow their pursuits in tranquility, in commerce or agriculture or any other occupation men may have; and he must see to it that a man is not afraid of improving his possessions for fear that they will be taken away from him, and another man is not afraid of starting a trade for fear of taxes; he must offer awards for anyone who wants to do these things and whoever comes up with ways of improving his city or his state. In addition, at the appropriate times of the year, he must keep his people occupied with festivities and spectacles; and because every city is divided into guilds or clans, he has to take these communities into consideration, meet with them once in a while, setting examples of humanity and munificence with his actions, always, nonetheless, maintaining the majesty of his dignity, because this cannot ever be lacking on any occasion.

CHAPTER 22

On the Private Advisers of Princes

To a prince, the choice of advisers is of no little importance; they may be good or not according to the prudence of the prince. And the first evaluation that is made of a prince and his intelligence is to observe the men that surround him; and when they are capable and loyal, he can always be considered wise, because he has recognized their capabilities and kept their loyalty; but when they are otherwise, one can form a bad opinion of him, because his first error is in this choice. There was no one who knew Messer Antonio of Venafro[1] as adviser to Pandolfo Petrucci, Prince of Siena, who did not judge Pandolfo himself as a most worthy man, because he had Antonio as his adviser. For there are three kinds

---

1 Messer Antonio Giordani da Venafro (1459–1530), a renowned lawyer.

of brains: one understands on its own, another understands what others explain, the third does not understand either on its own or through others; the first is most excellent, the second is excellent, the third is harmful. It follows, therefore, of necessity, that if Pandolfo were not in the first group, he must have been in the second; because every time that someone has the discernment to recognize the good and the evil that another does and says, even though he may have no innate ability to discern them on his own, he can recognize the good deeds and the bad ones of his adviser, and he praises the former and corrects the latter, and his adviser cannot hope to deceive him, and maintains his good behaviour. But as to how a prince can judge his adviser, there is a way that never fails: when you notice that an adviser thinks more of himself than of you, and that in every action he looks for his own self-interest, such a man as this will never be a good adviser, you will never be able to trust him. For he who has the state of a prince in his hands must never think of himself, but always of his prince, and must never think of anything that does not concern him; on the other hand, in order to keep him good, the prince must think of his adviser—by honouring him, making him wealthy, making him indebted to him, sharing with him honours and responsibilities—so that the adviser realizes that he cannot be without the prince, and the many honours will not make him wish for more, the many riches will not make him wish for more, the many responsibilities will make him fearful of changes. When, therefore, advisers and princes are of such a nature when they interact, they can trust each other; when they are otherwise, the end result will always be harmful both for one and the other.

CHAPTER 23

On How to Avoid Flatterers

I do not wish to leave out an important point and an error from which princes defend themselves with difficulty if they are not very prudent and if they do not make good choices; and these are the flatterers, who fill the courts; because men are so pleased with their own affairs and so deceive themselves when they are concerned, that they defend themselves from this plague with difficulty. And if they wish to defend themselves from it, they run the risk of becoming contemptible, because there is no way of guarding against flattery other than making men understand that they do not offend you when they tell you the truth; but when everyone can tell you the truth, you lose their respect. Therefore, a prudent prince should adopt a third way, choosing wise men in his state and to them alone give permission to speak the truth to him, and only about subjects he raises, and not anything else; but he must consult with them on everything, and listen to their opinions, and afterwards decide by himself in his own way. And in these counsels and with each adviser he should conduct himself in such a way that each of them will know that the more freely he speaks, the more consideration he will be given; outside of these, he should not want to hear from anybody, he should act on the matter that has been deliberated and be steadfast in his decisions. Anyone who does otherwise, is either ruined by flatterers or changes his mind often because of the variety of opinions, which results in losing respect.

I wish to quote a modern example in connection with this. Father Luca,[1] at the service of Maximilian, the present Emperor, speaking of His Majesty, said that he did not seek anybody's advice, yet he never did anything his way; this came about because he did the opposite of what was said above; for the Emperor is a secretive man, does not reveal his plans to anyone, does not consider others' opinions; however, as he begins to put his plans into effect and they come to be known and uncovered, they begin to be opposed by those he keeps around him, and he, being easily influenced, is dissuaded from carrying them out. It follows that those things he accomplishes one day, he destroys the next, no one understands what he wants or proposes to do, and one cannot rely on his deliberations.

A prince, therefore, must always seek advice, but only when he wishes to, not when others want him to; on the contrary, he should discourage everyone from offering advice on anything unless he asks; but he must be a great questioner and then, on the matters he raises, a patient listener to the truth; indeed, if he learns that anyone, for any reason, has not told him the truth, he should get angry. And since many think that any prince, who establishes a reputation for himself as a prudent man, is considered to be so not because of his nature but because of the good advisers he has around him, without doubt they are mistaken; for this is a general rule that never fails: a prince who is not wise in his own right cannot be counselled well, unless by chance he has put his trust in one adviser alone who governs him in everything,

---

1 Luca Rinaldi, bishop of Trieste (1459–1519).

and is a most prudent man; in this case, it could very well be, but it would not last long, because that governor of his would, in a short time, take his state from him. But seeking advice from more than one man, a prince who is not wise will never get consistent advice, and he, by himself, would never know how to combine them; each of his advisers will think of his own interests; he will not know either how to correct them or understand them; and one cannot find advisers who behave otherwise, because men will always turn out wicked for you, unless some necessity makes them good. Therefore, the conclusion is that good advice, wherever it may come from, must arise from the prudence of the prince, and not the prudence of the prince from good advice.

CHAPTER 24

Why the Princes of Italy Lost Their States

All that has been written above, if prudently followed, will make a new prince appear to be a well-established prince and will immediately render him more secure and stable in his rule than if he had been in power for many generations; for a new prince is more closely observed in his actions than a hereditary one, and when his deeds are recognized as ingenious (*virtuose*), they win men over to his side and bind them tightly to him much more than ancient blood can do; because men are much more taken by present matters than by past ones and when they find good in the present ones, they enjoy them and look no further; in fact, they will take up any defence for the new prince, provided he is not lacking in all his other duties; and so he will double his glory, for having brought into being a principality and for having adorned it by fortifying it with good laws, good armies, and good examples; just as the other will double his shame, for, having been born a prince, he lost his status for his lack of prudence.

And if one will consider those rulers who, in Italy, have lost their states in our time, such as the King of Naples,[1] the Duke of Milan,[2] and others, one will find in them, first, a common defect as it pertains to arms, for the reasons discussed above; then, one will see that some of them either had the people as their enemy, or, if they had the people as their friends, they could not secure

---

1 Frederick I of Aragon (r. 1496–1501).
2 Ludovico (il Moro) Sforza.

themselves against the nobles; for without these defects, states that are strong enough to put an army in the field are not lost. Philip of Macedonia—not the father of Alexander but the one who was defeated by Titus Quintius—did not have much of a state compared to the greatness of Rome and of Greece that attacked him; nonetheless, because he was a military man who knew how to win the favour of the people and secure himself against the nobles, he sustained the war against them for many years, and if in the end he lost control of a few cities, yet he was able to keep his kingdom. Therefore, these princes of ours, who had been established in their principality for many years, if they lost it later, should not blame Fortune but their own indolence and lack of initiative, for in quiet times they never thought that things could change (it is a common defect of men not to anticipate a storm in good weather), and when times of adversity came upon them, they thought of fleeing and not of defending themselves; and they hoped that the people, irritated by the insolence of the of the victors, would call them back. This decision, when all others are impossible, is a good one, but it is indeed bad to have neglected all other remedies for this; one would never want to fall down because he believes that he will find someone to pick him up; this either does not happen, or, if it happens, it does not afford you security, because that is a dishonourable defence since it is not dependent on you alone; and only those defences are good, are certain, are long-lasting that depend on yourself and on your ingenuity (*virtù*).

CHAPTER 25

How Much Fortune Can Affect Human Affairs and How We Can Resist It

It is not unknown to me that many have held and still hold the opinion that the affairs of this world are governed by Fortune and by God in such a manner that men, with all their prudence, cannot keep them under their control, indeed have no remedy at all for them; and for this reason, they might judge that one need not sweat much over matters, but let oneself be governed by fate. This opinion has been accepted more in our own times because of the tumultuous variability in circumstances that we have seen and see every day, beyond all human conjecture. Thinking of this, I have sometimes convinced myself of their opinion somewhat; nevertheless, so as not to extinguish our free will, I judge it to be possibly true that Fortune is the arbiter of half of our actions, but that she also leaves the other half, or just about, to be governed by us. And I compare her to one of these ruinous rivers that, when they become enraged, flood the plains, knock down trees and buildings, carrying off earth from this spot and depositing it in another; everyone flees before them, everyone yields to their violence, unable to oppose them in any way. And although they are like that, it is not to say that men cannot, in times of calm, take precautions, with embankments and dikes, so that when they rise again, either they are channelled off or their violence is neither so unrestrained nor so destructive. The same happens with Fortune, which shows her power where there is no ingenuity (*virtù*) intended to resist her, and she turns her force there where she knows that dikes and embankments were not erected to restrain her. And if you consider Italy, which is the seat of these calamities and the one that put them in motion, you will see she is a land without embankments and no protection at all, whereas, if she were protected by suitably sagacious means (*virtù*), like Germany, Spain and France, either this flood would not have produced the great damages that it has, or it would not have befallen us at all.

And I want this to be sufficient discussion about opposing Fortune in general terms. But restricting myself more to particulars, I say that one sees a prince prosper today and come to ruin tomorrow without ever having seen him change his nature or any of his character traits. This I believe derives firstly from the reasons debated at length earlier, that is, that the prince who relies completely on Fortune comes to ruin as that Fortune changes. I also believe that the prince whose modes of action are in tune with the nature of his times will prosper, and similarly the prince whose actions are discordant with the times will fail, for one sees that, in the affairs that drive them to the goal that each has before him—that is, glory and wealth—men proceed in different manners: one with caution, the other with impetuousness, one with violence, the other with craftiness, one with patience, the other with its opposite; and each may attain their goal in these different manners. One can further see two cautious men, one reaching his goal, the other not; and similarly, one can see two men prosper equally who have different behaviours, one being cautious and the other impetuous. This arises from nothing else but the nature of the times that may or may not conform with their course of action. From this follows what I said, that two men operating differently may achieve the same result, while two operating in the same manner, may not, one achieving his goal, the other not. On this also depends the variability of what is effective or not: for, if a man governs himself with caution and patience, and the times and circumstances turn in such a way that his conduct is effective, he will prosper; but if the times and circumstances change, he will come to ruin, because he will not change his modes of action. Nor may one find a man so prudent as to know how to adapt to this, both because one cannot deviate from that to which nature inclines him, but also because, having always flourished by following one path, he cannot be persuaded to depart from it. And therefore, the cautious man, when it is time to become impetuous, does not know how; hence, he comes to ruin. For, if he could change his nature with the times and the circumstances, his fortune would not change. Pope Julius II proceeded impetuously in all his affairs and found both the times and the circumstances so suitable to his course of action that he always achieved a successful outcome. Consider his first campaign against Bologna,[1] when Messer Giovanni Bentivoglio was still alive. The Venetians were not happy about it, nor was the King of Spain; Julius held discussions on that same campaign with France. Nevertheless, with his usual ferocity and impetuousness, he personally set out on that expedition. Such a move made Spain and the Venetians hesitate and kept them still, the latter out of fear, the former out of the desire to recapture the entire Kingdom of Naples; on the other hand, Julius dragged into it the King of France who, having seen Julius make his move and desiring his friendship in order to bring down the Venetians, judged that he could not deny him his troops without openly offending him. Julius, therefore, with his impetuous move, accomplished what no other pontiff, with all his human prudence, would have ever accomplished, because had he waited to leave Rome with firm conclusions and all affairs in order, as any other pontiff would have done, he would have never succeeded, since the King of France would have had a thousand excuses and the others would have instilled in him a thousand fears. I wish to leave aside his other deeds, which were all similar to this and all brought him success; the brevity of his life spared him from experiencing the opposite, because, if times had changed, requiring cautious ways, his ruin would have followed, nor would he have ever deviated from the ways to which he was inclined by nature.[2]

---

1 Julius II ousted the Bentivoglio family that ruled Bologna in 1506. See *Discourses on Livy* 1.27, where Machiavelli describes how risky Julius's actions were.

2 See *Discourses on Livy* 3.9.

I conclude, therefore, that since Fortune changes and men persevere stubbornly in their ways, men are successful when the two act in harmony and unsuccessful when the two are discordant. And I judge this to be true, that it is better to be impetuous than cautious, because Fortune is a woman, and it is necessary, in order to keep her down, to beat her and strike her. It is clear that she lets herself be won over more by impetuous men than by men who proceed coldly; and thus, as a woman, she is the friend of young men, for they are less cautious, more ferocious and command her more boldly.

CHAPTER 26

Exhortation to Liberate Italy from the Barbarians

Having considered, therefore, all of the things discussed above and thinking to myself about whether at the present in Italy the time is ripe to honour a new prince, and whether there is matter likely to give the opportunity, to a prudent and sagacious (*virtuoso*) prince, to introduce into it a form that would bring him honour and well-being to the community of men living in Italy, it seems to me that so many factors concur in favour of a new prince, that I know of no other time more appropriate than the present. And if, as I said,[1] it was necessary that the people of Israel should be enslaved in Egypt so as to see the worth (*virtù*) of Moses; that the Persians should be oppressed by the Medes so as to know the greatness of spirit in Cyrus; that the Athenians should be scattered so as to demonstrate the excellence of Theseus; likewise, at the present moment, so as to realize the genius (*virtù*) of an Italian spirit, it was necessary that Italy be reduced to her present conditions and that she be more enslaved than the Hebrews, more oppressed than the Persians, more scattered than the Athenians, without a leader, without order, beaten, despoiled, torn apart, overrun; she had to have endured every sort of calamity. And although before now a glimmer of hope had appeared in a man,[2] so that it was possible to think that he might have been ordained by God for Italy's redemption, nevertheless we have seen later how, at the very height of his career, he was refused by Fortune; so now, left lifeless, she awaits he who might heal her wounds and might put an

---

1 See chapter 6.
2 Cesare Borgia.

end to the pillaging in Lombardy, the extortions in the Kingdom of Naples and in Tuscany, and cure her of those sores that have been festering for a long time. Behold how she prays God to send her someone that might redeem her from these barbarous cruelties and insults. Behold how she is completely eager and willing to rally to a banner if only there be someone to raise it.

Nor can one see at the present what more she could hope for other than that your illustrious House, endowed with fortune and power (*virtù*), favoured by God and by the Church, of which it is now prince,[1] place itself at the head of her redemption; this will not be very difficult to do, if you keep before you the actions and lives of those named above; and although those men are extraordinary and marvelous, yet nevertheless they were men; and each one of them had less of an opportunity than the present one, because their undertakings were not more just than this, nor were they easier, nor was God more their friend than He is yours. Here is a great and just cause, for "war is just for those who find it necessary and sacred are the arms if there is no hope but in arms."[2] Here there is the greatest willingness, nor can there be great difficulty where there is great willingness, if only your House would seek inspiration from those men I have proposed as your models. Besides this, here we see extraordinary, unparalleled wonders performed by God: the sea has been opened, a cloud has shown you the way, the rock has gushed forth water, manna has rained here[3]—everything has converged for your greatness. The rest you must do yourself. God does not wish to do everything Himself in order not to take free will away from us and part of that glory that belongs to us.

It is no wonder that none of the Italians mentioned before was able to do what it is hoped your illustrious House will do, and if in so many revolutions in Italy and in so many campaigns it always appears that military prowess (*virtù*) is dead, this is because her ancient political orders were not good and there has been no one able to institute new ones; and nothing brings as much honour to a new man on the rise as new laws and new orders instituted by him. When these things are well founded and have greatness in them, they make him revered and admirable. And Italy has no lack

---

1 Giovanni de' Medici ruled the Church as Pope Leo X from 1513 to 1521.

2 Quoted with liberties from Livy, *History of Rome* 9.1.

3 Miracles that aided the Hebrew people in their flight from oppression in Egypt, as recounted in Exodus 14:21, 13:21, 17:6, and 16:14–15.

of matter to shape into any form; here there is great ability (*virtù*) in the limbs, if it were not lacking in the heads; consider duels and combats involving just a few men and see how much superior Italians are in strength, dexterity, and ingenuity; but when it comes to armies, they are outdone; all this comes from the ineffectiveness of her leaders; for those who know, are not followed; and each one of them thinks he knows, but so far no one has known how to emerge above the rest, either because of wits (*virtù*) or Fortune, and have the others yield to him. From this it follows that during so much time and in so many wars fought in the last twenty years, when an army was made up completely of Italians, it always had a poor showing. As proof of this, there is Taro, then Alexandria, Capua, Genoa, Vailà, Bologna, and Mestri.[1]

Therefore, if your illustrious House wishes to follow those excellent men who redeemed their lands, before all else it is necessary, as the true foundation of every undertaking, to provide yourself with your own army, because you could not have more loyal, truer or better soldiers; and although each one of them is brave in his own right, all united they will become better, when they will find themselves under the command of their prince and honoured and gratified by him. It is necessary, then, to prepare yourself with such an army in order to be able to defend yourself with Italian strength (*virtù*); and although Swiss and Spanish infantry may be considered terrifying, nevertheless there is a defect in both, so that a third army could not only oppose them but be confident that they would overcome them. Because the Spaniards cannot withstand an attack by the cavalry, and the Swiss end up fearing foot soldiers when they find them as determined in combat as they themselves are. Therefore, experience has shown and will show that the Spaniards cannot withstand French cavalry, and the Swiss are ruined by Spanish infantry. And although we have not seen a complete instance of this last situation, we have nevertheless seen some evidence of it in the battle of Ravenna,[2] when the Spanish infantrymen clashed with German battalions, who follow the same order as the Swiss. There the Spanish soldiers, with their agile bodies and the aid of their bucklers, got in under the pikes of the Germans and were safe to inflict damage on them, without the Germans' having any remedy against them; and if it had not been for the charge of the cavalry, the Spaniards would have destroyed

---

1 Italian forces lost these battles in 1495, 1499, 1501, 1507, 1509, 1511, and 1513, respectively.
2 11 April 1512. See chapter 13.

them all. It is possible, then, having understood the defects of both kinds of troops, to institute a new type that could withstand the cavalry and not fear the infantry; this will be brought about by the choice of arms and a change in the disposition of the troops. And these are things that, when first introduced, give reputation and greatness to a new prince.

Therefore, this is an opportunity that cannot be passed over, so that Italy might behold her redeemer at last. Nor can I fully express with what love he would be received in those provinces that have suffered from the floods of foreigners invading them; with what thirst for vengeance, with what obstinate loyalty, with what devotion, with what tears! What doors would be closed to him? Which people would deny him obedience? What jealousy would oppose him? What Italian would deny him homage? The stench of this barbarous dominion is unbearable to everyone. May your illustrious House, therefore, take on this task with that courage and that hope distinctive of just causes, so that under your banner this country may be ennobled and under your auspices those words of Petrarch may come true:

> Valour against fury
> Will take up arms, and cut short the battle,
> For ancient courage
> In Italian hearts is not yet dead.[1]

---

1 Petrarch, *Italia Mia*, lines 93–96.

Appendix A: Selections from Discourses on Livy[1]

[Like *The Prince*, the *Discourses on Livy* was published posthumously, in 1531, a year before *The Prince*. At present, scholars do not know definitively when the *Discourses* was written, although Machiavelli alludes to his work on republics in chapter 2 of *The Prince*, suggesting that he was working in some capacity on the two manuscripts simultaneously. There is general consensus that the *Discourses* was written between 1513 and 1519, and certainly the book was completed after the presentation of *The Prince* in 1515.

In contrast to *The Prince*, which was dedicated to Lorenzo de' Medici, the *Discourses on the First Ten Books of Titus Livy* is dedicated to Zanobi Buondelmonti and Cosimo Rucellai, friends of Machiavelli from the humanist gatherings in the Orti Oricellari gardens, whom he lamented are not princes but deserve to be. The choice of dedication is in keeping with the subject matter; whereas *The Prince*, a monograph on princely rule, was dedicated to the newly minted ruler of Florence, Lorenzo de' Medici, the *Discourses on Livy*, a treatise on republics, is dedicated to two private citizens of Florence.

Despite being devoted to the theme of republics, there is much overlap between the two texts. Overlap does not mean repetition, however, and when Machiavelli revisits themes such as the ruler's contest with Fortune, how to make a state endure, and his analysis of religion and critique of Christianity, these themes are explored more deeply and expanded upon in the *Discourses on Livy*. Often, there is a different tone to these themes as well, undoubtedly due to the evolution of Machiavelli's thought but also likely the result of an awareness on the part of Machiavelli as to who his initial audiences were. For example, his account of the ruler's relationship with Fortune is more pessimistic in the *Discourses on Livy*; his proclamations that great leaders always need Fortune's favour, even if only for the opportunity to display their *virtù*, and that the most any ruler can do is work within

---

1 Translated from the Italian by Christian E. Detmold, from *The Historical, Political, and Diplomatic Writings of Niccolo Machiavelli* (James R. Osgood and Company, 1882), modernized by Michel Pharand.

Fortune's plans, never defying them (*DL* 2.29), are darker than the optimistic pep talk in chapter 25 of *The Prince* that suggests Fortune can be not only thwarted through prudence but also mastered through audacity and force. In fact, while prudence is a theme which permeates the *Discourses on Livy*, when it comes to the individual's encounter with Fortune, Machiavelli's advice is to maintain a Stoic disposition (*DL* 3.31). The lone ruler seeking glory and recognition wants words of praise and encouragement and to be told that nothing is beyond reach, not a tale of caution, limits, and the reality that success is ultimately out of their hands. Likewise, Machiavelli's analysis of a state's longevity being dependent on a prince relinquishing power and transforming his principality into a republic (*DL* 1.19–20) is not the counsel a monarch struggling to survive wants to hear. Lastly, Machiavelli's critique of Christianity, which was largely limited to a single chapter (11) in *The Prince*, expands to encompass several chapters in the *Discourses on Livy* (1.11–13, 2.2, and 3.1) and goes further than presenting an account of papal power in Machiavelli's day and discussing the pope as merely a secular prince with an army; it offers a critique of how Christianity has been interpreted and practiced, including a condemnation of Saints Francis and Dominic, and how all this has led to Italy's weakened state, in conjunction with an analysis of how politically useful the pagan religions of ancient Rome have been.

Machiavelli also introduces new themes that explain the relationship between his two political masterpieces, which has caused careless readers to see an incompatibility between the two texts. The introduction of the cyclical conception of history (*DL* 1.2 and 3.1), which he took from Polybius and which also appears in the *Tercets on Fortune*, *The Florentine Histories*, and his unfinished poem *The Golden Ass*, provides an explanation for why a well-ordered and long-lived state must be a republic. There are the necessary exceptions of the origins of the state (*DL* 1.9–10) as well as the inevitability of corruption and crisis (*DL* 1.34), which call for a lone political actor, be it a prince or a dictator, to deal with these problems as only they can: swiftly, brutally, and unencumbered by procedural considerations. However, even with this admission, Machiavelli makes it clear that the dictator's role and power must be prescribed by law in a republic if the dictator is to remove corruption as opposed to strengthen it, and the prince is only necessary when a state is so ruined that rejuvenation is no longer possible. In light of Machiavelli's cyclical account of history, including his admission that all states will suffer corruption that, if not caught early, will require the state to be rejuvenated by extraordinary means, there is little tension between *The Prince* and the *Discourses on Livy*. The two texts provide a complete guide as to how a leader should rule—according to law in times of peace and good order, which is the model in a well-governed and long-lived state, and according to the cunning of the fox and the strength of the lion in times of disorder and chaos that threaten that norm.]

First Book

Introduction

Although the envious nature of men, so prompt to blame and so slow to praise, makes the discovery and introduction of any new principles and systems almost as dangerous as the exploration of unknown seas and continents, yet, wishing to do what may prove for the common benefit of all, I have resolved to open a new route, which has not yet been followed by anyone and may prove difficult and troublesome, but may also bring me some reward in the approval of those who will kindly appreciate my efforts. And if my poor talents and my little experience of the present and insufficient study of the past should make the result of my labours defective and of little use, I shall at least have shown the way to others, who will carry out my plans with greater ability, eloquence, and judgment, so that if I do not deserve praise, I ought at least not to incur disapproval.

When we consider the general respect for antiquity, and how often—to say nothing of other examples—a great price is paid for some fragments of an antique statue, which we are anxious to possess to ornament our houses, or to give to artists who strive to imitate them in their own works; and when we see, on the other hand, the wonderful examples which the history of ancient kingdoms and republics presents to us, the prodigies of virtue and of wisdom displayed by the kings, generals, citizens, and legislators who have sacrificed themselves for their country—when we see these more admired than imitated.... we cannot but be at the same time as much surprised as disappointed. The more so as in the differences which arise between citizens, or in the illnesses to which they are subjected, we see these same people consult the judgments and remedies prescribed by the ancients. The civil laws are in fact nothing but decisions given by their judges, and which, reduced to a system, direct our modern jurists in their decisions. And what is the science of medicine except the experience of ancient physicians, which their successors have taken for their guide? And yet to found a republic, maintain states, to govern a kingdom, organize an army, conduct a war, dispense justice, and extend empires, you will find neither prince, nor republic, nor captain, nor citizen, who consults the examples of antiquity! This neglect, I am convinced, is due less to the weakness to which the vices of our education have reduced the world or to the evils caused by the proud indolence which prevails in most of the Christian states, than to the lack of real knowledge of history, whose true sense is not known and whose spirit they do not understand. Thus the majority of those who read it take pleasure only in the variety of the events which history relates, without ever thinking of imitating the noble actions, deeming it not only difficult but impossible to do so; as though heaven, the sun, the elements, and men had changed the order of their motions and power, and were different from what they were in ancient times.

Wishing, therefore, as much as I can, to draw mankind from this error, I have thought it proper to write upon those books of Titus Livius that have come to us in their entirety despite the malice of time;[1] touching upon all those matters which, after a comparison between the ancient and modern events, may seem to me necessary to facilitate their proper understanding. In this way those who read my remarks may derive those advantages which should be the aim of all study of history; and although the undertaking is difficult, yet, helped by those who have encouraged me in this attempt, I hope to carry it sufficiently far so that only little may remain for others to carry it to its destined end.

Chapter I

Of the beginning of cities in general, and especially that of the city of Rome.

Those who read about the beginning of Rome and about her lawgivers and her organization will not be astonished that so much virtue should have maintained itself during so many centuries, and that so great an empire should have sprung from it afterwards. To speak first of her origin, we should note that all cities are founded either by natives or by strangers. The little security which the inhabitants found in living dispersed; the impossibility for each to resist isolated, either because of the situation or because of their

---

1 Only books 1–10 and 21–45 were known to exist in Machiavelli's day.

small number, the attacks of any enemy that might present himself; the difficulty of uniting in time for defence at his approach, and the necessity of abandoning the greater number of their retreats, which quickly became a prize to the invader: such were the motives that caused the first inhabitants of a country to build cities for the purpose of escaping these dangers. They resolved, of their own accord, or by the advice of someone who had most authority among them, to live together in a place of their choice that might offer them greater conveniences and greater defence capability. Thus, among many others, were Athens and Venice....

The second case is when a city is built by strangers; these may be either freemen, or subjects of a republic or of a prince, who, to relieve their states from an excessive population, or to defend a newly acquired territory which they wish to preserve without expense, send colonies there. The Romans founded many cities in this way within their empire. Sometimes cities are built by a prince, not for the purpose of living there, but merely as monuments to his glory; such was Alexandria, built by Alexander the Great.[1] But as all these cities are at their very origin deprived of liberty, they rarely succeed in making great progress, or in being counted among the great powers. Such was the origin of Florence....

The founders of cities are independent when they are people who, under the leadership of some prince, or by themselves, have been obliged to escape the pestilence, war, or famine that was devastating their native country and are seeking a new home. These either inhabit the cities of the country of which they take possession, as Moses did, or they build new ones, as did Aeneas.[2] In such cases we are able to appreciate the talents of the founder and the success of his work, which is more or less remarkable depending on how much wisdom and skill he displays in founding the city. Both of these are recognized by his selection of a location for the city, and by the nature of the laws which he establishes in it. And as men work either from necessity or from choice, and as it has been shown that ability has more sway where labour is the result of necessity rather than of choice, it is a matter of consideration whether it might not be better to establish a city in a sterile region,

---

1 Alexander III of Macedon (356–323 BCE) founded the city of Alexandria in 331 BCE after driving the Persians out of Egypt.

2 Aeneas was a mythological character, featured in Homer's *Iliad* as a Trojan lieutenant and in Virgil's *Aeneid* where his travels after the fall of Troy lead him to Italy, where Virgil portrays him as the progenitor of Romulus and Remus, the legendary founders of Rome.

where the people, compelled by necessity to be industrious, and therefore less prone to idleness, would be more united and less exposed, given the poverty of the country, to occasions for conflict…. Such a site selection would doubtless be more useful and wise if men were content with what they possess, and did not wish to exercise command over others.

Now, as people cannot make themselves secure except by being powerful, in founding a city one must avoid a sterile country. On the contrary, a city should be located in a region where the fertility of the soil affords the means of becoming great and of acquiring strength to repel all who might attempt to attack it or oppose the development of its power. As for the idleness which the fertility of a country tends to encourage, the laws should compel men to work where the sterility of the soil does not do so, as was done by those skilful and wise legislators who have lived in very agreeable and fertile countries, such as are apt to make men idle and unfit for the exercise of valour. These, by way of an offset to the pleasures and softness of the climate, imposed upon their soldiers the rigors of a strict discipline and severe exercises, so that they became better warriors than what nature produces in the harshest climates and most sterile countries…. I say, then, that to establish a city, it is wisest to select the most fertile spot, especially as the laws can prevent the ill effects that would otherwise result from that very fertility….

… If we accept the opinion that Aeneas was the founder of Rome, then we must count that city as one of those built by strangers; but if Romulus is taken as its founder, then it must be classed with those built by the natives of the country. Either way it will be seen that Rome was from the first free and independent, and we shall also see (as we shall show further on) to how many privations the laws of Romulus, of Numa,[1] and of others subjected its inhabitants; so that neither the fertility of the soil, nor the proximity of the sea, nor their many victories, nor the greatness of its empire, could corrupt them during several centuries, and they maintained there more ability than has ever been seen in any other city or republic….

---

1 Numa Pompilius (753–673 BCE) succeeded Romulus to become the second king of Rome, reigning from 715 BCE until his death.

Chapter II

Of the different kinds of republics, and of what kind the Roman Republic was.

I will speak only of those whose origin has been independent, and which from the first governed themselves by their own laws.... Some have had at the very beginning, or soon after, a legislator, who, like Lycurgus with the Spartans,[1] gave them by a single act all the laws they needed. Others have owed theirs to chance and to events, and have received their laws at different times, as Rome did. It is very fortunate for a republic to have a legislator sufficiently wise to give her laws so regulated that, without needing to correct them, they afford security to those who live under them. Sparta observed her laws for more than eight hundred years without altering them and without experiencing a single dangerous disturbance.... Those republics, on the other hand, that began without having a perfect constitution, but made a fair beginning and are capable of improvement, such republics may perfect themselves with the help of unexpected events. It is very true, however, that such a republic will never reform itself without risk, for the majority of men never willingly adopt any new law tending to change the constitution of the state, unless the necessity of the change is clearly demonstrated, and as such a necessity cannot make itself felt without being accompanied by danger, the republic may easily be destroyed before having perfected its constitution....

... I must at the outset observe that some of the writers on politics distinguished three kinds of government: principality, aristocracy, and democracy. They also maintain that the legislators of a people must choose from these three the one that seems to them most suitable. Other authors, wiser according to the opinion of many, count six kinds of governments, three of which are very bad and three good in themselves but so liable to be corrupted that they become absolutely bad. The three good ones are those we have just named; the three bad ones result from the degradation of the other three, and each of them resembles its corresponding original, so that the transition from the one to the other is very easy. Thus the principality becomes a tyranny, aristocracy

---

1 Lycurgus (d. 730 BCE) was a legendary early king of Sparta credited with instituting social and legal reforms which transformed Sparta from a mundane settlement into a powerful military aristocracy.

degenerates into oligarchy, and democracy lapses readily into anarchy. So that a legislator who gives to a state which he founds any of these three forms of government constitutes it but for a brief time, for no precautions can prevent any one of the three that are reputed good from degenerating into its opposite kind, so great is the similarity between the virtue and the vice.[1]

Chance has given birth to these different kinds of governments among men; for at the beginning of the world the inhabitants were few in number and lived for a time dispersed, like beasts. As the human race increased, the necessity to unite themselves for defence made itself felt; the better to do so, they chose the strongest and most courageous from among themselves and placed him at their head, promising to obey him. Thence they began to know the good and the honest, and to distinguish them from the bad and the vicious; for seeing a man injure his benefactor aroused at once two sentiments in every heart: hatred against the ingrate and love for the benefactor. They blamed the first, and on the contrary honoured those the more who showed themselves grateful, for each felt that he in turn might fall victim to a similar wrong; and to prevent similar evils, they set to work to make laws, and to institute punishments for those who contravened them. Such was the origin of justice. This caused them, when they later had to choose a prince, neither to look to the strongest nor bravest, but to the wisest and most just. But when they began to make sovereignty hereditary and not by election, the children quickly degenerated from their fathers; and, rather than try to equal their virtues, they considered that a prince had nothing else to do than to excel everyone in luxury, indulgence, and every other variety of pleasure. The prince consequently soon drew hatred upon himself. As an object of hatred, he naturally felt fear; fear in turn compelled him to precautions and violent wrongs, and thus tyranny quickly developed. Such were the beginning and causes of disorders, conspiracies, and plots against the sovereigns, instigated not by the weak and timid, but by those citizens who, surpassing the others in grandeur of soul, in wealth, and in courage, could not submit to the outrages and excesses of their prince. Under such powerful leaders the masses armed themselves against the tyrant, and, after having rid themselves of him, submitted to these chiefs as their liberators. These, abhorring the very name of prince, formed a new government; and at first, bearing in mind the past tyranny,

---

1 Machiavelli's categorization and analysis of regimes is heavily influenced by book 6 of Polybius's *Histories*.

they governed in strict accordance with the laws which they had established themselves, preferring public interests to their own and administered and protected with greatest care both public and private affairs. Then the children succeeded their fathers, and ignorant of the changes of fortune, having never experienced its reverses, and indisposed to remain content with this civil equality, they in turn gave in to cupidity, ambition, licentiousness, and violence, and soon caused the aristocratic government to degenerate into an oligarchic tyranny, oblivious to all civil rights. They soon, however, experienced the same fate as the first tyrant: the people, disgusted with their government, placed themselves at the command of whoever was willing to attack them, and this disposition soon produced an avenger, who was sufficiently well supported to destroy them. The memory of the prince and the wrongs committed by him being still fresh in their minds, and having overthrown the oligarchy, the people were not willing to return to the government of a prince. A popular government was therefore resolved upon, and it was organized in such a way that the authority should not again fall into the hands of a prince or a small number of nobles. And as all governments are at first looked up to with some degree of reverence, the popular state also maintained itself for a time, albeit never for very long, and lasted generally only about as long as the generation that had established it, for it soon ran into that kind of license which inflicts injury upon public as well as private interests. Each individual consulted only his own passions, and a thousand acts of injustice were daily committed, so that, constrained by necessity, or directed by the counsels of some good man, or for the purpose of escaping from this anarchy, they returned again to the government of a prince, and from this they generally lapsed again into anarchy, step by step, in the same manner and from the same causes we have indicated.

Such is the circle which all republics are destined to run through. Seldom, however, do they come back to the original form of government, because their duration is not sufficiently long to enable them to undergo these repeated changes and preserve their existence. But it may well happen that a republic lacking strength and good counsel in its difficulties becomes subject after a while to some neighboring state that is better organized than itself; and if such is not the case, then they revolve indefinitely in this circle of revolutions. I say, then, that all kinds of government are defective: those three which we have qualified as good because they are too short-lived, and the three bad ones because of their inherent viciousness. Thus wise legislators, knowing the vices of each of these systems of government by themselves, have chosen one that should partake of all of them, judging it to be the most stable and solid. In fact, when there is combined under the same constitution a prince, a nobility, and the power of the people, then these three powers will watch and keep each other reciprocally in check.

...

Chapter IV

The disunion of the Senate and the people renders the republic of Rome powerful and free.

I shall not pass over in silence the disturbances that occurred in Rome from the time of the death of the Tarquins to that of the creation of the Tribunes....

... I maintain that those who blame the quarrels of the nobles and the people of Rome condemn that which was the very origin of liberty, and that they were probably more impressed by the cries and noise which these disturbances occasioned in public places than by the good effects they produced. Moreover, they do not consider that in every republic there are two parties, that of the nobles and that of the people, and all the laws that are favourable to liberty result from the opposition of these parties to each other, as may easily be seen from the events that occurred in Rome. From the time of the Tarquins to that of the Gracchi,[1] that is to say, within the space of over three hundred years, the differences between these parties caused but very few exiles, and cost still less blood.... Nor can we consider a republic disorderly where so many virtues were seen to shine. For these good examples are the result of good education, and good education is due to good laws; and good laws in their turn spring from those very agitations which have been so inconsiderately condemned by many. For

---

1   Machiavelli refers to the period of time between the exile of the Tarquin kings from Rome in 510 BCE and the politically motivated murders of the Gracchi brothers, Tiberius (163–133 BCE) and Gaius (153–121 BCE). The Gracchi each served as tribune of the plebs and introduced radical laws which, among other reforms, sought to redistribute land and grain within Roman society. As a result, each brother became increasingly powerful, inciting fear and hatred in the upper classes, who had them killed. Their murders by the Roman nobility ended a relatively peaceful political milieu and set a precedent for the use of violence in Roman politics.

whoever will carefully examine the result of these agitations will find that they have neither caused exiles nor any violence prejudicial to the general good, and will be convinced even that they have given rise to laws and institutions that were to the advantage of public liberty.... The demands of a free people are rarely harmful to their liberty: they are generally inspired by oppressions, experienced or feared. And if their fears are ill founded, it can resort to public assemblies, where the mere eloquence of a single good and respectable man will make them realize their error. "The people," says Cicero, "although ignorant, are still capable of appreciating the truth, and yield to it readily when it is presented to them by a man whom they esteem worthy of their confidence."[1]

...

Chapter V

To whom can the guardianship of liberty more safely be confided: to the nobles or to the people? And which of the two have most cause for creating disturbances: those who wish to acquire or those who desire to conserve?

All the legislators that have given wise constitutions to republics have deemed it an essential precaution to establish a guard and protection for liberty, and depending on how this was more or less wisely placed, liberty endured a longer or shorter period of time. As every republic was composed of nobles and people, the question arose as into whose hands it was best to place the protection of liberty.... If we consider the goals of the nobles and of the people, we must see that the first have a great desire to dominate, while the latter only wish not to be dominated, and thus a greater desire to live in the enjoyment of liberty; so that when the people are entrusted with the care of any privilege or liberty, being less disposed to encroach upon it, they will necessarily take better care of it, and being unable to take it away themselves, will prevent others from doing so.

... And, truly, whoever weighs all these reasons accurately may well remain in doubt as to which of the two classes he would choose as the guardians of liberty, not knowing which would be the least dangerous: those who seek to acquire an authority which they have not, or those who desire to preserve that which they

---

1 See Cicero, *De amicitia*, chapter 25.

already possess. After careful examination, this is what I think may be concluded from it. The question refers either to a republic that wishes to extend its empire, such as Rome, or to a state that limits itself merely to its own preservation. In the first case Rome should be imitated, and in the second the example of Sparta and Venice should be followed.[1] In the next chapter we shall see the reasons why and the means by which this is to be done.

To return now to the question as to which men are most dangerous in a republic, those who wish to acquire power or those who fear to lose that which they possess…. It appears that such upheavals are most frequently occasioned by those who possess; for the fear to lose stirs the same passions in men as the desire to gain, as men do not believe themselves sure of what they already possess except by acquiring still more. Moreover, these new acquisitions provide many means of strength and power for abuses, and what is still worse is that the haughty manners and insolence of the nobles and the rich excite in the breasts of those who have neither birth nor wealth not only the desire to possess, but also the wish to revenge themselves by depriving the former of those riches and honours which they see them employ so badly.

Chapter VI

Whether it was possible to establish in Rome a government capable of ending the hostilities between the nobles and the people.

… It seems to me important to examine whether it was possible to establish a government in Rome that could prevent all these quarrels, and to do this well we must necessarily examine those republics that have maintained their liberties without such hostilities and disturbances; we must examine what form their governments took and whether such a government could have been introduced in Rome.

In Sparta we have an example among the ancients and in Venice among the moderns; to both these states I have already referred above. Sparta had a king and a senate, few in number, to govern her; Venice had no such distinctions and gave the name 'gentlemen' to all who were entitled to take part in the administration of the government….

In examining all these circumstances, we see that the legislators of Rome had to do one of two things to ensure their republic

---

1 Venice and Sparta entrusted liberty to their nobles.

possessed the same tranquility as that enjoyed by the two republics of which we have spoken; namely, either not to employ the people in the armies, like the Venetians, or not to open the doors to foreigners, as had been the case in Sparta. But the Romans in both cases took just the opposite course, which gave to its people greater power and increased numbers and countless opportunities for disturbances. But if the republic had been more tranquil, it would necessarily have been weaker, and she would have lost her energy and consequently the ability of achieving that high degree of greatness to which she attained. Hence to have removed the cause of trouble from Rome would have been to deprive her of her power of expansion. And thus we see in all human affairs, upon careful examination, that you cannot avoid one inconvenience without incurring another. If therefore you wish to make a people numerous and warlike, so as to create a great empire, you will have to constitute it in such a way that will cause you more difficulty in managing it, and if you keep it either small or unarmed and you acquire other colonies, you will not be able to hold them, or you will become so weak that you will fall victim to whoever attacks you. And therefore in all our decisions we must consider well what presents the least inconveniences, and then choose that as the best path, for we shall never find any course entirely free from objections.... If anyone therefore wishes to establish an entirely new republic, he will have to consider whether he wishes to have her expand in power and size like Rome, or whether he intends to confine her within narrow limits. In the first case, it will be necessary to organize her as Rome was, and submit to dissent and troubles as best he can; for without a great number of men, and these well-armed, no republic can ever increase in size. In the second case, he may organize her like Sparta and Venice, but as expansion is the poison of such republics, he must by every means in his power prevent her from making conquests, for such acquisitions by a weak republic always prove their ruin, as happened to both Sparta and Venice. The first, having subjected to her rule nearly all of Greece, exposed its weak foundations at the slightest accident, for when the rebellion of Thebes occurred, which was led by Pelopidas, the other cities of Greece also rose up and almost ruined Sparta.[1] Similarly, Venice, having obtained possession of a great part of Italy, and most of it not by war but by

---

1 The rebellion began in 379 BCE and led to the decisive military defeat of Sparta by Thebes at the Battle of Leuctra in 371 BCE, shattering Sparta's military supremacy.

means of money and fraud, when it came time for her to prove her strength, she lost everything in a single battle.[1]

... But as all human things are kept in perpetual movement and can never remain stable, states naturally either rise or decline, and necessity compels them to act unreasonably; so that, having organized a republic competent to maintain herself without expanding, if forced by necessity to extend her territory, we shall see her foundations give way and herself quickly brought to ruin. And thus, on the other hand, if Heaven favours her so as never to be involved in war, the continued tranquillity would weaken her or provoke internal dissensions, which together, or either of them separately, will be apt to prove her ruin. Seeing then the impossibility of establishing in this respect a perfect equilibrium, and that a precise middle course cannot be maintained, it is proper when organizing a republic to select the most honourable course and to constitute her so that, even if necessity should compel her to expand, she may yet be able to preserve her acquisitions....

Chapter IX

To found a new republic, or to entirely reform the old institutions of an existing one, must be the work of one man only.

... We must assume, as a general rule, that it never or rarely happens that a republic or monarchy is well organized, or its old institutions entirely reformed, unless this is done by a single individual. It is even necessary that he whose mind has conceived such an organization should be alone in carrying it into effect. A republic's wise legislator, therefore, whose goal is to promote the public good and not his private interests, and who prefers his country to his own successors, should concentrate all authority in himself. Moreover, a wise mind will never criticize anyone for having used any unlawful means to establish a kingdom or organize a republic. It is well that when the act accuses him, the result should excuse him; and when the result is good, as in the case of Romulus,[2] it will always absolve him from blame. For he who commits violence for the purpose of destroying should be rebuked, but not he who employs it for beneficent purposes. The lawgiver should, however,

---

1   The Battle of Agnadello (1509) in which Venice suffered a humiliating loss to the League of Cambrai, consisting of Pope Julius II, Louis XII of France, Ferdinand II of Aragon, and the Holy Roman Emperor Maximilian I, mentioned in *The Prince* 12 and *Florentine Histories* 1.29.
2   The founding of the Roman Republic.

be sufficiently wise and virtuous not to leave this authority which he has assumed either to his heirs or to anyone else; for mankind being more prone to evil than to good, his successor might employ for evil purposes the power which he had used only for good ends. Besides, although one man alone should organize a government, it will not last long if its administration remains on the shoulders of a single individual; but it will survive when it is the responsibility of many, and when many are required to sustain it. Therefore, as the organization of anything cannot be made by many, because the divergence of their opinions hinders them from agreeing as to what is best, yet once they do understand it, they will not readily agree to abandon it. That Romulus deserves to be excused for the death of his brother and that of his associate, and that what he did was for the general good and not for the gratification of his own ambition, is proved by the fact that he immediately instituted a Senate with which to consult and according to whose opinions he might form his resolutions. And on carefully considering the authority which Romulus reserved for himself, we see that all he kept was the command of the army in case of war and the power of convening the Senate....

The above views might be corroborated by any number of examples, such as those of Moses, Lycurgus, Solon,[1] and other founders of monarchies and republics who were able to establish laws suitable for the general good only by keeping for themselves an exclusive authority; but all these are so well known that I will not further refer to them....

Chapter X

Just as the founders of a republic or monarchy deserve praise, so do the founders of a tyranny deserve contempt.

Of all men who have been eulogized, those who have been the authors and founders of religions deserve it most; next come those who have established republics or kingdoms. After these the most celebrated are those who have commanded armies and have extended the possessions of their kingdom or country. To these may be added literary men, but, as these are of different kinds, they are celebrated according to their respective degrees of excellence.

---

1 Solon (630–560 BCE) was an Athenian politician and poet who is credited with legal and social reforms that formed the basis of Athenian democracy.

All others—and their number is infinite—receive such share of praise according to the exercise of their arts and professions. On the contrary, those who have destroyed religions, who have ruined their republics and kingdoms, who are enemies of virtue, of letters, and of every art that is useful and honourable to mankind, are doomed to infamy and universal contempt. Such are the impious and violent, the ignorant, the idle, the vile and degraded. And there are none so foolish or so wise, so wicked or so good, that, in choosing between these two qualities, they do not praise what is praiseworthy and blame what deserves blame. And yet nearly all men, deceived by a false good and a false glory, allow themselves voluntarily or ignorantly to be drawn towards those who deserve more blame than praise. For example, those who by establishing a republic or kingdom could earn eternal glory for themselves turn to tyranny, without perceiving how much glory, how much honour, security, satisfaction, and tranquillity of mind they forfeit, and what infamy, disgrace, blame, danger, and anxiety they will suffer.... Let him also note how much more praise those emperors deserved who, after Rome became an empire, conformed to the laws like good princes, than those who took the opposite course, and he will see that Titus, Nerva, Trajan, Hadrian, Antoninus, and Marcus Aurelius[1] did not require the Praetorian Guard or the countless legions to defend them, because they were protected by their own good conduct, the good will of the people, and by the love of the Senate. He will also see that neither the Eastern nor the Western armies were enough to save Caligula, Nero, Vitellius,[2] and so many other wicked emperors, from the enemies which their bad conduct and evil lives had raised up against them.

And if the history of these men were carefully studied, it would prove an ample guide to any prince and show him the way to glory or to infamy, to security or to perpetual apprehension. For of the twenty-six emperors that reigned from the time of Caesar to that of Maximinus,[3] sixteen were assassinated and only ten died

---

1 Titus (39–81 CE) r. 79–81, Nerva (30–98) r. 96–98, Trajan (c. 53–117) r. 98–117, Hadrian (76–138) r. 117–38, Antoninus (86–161) r. 138–61, and Marcus Aurelius (121–80) r. 161–80.
2 Caligula (12–41 CE) r. 37–41, Nero (37–68) r. 54–68, and Vitellius (15–69) r. 69.
3 Gaius Julius Caesar (100–44 BCE) heralded the end of the Roman Republic when he crossed the Rubicon river with his army in violation of Roman law in 49 BCE, starting a civil war which effectively ended the republican phase of Rome. Maximinus was emperor of Rome from 235 to 238 CE when he was murdered by his own troops.

a natural death; and if, among those who were killed, there were one or two good ones, like Galba and Pertinax,[1] their death was the consequence of the corruption which their predecessors had produced among the soldiers. And if among those who died a natural death there were some wicked ones, like Severus,[2] it was due to their extraordinary good fortune and courage, two qualities which men rarely possess....

And surely, if a prince is a man, he will be shocked at the thought of re-enacting those evil times and be fuelled with an intense desire to follow the example of the good. And truly, if a prince is anxious for glory and the good opinion of the world, he should rather wish to possess a corrupt city, not to ruin it completely as Caesar did, but to reorganize it as Romulus did. For certainly the heavens cannot offer a man a greater opportunity of glory, nor could men desire a better one....

Chapter XI

Of the religion of the Romans.

Although the founder of Rome was Romulus, to whom, like a daughter, she owed her birth and her education, yet the gods did not judge the laws of this prince sufficient for so great an empire, and therefore inspired the Roman Senate to elect Numa Pompilius[3] as his successor, so that he might regulate all those things that Romulus had not. Numa, finding a very savage people, and wishing to reduce them to civil obedience by the arts of peace, turned to religion as the most necessary and guaranteed support of any civil society, and he established it upon such foundations that for many centuries nowhere but in that republic was there more fear of the gods, which greatly facilitated all the enterprises

---

1 Servius Galba Ceasar Augustus (3 BCE–69 CE) was emperor of Rome for seven months in 68–69 CE, after Nero's death. Publius Helvius Pertinax (126–193 CE) was emperor of Rome for a few months in 193. Both were unpopular for introducing reforms which reined in the excesses of previous emperors, and both were murdered for their efforts, although Galba also made many mistakes during his short rule. Machiavelli discusses Pertinax in *The Prince*, chapter 19.

2 Lucius Septimius Severus (145–211 CE) was emperor of Rome from 193 to 211, when he died of natural causes. Machiavelli discusses him in *The Prince*, chapter 19.

3 Numa Pompilius, the second king of Rome, reigned from 715 to 673 BCE.

which the Senate or Rome's great men attempted. Whoever examines the actions of the people of Rome as a body or of many individual Romans will see that these citizens were much more afraid of breaking an oath than the laws, because they respected the power of the gods more than that of men.... And whoever reads Roman history attentively will see to what degree religion served, in commanding armies, in uniting the people and keeping them well behaved, and in covering the wicked with shame. So that if the question were discussed whether Rome was more indebted to Romulus or to Numa, I believe that the highest merit would go to Numa; for where religion exists it is easy to introduce armies and discipline, but where there are armies and no religion it is difficult to introduce discipline. And although we have seen that Romulus could organize the Senate and establish other civil and military institutions without the help of divine authority, yet this was very necessary for Numa, who pretended to speak with a nymph who advised him about everything he wished to persuade the people of;[1] and the reason for all this was that Numa mistrusted his own authority, fearing it would prove insufficient to enable him to introduce new and unaccustomed legislation in Rome. In truth, there never was any remarkable lawgiver among any people who did not resort to divine authority, as otherwise his laws would not have been accepted by the people. For there are many good laws whose importance is known to the prudent lawgiver, but whose reasons are not sufficiently evident to enable him to persuade others to submit to them. Thus do wise men, for the purpose of removing this difficulty, resort to divine authority. Thus did Lycurgus and Solon,[2] and many others who aimed at the same thing.

... With all these things in mind, I conclude that the religion introduced by Numa into Rome was one of the chief causes of the prosperity of that city, for this religion gave rise to good laws, and good laws bring good fortune, and from good fortune comes happy success in all enterprises. And just as observing divine institutions is the cause of the greatness of republics, so does disregarding them cause the ruin of republics; for where the fear of God is lacking, there the country will come to ruin, unless it be

---

1 The water-nymph Egeria allegedly met with Numa by night and instructed him in matters of statesmanship and religion.
2 Lycurgus (d. c. 730 BCE) was king of Sparta, and Solon (d. c. 560 BCE) was a prominent politician in Athens. Both instituted reforms that strengthened their respective states.

sustained by the fear of the prince, which may temporarily supply the lack of religion. But as the lives of princes are short, the kingdom will necessarily perish as the prince fails in ability. Hence kingdoms which depend entirely upon the ability of one man endure only for a brief time, for his ability dies with his life, and it rarely happens that it is renewed in his successor, as Dante so wisely says.[1] ...

The welfare, then, of a republic or a kingdom does not consist in having a prince who governs it wisely during his lifetime, but in having one who will give it such laws that it will maintain itself even after his death.

Chapter XII

The importance of giving religion a prominent influence in a state, and how Italy was ruined because she failed in this respect through the conduct of the Church of Rome.

Princes and republics who wish to remain free from corruption must above all preserve the purity of all religious observances and treat them with proper reverence; for there is no greater indication of the ruin of a country than to see religion scorned.... It is therefore the duty of princes and heads of republics to uphold the foundations of their country's religion, for then it is easy to keep their people religious and consequently well behaved and united. And therefore everything that tends to favour religion, even though they believe it to be false, should be received and used to strengthen it, and this should be especially done the more prudent the rulers are and the better they understand the natural course of things. Such was, in fact, the practice observed by wise men, which has given rise to the belief in the miracles that are celebrated in religions, however false they may be. For prudent rulers have given these miracles increased importance, no matter where or how they originated, and their authority afterwards gave them credibility with the people. Rome had many such miracles and one of the most remarkable was that which occurred when the Roman soldiers sacked the city of Veii;[2] some of them entered the temple of Juno, and, placing themselves before her statue, said to her, "Do you wish to come to Rome?" Some imagined that

---

1 In a section omitted from this edition, Machiavelli refers to and takes liberty with a passage from Dante's *Purgatorio* 7.121–23.
2 396 BCE.

they saw the statue make a sign of assent, and others claimed to have heard her reply, "Yes." Now these men, being very religious, according to Titus Livius, having entered the temple quietly, filled with devotion and reverence, might really have believed that they had heard a reply to their question, such as perhaps they could have presumed. This opinion and belief was advocated and magnified by Camillus[1] and the other Roman leaders.

And certainly if the Christian religion had from the beginning been maintained according to the principles of its founder, the Christian states and republics would have been much more united and happy than they are.... But as some believe that the well-being of Italian affairs depends upon the Church of Rome, I will present such arguments against that opinion as occur to me, two of which are most important and I believe cannot be refuted. The first is that the evil example of the court of Rome has destroyed all piety and religion in Italy, which leads to infinite improprieties and disorders; for as we may presuppose all good where religion prevails, so where it is lacking we have the right to suppose the very opposite. We Italians then owe to the Church of Rome and to her priests our having become irreligious and bad. However, we owe her a still greater debt and one that has ruined us, namely, that the Church has kept and still keeps our country divided. And certainly a country can never be united and happy unless it obeys wholly one government, whether a republic or a monarchy, as is the case in France and in Spain, and the sole reason why Italy is not in that condition and not governed by either one republic or one sovereign is the Church. For having acquired and held a temporal supremacy, she has never had sufficient power or courage to seize the rest of the country and make herself sole sovereign of all Italy. On the other hand, she has not been so weak that the fear of losing her temporal power prevented her from enlisting the aid of a foreign power to defend her against whoever had become too powerful in Italy. This was seen in former days by many sad experiences, when through the intervention of Charlemagne she drove out the Lombards, who were masters of nearly all Italy,[2]

---

1   Marcus Furius Camillus (d. 365 BCE) was a Roman soldier and statesman who won numerous military campaigns and served five times as dictator. Livy calls him the second founder of Rome for his freeing Rome from the Gauls c. 390 BCE. See Livy 5.49.

2   Pope Stephen II (d. 757), who served as pope from 752 to 757, enlisted the help of the Frankish king Pippin III to help eliminate the threat the expanding Lombard presence in Italy posed to the papacy. Pippin's son Charlemagne (Charles the Great) defeated the Lombards

and when in our times she crushed the power of the Venetians with the help of France, and afterwards with the assistance of the Swiss in turn drove out the French.[1] The Church, then, not having been powerful enough to be able to master all Italy, nor having allowed any other power to do so, has been the reason Italy has never been able to unite under one head, but has always remained under a number of princes and lords, which caused her so many dissensions and so much weakness that she fell victim not only to powerful barbarians, but to whoever chose to attack her. This we Italians owe to the Church of Rome and to nobody else....

Chapter XIII

How the Romans used religion to preserve order in their city and to carry out their enterprises and suppress disturbances.

I would like to mention here some examples to show how the Romans employed religion to reorganize their city and to further their enterprises. And although there are many instances to be found in the writings of Titus Livius, I will limit myself to the following. The Romans, having created the Tribunes with consular powers and selected all but one from the plebeian order, and after a pestilence and famine occurred in that year accompanied by some extraordinary phenomena, the nobles took advantage of this new creation of the Tribunes by saying that the gods were angry because Rome had been lacking in respect to the majesty of her empire, and that there was no other way of placating the gods but by restoring the election of the Tribunes to its original plan. The result was that the people, under the influence of religious fear, selected the Tribunes altogether from among the nobles.

It was also seen at the siege of the city of Veii that the captains of the Roman army used religion to keep their soldiers predisposed

---

in 774. Pope Leo III (d. 816), who served as pope from 795 to 816, cemented this alliance by proclaiming Charlemagne emperor in 800. Machiavelli discusses these events in *Florentine Histories*, 1.10 and 11, although he erroneously identifies Pope Stephen II as Pope Gregory III.

1 The Church formed the League of Cambrai in 1508 (consisting of Louis XII of France, the Emperor Maximilian I, Pope Julius II, King Henry VII of England, King Ferdinand of Spain, and King Ladislas II of Bohemia and Hungary) to suppress the Venetians and then turned on France by forming the Holy League in 1511 (consisting of Pope Julius II, King Ferdinand of Spain, Venice, the Swiss, and King Henry VIII of England, with the Emperor Maximilian I joining in 1512) to force the French out of Italian territory.

to any enterprise; for when Lake Albanus rose that year in a very extraordinary manner, and the soldiers, tired of the long siege, wished to return to Rome, the leaders invented the story that Apollo and certain other oracles had predicted that the city of the Veientians would be taken in the year when Lake Albanus would overflow its banks.[1] The soldiers, having taken new hope from these predictions so as to capture the city, bore the exhaustion of the war and the siege cheerfully, and pushed the assault with so much energy that Camillus, who had been made Dictator, succeeded in taking that city after a ten-year siege.[2] And thus religion, judiciously used, promoted the capture of Veii and the restitution of the tribunate to the nobility, either of which would have been with difficulty accomplished without it....

...

Chapter XVI

A people accustomed to living under a prince preserves its liberties with difficulty if by accident it has become free.

Many examples in ancient history prove how difficult it is for a people accustomed to living under the government of a prince to preserve its liberty, if by some accident it has recovered it, as was the case with Rome after the expulsion of the Tarquins.[3] And this difficulty is a reasonable one, for such a people may well be compared to some wild animal, which, although by nature ferocious and savage, has been as it were subdued by having been always kept imprisoned and in servitude, and being let out into the open fields, not knowing how to provide food and shelter for itself, becomes an easy prey to the first one who attempts to chain it up again. The same thing happens to a people unaccustomed to self-government, for, ignorant of all public affairs, of all means of defence or offence, neither knowing the princes nor being known by them, it soon relapses under a yoke, often much heavier than the one it had only just shaken off. This difficulty occurs even when the body of the people is not wholly corrupt; however, when corruption has taken possession of the whole people, then it cannot preserve its free condition even for the shortest possible

---

1 See Livy 5.15–16.
2 See Livy 5.19–21.
3 510 BCE.

time, as we shall see further on. Thus our argument refers to a people where corruption has not yet become general, and where the good still prevails over the bad. To the above comes another difficulty, which is that the state that becomes free makes enemies for itself and not friends. All those become its enemies who benefited from the tyrannical abuses and fattened upon the treasures of the prince, and who, being now deprived of these advantages, cannot remain content and are therefore driven to attempt to re-establish the tyranny so as to recover their former authority and advantages. As I have said, a state that becomes free makes no friends; for free governments bestow honours and rewards only according to certain honest and fixed rules, beyond which there are neither the one nor the other. And those who obtain these honours and rewards do not consider themselves obliged to anyone, because they believe that they were entitled to them by their merits. Besides the advantages that result to the mass of the people from a free government—such as to be able freely to enjoy one's possessions without apprehension, to have nothing to fear for the honour of his wife and daughters, or for himself—all these advantages are not appreciated by anyone while he enjoys them; for no one will confess himself under obligation to anyone merely because he has not been injured by him.

Thus a state that has freshly achieved liberty makes enemies and no friends. And to prevent this inconvenience and the disorders which are apt to come with it, there is no remedy more powerful, valid, healthful, and necessary than the killing of the sons of Brutus,[1] who, as history shows, had conspired with other Roman youths for no other reason than because under the consuls they could not have the same extraordinary advantages they had enjoyed under the kings; so that the liberty of the people seemed to have become their bondage. Whoever undertakes to govern a people under the form of either republic or monarchy, without protecting himself against those opposed to this new order of things, establishes a government of very brief duration. It is true that I consider unfortunate those princes who, to safeguard their government to which the mass of the people is hostile, are obliged to resort to extraordinary measures; for he who has but a few enemies can easily constrain them without great scandal, but he to whom the masses are hostile cannot, and the more cruelty he employs the weaker his authority becomes, so that his best remedy is to try and secure the good will of the people. Although

1 See Livy 2.3–5.

I have departed in this discourse from my subject, in speaking sometimes of a republic and sometimes of a prince, yet I will say a few more words so as not to have to return to this matter.

A prince, then, who wishes the good will of a people that is hostile to him (I mean such princes as have been tyrants in their country) should first of all ascertain what the people really desire, and he will always find that they want two things: to revenge themselves on those who have been the cause of their enslavement, and to recover their liberty. The first of these desires the prince may satisfy entirely, and the second in part....

Chapter XIX

If an able and vigorous prince is succeeded by a weak one, the latter may for a time be able to maintain himself; but if his successor is also weak, then the latter will not be able to maintain his state.

In carefully examining the characters and conduct of Romulus, Numa, and Tullus,[1] the first three kings of Rome, we see that she was favoured by the greatest good fortune in having her first king courageous and warlike, her second peace-loving and religious, and her third equally courageous as Romulus, and preferring war to peace. For it was important for Rome that at the outset there should arise a legislator capable of endowing her with civil institutions, but then it was essential that the succeeding kings should equal Romulus in ability and valour; otherwise the city would have become effeminate and a prey to her neighbours. Thus we may note that a successor of less vigor and ability than the first king may yet be able to maintain a state established by the genius and courage of his predecessor, and may enjoy the fruits of his labours. But if he should live a long life, or his successor not have the same good qualities and courage as the first king, then the government will necessarily go to ruin. And so, on the contrary, if one king succeeds another of equally great abilities and courage, then it will often be seen that they achieve extraordinary greatness for their state, and that their fame will rise to the very heavens....

I say then, that, according to these examples, the successor of a wise and vigorous prince, though weak himself, may maintain a kingdom, but if the successor of a weak prince is also weak, no kingdom can be maintained, unless it were constituted like France, which is maintained by the force of its ancient

---

1   Romulus, Numa Pompilius, and Tullus Hostilius.

institutions; and I call that prince weak who is incapable of waging war.... Let all princes then who govern states take note, that he who follows the course of Numa may keep or lose his throne, according to chance and circumstances; but he who imitates the example of Romulus, and combines valour with prudence, will retain his throne, unless it is taken from him by some persistent and excessive force. And we may certainly assume that, if Rome had not chanced to have for her third king a man who knew how by force of arms to restore her original reputation, she would not have been able, except with greatest difficulty, to gain a firm foothold and achieve the great things she did. And thus so long as she was governed by kings, she was exposed to the danger of being ruined by a weak or a wicked one.

Chapter XX

Two continuous successions of able and virtuous princes will achieve great results; and as well-constituted republics have, in the nature of things, a succession of virtuous rulers, their acquisitions and extension will consequently be very great.

After Rome had expelled her kings, she was no longer exposed to the dangers, which we have spoken of above, resulting from a succession of weak or wicked kings; for the sovereign authority was vested in the consuls, who obtained that authority not by inheritance, or fraud, or violent ambition, but by the free votes of the people, and were generally most excellent men. Rome, with the benefit of the virtue and good fortune of these men, was thus able to attain her utmost grandeur in no greater length of time than she had existed under the rule of kings. For if, as has been seen, two successive good and valorous princes are sufficient to conquer the world, as was the case with Philip of Macedon and Alexander the Great,[1] a republic should be able to do still more, having the power to elect not only two successions, but an infinite number of

---

1 Philip II (382–336 BCE) turned Macedon from a weak state beleaguered militarily by its neighbours into an economic and military powerhouse that controlled all of Greece and had designs on Persia. He was succeeded by his son Alexander III (the Great), who extended Macedonian power throughout the Mediterranean region and not only fulfilled but exceeded his father's ambitions in Asia. Alexander's children, who were placed on the throne after his death and lacked his intelligence and political intuition, were murdered, and the empire was fractured into a number of successor states.

most competent and virtuous rulers one after the other; and this system of electing a succession of virtuous men should always be the established practice of every well-ordered republic.

...

Chapter XXVI

A new prince in a city or province conquered by him should organize everything anew.

Whoever becomes prince of a city or state, especially if the foundation of his power is weak and he does not wish to establish there either a monarchy or a republic, will find the best means of controlling that principality by organizing the government entirely anew (he being himself a new prince there); that is, he should appoint new governors with new titles, new powers, and new men, and he should make the poor rich, as David did when he became king, "who heaped riches upon the needy, and dismissed the wealthy empty-handed."[1] In addition, he should destroy the old cities and build new ones, and relocate the inhabitants from one place to another; in short, he should leave nothing unchanged in that province, so that there be neither rank, nor grade, nor honour, nor wealth that should not be recognized as coming from him. He should take Philip of Macedon, father of Alexander, for his model, who by proceeding in this manner went from being a petty king to master of all Greece. And his historian tells us that he relocated the inhabitants from one province to another, as shepherds move their flocks from place to place. Doubtless these means are cruel and destructive of all civilized life, and neither Christian nor even human, and should be avoided by everyone. In fact, the life of a private citizen would be preferable to that of a king at the expense of the ruin of so many human beings. Nevertheless, whoever is unwilling to adopt the first and humane course must, if he wishes to maintain his power, follow the latter evil course. But men generally decide upon a middle course, which is most hazardous, for they know neither how to be entirely good or entirely bad....

...

---

1 Luke 1:53. Machiavelli distorts this passage, either intentionally or unintentionally, by attributing the deeds to King David, as opposed to God.

Chapter XXXIV

The authority of the dictatorship has always proved beneficial to Rome and never injurious; it is the authority which men usurp, and not that which is given to them by the free votes of their fellow-citizens, that is dangerous to civil liberty.

Some writers have blamed those Romans who first introduced the practice of creating Dictators, as this in time led to despotism in Rome, alleging that the first tyrant of that city governed her under the title of Dictator and saying that, if it had not been for this office, Caesar[1] never could under any other public title have imposed his tyranny upon the Romans. Evidently the subject could not have been thoroughly considered by those who advance this opinion, so generally adopted without good reasons; for it was neither the name nor the rank of the Dictator that subjected Rome to servitude, but rather the authority which citizens usurped through prolonging their time in the government. And if the title of Dictator had not existed in Rome, some other would have been taken; for power can easily acquire a name, but a name cannot acquire power. And it is seen that the Dictator, whenever created according to public law and not usurped by individual authority, always proved beneficial to Rome; it is the judicial courts and the powers created by illegitimate means that harm a republic, and not those appointed in the regular way, as was the case in Rome, where in the long course of time no Dictator ever failed to prove beneficial to the republic.... Dictators were appointed only for a limited term, not in perpetuity, and their power to act was confined to the particular occasion for which they were created. This power consisted in being able to decide alone which measures to adopt for averting the pressing danger, to do whatever he deemed proper without consultation, and to inflict punishment upon anyone without appeal. But the Dictator could do nothing to alter

---

1 Upon returning to Rome after defeating the forces of his political rival, Pompey, Caesar was proclaimed dictator for life in 44 BCE, and while many of his reforms were beneficial and made him popular with the people, his consolidation of power was seen by the patricians as reminiscent of monarchy and incompatible with the spirit of the Roman Republic. He was assassinated on 15 March, the Ides of March, by a group of at least sixty conspirators as he made his way to the Senate. With its republican institutions in tatters, Rome descended into civil war in the wake of Caesar's death, and the Roman Republic became the Roman Empire. See also p. 148, n. 3.

the form of the government, such as to diminish the powers of the Senate or the people, or to abrogate existing institutions and create new ones. So that, considering the short period for which he held the office and the limited powers which he possessed, and the fact that the Roman people were as yet uncorrupted, it is evident that it was impossible for the Dictator to exceed his powers and to harm the republic, which on the contrary, as all experience shows, was always benefited by him.

And truly, of all the institutions of Rome, this one deserves to be counted among those to which she was most indebted for her greatness and supremacy. For without such an institution Rome would with difficulty have escaped the many extraordinary dangers that befell her; for the customary proceedings of republics are slow, no magistrate or council being permitted to act independently but in almost all instances being obliged to act cooperatively, so that often much time is required to harmonize their many opinions; and belated measures are most dangerous when the occasion requires prompt action. Thus all republics should have some institution similar to the office of Dictator.... And when a republic lacks some such system, a strict observance of the established laws will expose her to ruin; or, to save her from such danger, the laws will have to be disregarded. Now in a well-ordered republic it should never be necessary to resort to extra-constitutional measures; for although they may be beneficial at the time, yet the precedent is pernicious, for if the practice is once established of disregarding the laws for worthy purposes, they will soon be disregarded under that pretext for evil purposes. Thus no republic will ever be perfect if she has not by law provided for everything, possessing a remedy for every emergency and fixed rules to apply it. Thus I will conclude by saying that those republics which in dangerous times cannot resort to a dictatorship, or some similar authority, will always be ruined when serious occasions occur....

Second Book

Introduction

Men always praise the ancient times and find fault with the present, though often without reason. They are such devotees of the past that they praise not only the times which they know only by the accounts of historians, but, having grown old, they also praise all they remember seeing in their youth. Their opinion is generally erroneous in that respect, and I think the reasons for this illusion are various. The first I believe to be the fact that we never know the whole truth about the past, and very frequently writers conceal events that would reflect disgrace upon their times, while they magnify and amplify those that enhance it. The majority of authors obey the fortune of conquerors to the degree that, by way of rendering their victories more glorious, they exaggerate not only the valiant deeds of the victor, but also of the vanquished, so that future generations of the countries of both will wonder at those men and times, and are obliged to praise and admire them to the utmost. Another reason is that men's hatreds generally spring from fear or envy. Now, these two powerful reasons for hatred do not exist for us with regard to the past, which can no longer inspire either apprehension or envy. But it is very different with the affairs of the present, in which we ourselves are either actors or spectators, and of which we have a complete knowledge, nothing being concealed from us. And knowing the good as well as many other things that are displeasing to us, we are forced to conclude that the present is inferior to the past, though in reality it may be much more worthy of glory and fame....

I repeat, then, that this practice of praising the past and denouncing the new exists, though it cannot be said that it is always incorrect; for sometimes our judgment is of necessity correct, human affairs being in a state of perpetual movement, always either ascending or declining. We see, for instance, a city or country with a government well organized by some man of superior ability; for a time it progresses and attains a great prosperity through the talents of its lawgiver. Now, if anyone living at such a period should praise the past more than the time in which he lives, he would certainly be deceiving himself, and this error will be caused by the reasons noted above. But should he live in that city or country at the period after it has passed the zenith of its glory and in the time of its decline, then he would not be wrong in praising the past.... I say that, if men's judgment is wrong about whether the present age be better than the past—of which the latter, owing to its antiquity, they cannot have such perfect knowledge as of their own period—the judgment of old men of what they have seen in their youth and in their old age should not be false, inasmuch as they have equally seen both one and the other. This would be true if men at different periods of their lives had the same judgment and the same appetites. But as these vary, though the times do not, things cannot appear the same to men who have other tastes, other delights, and other considerations in old age from what they had in youth. For as men when they age lose their strength and energy, while their prudence and judgment improve, so the same things that in youth appeared to them supportable and good, will necessarily, when they have grown old, seem to them unbearable and evil; and when they should blame their own judgment they find fault with the times. Moreover, as human desires are insatiable (because nature makes it possible to desire everything, while Fortune limits what can be attained), this gives rise to a constant discontent in the human mind and a weariness of the things possessed; and it is this which makes men denounce the present, praise the past, and desire the future, and all this without any reasonable motive. I do not know, then, whether I deserve to be classed with those who deceive themselves, if in these *Discourses* I shall praise too much the times of ancient Rome and criticize those of our own day. And truly, if the virtues that ruled then and the vices that prevail now were not as clear as the sun, I should be more reticent in my expressions, lest I should fall into the very error for which I reproach others. But the matter being so obvious that everybody sees it, I shall boldly and openly say what I think of the ancient times and of the present, so as to excite in the minds of the young men who may read my writings the desire to avoid the evils of the latter, and to prepare themselves to imitate the virtues of the former, whenever Fortune offers them the opportunity. For it is the duty of an honest man to teach others that good which the malignity of the times and of Fortune has prevented him from accomplishing, so that among the many capable ones whom he has instructed, someone perhaps more favoured by Heaven, may succeed in performing it.

...

Chapter II

What nations the Romans had to contend against, and with what obstinacy these nations defended their liberty.

Nothing required so much effort on the part of the Romans to subdue the nations around them, as well as those of more distant countries, as the love of liberty which these people cherished in those days, and which they defended with so much obstinacy that nothing but the exceeding ability of the Romans could ever have conquered them. For we know from many instances to what danger they exposed themselves in order to preserve or recover their liberty, and what vengeance they unleashed upon those who had deprived them of it. The lessons of history also teach us, on the other hand, the injuries peoples and cities suffer from servitude. And while in our own times there is only one country in which we can say that free communities exist,[1] in those ancient times all countries contained numerous cities that enjoyed entire liberty. In the times we are now speaking about, in Italy from the mountains that divide the present Tuscany from Lombardy, down to the extreme point, all the peoples were free, such as the Etruscans, the Romans, the Samnites, and many others that inhabited the rest of Italy.... And it is easy to understand from where that affection for liberty arose in the people, for they had seen that cities never increased in supremacy or wealth unless they were free. And certainly it is wonderful to think of the greatness which Athens attained within the space of a hundred years after having freed herself from the tyranny of Pisistratus and still more wonderful to reflect upon the greatness which Rome achieved after she was rid of her kings. The cause of this is obvious, for it is not individual prosperity, but rather the common good, that makes cities great; and certainly the common good is esteemed nowhere but in republics, because whatever they do is for the common benefit; and should it happen to cause injury to one or more individuals, those for whose benefit the thing is done are so numerous that they can always carry the measure against the few who are injured by it. But the very reverse happens where there is a prince whose private interests are usually in opposition to those of the city, while the measures taken for the benefit of the city are seldom deemed personally advantageous by the prince. This state of things soon leads to a tyranny, the least evil of which is to halt the advance of the city in its career of prosperity, so that it grows neither in power nor wealth, but on the contrary rather retrogrades. And if fate should have it that the tyrant is enterprising, and by his courage and valour extends his dominions, it will never be for the benefit of the city, but only for his own; for he will never bestow honours and positions upon the good and brave citizens over whom he tyrannizes, so that he may have no occasion to suspect and fear them. Nor will he make the states which he conquers subject or tributary to the city of which he is the despot, because it would not be to his advantage to make that city powerful, while it will always be in his interest to keep the state disunited, so that each place and country shall recognize him alone as master; thus he

---

1 Germany.

alone, and not his country, profits by his conquests. Those wishing to have this opinion confirmed by many other arguments need only read Xenophon's treatise "On Tyranny."[1]

It is no wonder, then, that the ancients hated tyranny and loved freedom, and that the very name of liberty was held in such esteem by them, as was shown by the Syracusans when Hieronymus, the grandson of Hiero, was killed.[2] When his death became known to his army, which was near Syracuse, it caused at first some disturbances, and they were about to perpetrate violence upon his murderers; however, when they learned that the cry of liberty had been raised in Syracuse, they were delighted and instantly returned to order. Their fury against the tyrannicides was quelled, and they thought only of how a free government might be established in Syracuse....

Thinking about why in ancient times people were more devoted to liberty than in the present, I believe that it stems from this: that men were stronger in those days, which I believe to be attributable to the difference in education, founded upon the difference between their religion and ours. For, as our religion teaches us the truth and the true way of life, it causes us to attach less value to the honours of this world; while the pagans, esteeming such honours as the highest good, were more energetic and ferocious in their actions. We may observe this also in most of their institutions, beginning with the magnificence of their sacrifices as compared with the humility of ours, which are gentle solemnities rather than magnificent ones, and have no energy or ferocity in them, while in theirs there was no lack of pomp and magnificence, to which was added the ferocious and bloody nature of the sacrifice by the slaughter of many animals, and the familiarity with this terrible sight inspired men to similar ferocity. In addition, the Pagan religion exalted only men who had achieved great worldly glory, such as commanders of armies and chiefs of republics, while ours glorifies more the humble and contemplative men than the men of action. Our religion, moreover, proclaims the supreme good to be humility, lowliness, and a contempt for worldly objects, while theirs, on the contrary, places the supreme good in grandeur of

---

1 Often translated as "Hiero the Tyrant," a dialogue between the poet Simonides and the tyrant Hiero. Simonides maintains that because Hiero rose to the position of Tyrant from the station of an ordinary citizen, he is in the best position to explain which position is better. Machiavelli praises Hiero's rise to power in *The Prince*, chapter 6.

2 Tyrant of Syracuse from 216 to 215 BCE, Hieronymus was murdered in 215 BCE.

soul, strength of body, and all such qualities that render men formidable. And if our religion demands we show fortitude of soul, it is more to enable us to suffer than to achieve great deeds.

These principles seem to me to have made the world weak and caused it to become an easy prey to evil-minded men, who can control it more securely seeing that the majority of men, for the sake of gaining access to Heaven, are more disposed to endure injuries than to avenge them. And although it would seem that the world has become effeminate and Heaven disarmed, yet this arises unquestionably from the baseness of men, who have interpreted our religion according to the promptings of sloth rather than those of vigorous ability. For if we were to reflect that our religion allows us to exalt and defend our country, we should see that according to it we ought also to love and honour our country, and prepare ourselves so as to be capable of defending her. It is this education, then, and this false interpretation of our religion, that is the cause of there not being so many republics nowadays as there were in ancient times, and that there is no longer the same love of liberty among the people now as there was then. I believe, however, that another reason for this will be found in the fact that the Roman Empire, by force of arms, destroyed all the republics and free cities, and although that empire was afterwards itself dissolved, yet these cities could not reunite themselves nor reorganize their civil institutions, except in a very few instances.

... Only those cities and countries that are free can achieve greatness. Population is greater in such states because marriages are more free and offer more advantages to the citizen; for people will gladly have children when they know that they can support them, that they will not be deprived of their patrimony, and that their children not only are born free and not slaves, but, if they have ability, can attain the highest honours of the state. In free countries we also see wealth increase more rapidly, both from agriculture and from industry and art; for everybody gladly multiplies those things and seeks to acquire those goods whose possession he can quietly enjoy. Hence men compete with each other to increase both private and public wealth, which consequently increase in an extraordinary manner. But the opposite of all this takes place in countries that are subject to another, and the more rigorous the subjection of the people, the more will they be deprived of all the good to which they had previously been accustomed. And the hardest of all servitudes is to be subject to a republic, and for these reasons: first, because it is more enduring, and there is no hope of escaping from it, and second, because republics aim to enervate and weaken all other states so as to increase their own power....

...

Chapter XXIX

Fortune blinds the minds of men when she does not wish them to oppose her plans.

If we observe carefully the course of human affairs, we shall often notice accidents and occurrences against which it seems to be the will of Heaven that we should not have prepared.... Therefore, men who habitually live in great adversity or prosperity deserve less praise or less blame, for it will generally be found that they have been brought to their ruin or their greatness by some great occasion offered by the heavens, which gives them the opportunity, or deprives them of the power, to conduct themselves with courage and wisdom. It certainly is the course of Fortune, when she wishes to effect some great result, to select for her instrument a man of such spirit and ability that he will recognize the opportunity which is afforded him. And thus, in the same way, when she wishes to effect the ruin and destruction of states, she places men at the head who contribute to and hasten such ruin; and if there is anyone powerful enough to resist her, she has him killed, or deprives him of all means of doing any good.... I repeat, then, as an incontrovertible truth, proved by all history, that men may assist Fortune but cannot oppose her; they may develop her plans, but cannot defeat them. Men should never despair on that account; for, not knowing the purpose of Fortune, which she pursues by dark and devious ways, men should always be hopeful, and never yield to despair, whatever troubles or ill fortune may befall them.

Third Book

Chapter I

To ensure the longevity of religious sects or republics, it is often necessary to bring them back to their original principles.

There is nothing more true than that all the things of this world have a limit to their existence; but those only run the entire course ordained for them by Heaven which do not allow their body to become disorganized, but keep it unchanged in the manner ordained, or if they change it, do so such that the change shall be for their advantage and not to their injury. And as I speak here of mixed bodies, such as republics or religious sects, I say that those changes are beneficial which bring them back to their original principles. And the best-constituted bodies with the longest existence are those that possess the intrinsic means of frequently renewing themselves, or that obtain this renewal as a result of some external accident. And it is a truth clearer than light that, without such renewal, these bodies cannot continue to exist, and the means of renewing them is to bring them back to their original principles. For, as all religions, republics and monarchies must have within themselves some goodness, by means of which they obtain their first growth and reputation, and as in the course of time this goodness becomes corrupted, it will necessarily destroy the body unless something intervenes to bring it back to its initial principles....

This return of a republic to its original principles is either the result of extrinsic accident or of intrinsic prudence. As an example of the first, we have seen how necessary it was that Rome should be taken by the Gauls,[1] as a means of her renovation or new birth; so that, being thus born again, she might take new life and vigor, and might resume the proper observance of justice and religion, which were becoming corrupt....

It is necessary then (as has been said) for men who live associated together under some kind of regulations often to be brought back to themselves, so to speak, either by external or internal occurrences. As to the latter, they are either the result of a law that obliges the citizens of the association often to render an account of their conduct, or some man of superior character arises among them whose noble example and virtuous actions will produce the same effect as such a law. This good, then, in a republic is due either to the excellence of some one man or to some law; and as to the latter, the institution that brought the Roman Republic back to its original principles was the creation of the tribunes of the people, the censors, and all the other laws that tended to repress the

---

1 The Gauls sacked Rome in 390 BCE. When Machiavelli refers to France from the perspective of his day, he uses the terms France and the French; however, because the Romans referred to the area and its people as Gaul and the Gauls, when Machiavelli is discussing them from the perspective of the Romans, he typically uses these terms.

insolence and ambition of men. But to give life and vigor to those laws requires a virtuous citizen, one who will courageously help in their execution against the power of those who transgress them.

On the same topic, it was said by the magistrates who governed Florence from 1434 until 1494 that it was necessary every five years to rejuvenate the government, and that otherwise it would be difficult to maintain it. By "rejuvenating the government" they meant to strike the people with the same fear and terror as they did when they first assumed the government, when they had inflicted the most extreme punishment upon those who, according to their principles, had conducted themselves badly. But as the recollection of these punishments fades from men's minds, they become emboldened to make new attempts against the government, and to defame it, and therefore it is necessary to provide against this by bringing the government back to its beginnings. Such a return to first principles in a republic is sometimes caused by the simple virtues of one man, without depending upon any law that incites him to inflict extreme punishments; and yet his good example has such an influence that the good men strive to imitate him, and the wicked are ashamed to lead a life so contrary to his example.... And certainly if at least some such striking enforcement of the laws as described above, or noble examples, had occurred in Rome every ten years, that city would never have become so corrupt; but as both became more rare, corruption increased more and more. In fact, after Marcus Regulus[1] we find not a single instance of such virtuous example; and although the two Catos arose,[2] yet there was so long an interval between Regulus and them, and between the one Cato and the other, and they were such isolated instances, that their example accomplished little good; in particular, the latter Cato found the citizens

---

1 Marcus Regulus, elected consul during the first Punic War between Rome and Carthage, died in 250 BCE. His death at the hands of the Carthaginians was mythologized, and he became an icon of Roman valour.

2 Cato the Elder (234–197 BCE) was a Roman censor, a distinguished position responsible for determining eligibility to serve in the Senate, including the power to remove members deemed to have engaged in inappropriate behaviour. His great-grandson Cato the Younger (95–46 BCE) fought to preserve the Roman Republic by siding with Pompey against Caesar in the civil war that ended the Roman Republic and ushered in the Roman Empire. In the wake of his defeat, he committed suicide rather than submit to Caesar's mercy, becoming a martyr of the Roman Republic. Both were renowned for their moral integrity and commitment to Roman values.

of Rome already so corrupt that he utterly failed to improve them by his example. Let this suffice so far as regards republics.

Now with regard to religions we shall see that revivals are equally necessary, and the best proof of this is furnished by our own, which would have been entirely lost had it not been brought back to its pristine principles and purity by Saint Francis and Saint Dominic;[1] for by their voluntary poverty and the example of the life of Christ, they revived the sentiment of religion in the hearts of men, where it had become almost extinct. The new orders which they established were so powerful that they became the means of saving religion from being destroyed by the licentiousness of the prelates and heads of the Church. They continued themselves to live in poverty, and by means of hearing confessions and preaching they obtained so much influence with the people that they were able to make them understand that it was wicked even to speak ill of wicked rulers, and that it was proper to render them obedience and to leave the punishment of their errors to God. And thus these wicked rulers do as much evil as they please, because they do not fear a punishment they do not see or believe in. This revival of religion, then, by Saint Francis and Saint Dominic has preserved it and maintains it to this day.

Monarchies also need renewing, and to bring their institutions back to first principles. The Kingdom of France shows us the good effects of such renewals, for this monarchy more than any other is governed by laws and ordinances. The parlements, and mainly that of Paris, are the conservators of these laws and institutions, which are renewed by them from time to time by taking action against some of the princes of the realm, and at times even by decisions against the King himself. And thus this kingdom has maintained itself up to the present time by its determined constancy in repressing the ambition of the nobles; for if it were to leave them unpunished, the disorders would quickly multiply and the end would doubtless be either that the guilty could no longer be punished without great danger, or that the kingdom itself would be broken up.

We may conclude, then, that nothing is more necessary for an association of men, either as a religious sect, republic, or

---

1 Saint Francis of Assisi (1181–1226) founded the Franciscan Order rooted in the principles of apostolic poverty and unquestioning loyalty to the Church in 1209. Saint Dominic (c. 1170–1221) founded the Dominican Order in 1216 to preach and promote orthodox Church doctrine, especially among non-Christians or those whom the Church considered to hold heretical beliefs.

monarchy, than to restore to it from time to time the power and reputation which it had in the beginning, and to strive to have either good laws or good men to bring about such a result, without the need of intervention by any extrinsic force. For although such may at times be the best remedy, as in the case of Rome (when captured by the Gauls), yet it is so dangerous that it is in no way desirable....

Chapter II

It may at times be the highest wisdom to feign folly.

No one over displayed so much wisdom, or was esteemed so wise on account of any distinguished act, as Junius Brutus[1] deserves to be esteemed for his simulation of folly. And although Titus Livius gives but one reason that induced him to this simulation, namely, that he might live in greater security and preserve his property, yet if we well consider his conduct we are led to believe that he had another reason, which was that by thus avoiding observation he would have a better chance of destroying the kings, and of liberating his country, whenever an opportunity arose. And that such was really his thought may be seen, first, from his interpretation of the oracle of Apollo,[2] when he pretended to have fallen and kissed the earth, hoping thereby to propitiate the gods to his projects; and afterwards, when on the occasion of the death of Lucretia,[3] in

---

1 Junius Brutus, often referred to as simply Brutus by Machiavelli, was nephew to the last king of Rome. He had many grievances against the king, including the death of his brother, and so he pretended to be of limited intelligence and agreeable to anything the king wanted lest he provide the king with reason to fear him or desire any of his possessions.

2 Brutus accompanied two of the king's sons to the oracle at Delphi, where they asked who would be the next king of Rome. The oracle's answer was that whichever one of those present was the first to kiss his mother would hold supreme power in the city. The king's sons took this prophecy literally and drew lots to determine which of them would kiss their mother upon their return home. However, Brutus interpreted the oracle's response differently: he pretended to slip, fell to the ground, and kissed the earth, which he viewed as the mother of all. After the expulsion of the Tarquin kings in 509 BCE, he and Collantius became the first consuls of the Roman Republic. See Livy 1.56.

3 Upon hearing his cousin Collantius boast of his wife Lucretia's beauty, Sextus Tarquinius, son of the seventh and last king of Rome, became obsessed with Lucretia and sexually assaulted her, using the threats of killing her and dishonouring her by placing her body in a compromising

the midst of the father, husband, and other relatives, he was the first to pluck the dagger from her breast and to make all present swear henceforth to suffer no king to reign in Rome.

All those who are dissatisfied with their ruler should take a lesson from this example of Brutus; they should measure and weigh well their strength, and if sufficiently powerful to be able to declare themselves his enemies and to make open war against the prince, then they should take that course as the least dangerous and most honourable. But if their condition be such that their forces do not suffice for open war against the prince, then they should seek by every art to win his friendship, and for this purpose employ all possible means, such as adopting his tastes and taking delight in all things that give him pleasure. Such intimacy will ensure you tranquillity without any danger, enable you to share the enjoyment of the prince's good fortune with him, and at the same time afford you every convenience for enacting your plans. True, some people say that one should not keep so close to princes as to be involved in their ruin, nor so far away that when they are ruined you cannot advance your own fortunes. This middle course would undoubtedly be the best to pursue, but as I believe that impossible, one of the above-described modes must be adopted: either to go away from them entirely or to attach yourself very closely to them. Whoever attempts any other way and is a personage of distinction, exposes himself to constant danger. Nor will it do for him to say, "I do not care for anything; I desire neither honour nor profit; all I want is to live quietly and without trouble,"—for such excuses would not be accepted. Men of position cannot choose their way of living, and even if they did choose it sincerely and without ambition, they would not be believed; and were they to attempt to adhere to it, they would not be allowed to do so by others.

It is advisable, then, at times to feign folly, as Brutus did; and this is sufficiently done by praising, speaking, seeing, and doing things contrary to your way of thinking and character, and merely to please the prince. And as I have spoken of the wisdom of Brutus in recovering the liberty of Rome, let me now speak of his severity in maintaining it.

---

position alongside a slave whom he would also kill to force her cooperation. To avoid this fate, she gave in to his sexual demands. Afterwards she revealed these events to her husband and, in order to restore her honour, committed suicide in front of him, her father, and their comrades, including Brutus. Brutus pulled the dagger from her chest and demanded that all present pledge themselves to immediately avenge Lucretia and rid Rome of both the Tarquins and kings. See Livy 1.57–59.

Chapter III

To preserve the newly recovered liberty in Rome, it was necessary that the sons of Brutus be executed.

The severity of Brutus was not only useful, but necessary for the maintenance of that liberty in Rome which he had restored to her; and certainly it is one of the rarest examples within recorded history for a father not only to sit in judgment and condemn his own sons, but actually to be present at their execution. Every student of ancient history well knows that any change of government, be it from a republic to a tyranny, or from a tyranny to a republic, must necessarily be followed by some terrible punishment of the enemies of the new order of things. And whoever makes himself tyrant of a state and does not kill Brutus, or whoever restores liberty to a state and does not slaughter the sons of Brutus, will not maintain his position long. Having already in another place treated this subject at length,[1] I refer to what I have said there and confine myself now to citing a single and most remarkable example, taken from the history of our own country. It is that of Piero Soderini,[2] who believed that he would be able by patience and gentleness to overcome the determination of the new sons of Brutus to return to another form of government, in which, however, he greatly deceived himself. And although his natural wisdom recognized the necessity of destroying them, and although the quality and ambition of his adversaries afforded him the opportunity, yet he had not the courage to do so. For he thought, and several times acknowledged it to his friends, that to boldly strike down his adversaries and all opposition would oblige him to assume extraordinary authority, and even legally to destroy equality among the citizens; and that, even if he did not afterwards use this power tyrannically, this course would so alarm the masses that after his death they would never again consent to the election of another gonfalonier for life,[3] which he deemed essential

---

1 See *DL* 1.16.
2 Piero di Tommaso Soderini (1452–1522) was elected in Florence as gonfalonier for life (see n. 3 below) in 1502 following the expulsion of the Medici. After ignoring Machiavelli's advice to break a treaty with France and side militarily with the papacy, he and Florence were punished by Pope Julius II with the reinstatement of the Medici in 1512, which forced Soderini into permanent exile.
3 Gonfalonier, or standard-bearer for life, was an elected position; he who held it functioned as the head of the Florentine Republic.

for the strengthening and maintaining of the government. This respect for the laws was most praiseworthy and wise on the part of Soderini. Still one should never allow an evil to persist out of respect for the law, especially when the law itself might easily be destroyed by the evil; and he should have borne in mind that as his acts and motives would have to be judged by the result, had he been fortunate enough to succeed and live, everybody would have attested that what he had done was for the good of his country, and not for the advancement of any ambitious purposes of his own. Moreover, he could have regulated matters so that his successors could not have used for evil the means he had used for beneficent purposes. But Soderini deceived himself, not understanding that malignity is neither effaced by time nor placated by gifts. So that by failing to imitate Brutus he lost at the same time his country, his state, and his reputation.

...

Chapter XXV

Of the poverty of Cincinnatus and that of many other Roman citizens.

We have argued elsewhere[1] that it is of the greatest advantage in a republic to have laws that keep her citizens poor. Although there does not appear to have been any special law to this effect in Rome (the agrarian law having met with the greatest opposition), yet experience shows that even as late as four hundred years after its foundation there was still great poverty in Rome. We cannot ascribe this fact to any other cause than that poverty was never allowed to stand in the way of the achievement of any rank or honour, and that virtue and merit were sought for under whatever roof they dwelt; it was this system that made riches naturally less desirable. We have clear proof of this when the Consul Minutius and his army were surrounded by the Aequi,[2] and all Rome was full of apprehensions lest the army should be lost, so that they resorted to the creation of a Dictator, their last remedy in difficult

---

1 See *DL* 1.37.
2 A neighbouring people which predated the founding of Rome. They inhabited territories along the Apennine mountains to the east of Rome. Early Rome faced repeated military conflict with the Aequi, until they were assimilated as Roman citizens without voting rights at the end of the Second Samnite War in 304 BCE.

times. They appointed Lucius Quinctius Cincinnatus,[1] who at the time was on his little farm, which he cultivated with his own hands.... Cincinnatus was engaged in ploughing his fields, which did not exceed four acres, when the messengers of the Senate arrived from Rome to announce his election to the dictatorship, and to point out to him the imminent danger to the Roman Republic. He immediately put on his toga, gathered an army, and went to the relief of Minutius, and having crushed and despoiled the enemy, and freed the consul and his army, he would not permit them to share the spoils, saying, "I will not allow you to participate in the spoils of those to whom you came so near falling prey." He deprived Minutius of the consulate and reduced him to the rank of legate, saying to him, "You will remain in this rank until you have learned to be consul."[2] Cincinnatus then chose for his master of cavalry Lucius Tarquinius, whose poverty had obliged him to fight on foot. Let us note here how Rome honoured poverty (as has been said) and how four acres of land sufficed for the support of so good and great a citizen as Cincinnatus....

...

Chapter XXIX

The faults of the people spring from the faults of their rulers.

Let not princes complain of the faults committed by the people subjected to their authority, for they result entirely from the prince's own negligence or bad example. In examining the people who in our day have been given to larceny and other vices of that kind, we see that these arise entirely from the faults of their rulers, who were guilty of similar abuses. Before Pope Alexander VI[3] had crushed the petty tyrants that ruled the Romagna, that country presented an example of all the worst crimes. The slightest causes gave rise to murder and every kind of plundering, and this was

---

1 Lucius Quinctius Cincinnatus (c. 519–c. 430 BCE) served as a Roman consul. He was appointed dictator in 458 BCE, after his retirement, and subsequently upheld as an exemplar of Roman virtue and civic-mindedness.
2 See Livy 3.29.
3 Pope Alexander VI (1431–1503), father of Cesare Borgia, served as pope from 1492 to 1503. Machiavelli discusses him in *The Prince*, chapters 3, 7, 11, and 18.

due exclusively to the wickedness of the princes and not to the evil nature of the people, as alleged by the former. For these princes, being poor, yet wishing to live in luxury like the rich, were obliged to resort to every variety of plundering. And among other dishonest means which they employed was the making of laws prohibiting one thing or another, and immediately afterwards they were themselves the first to encourage their non-observance, leaving such transgressions unpunished until a great number of persons had been guilty of it, and then suddenly they turned to prosecute the transgressors, not from any zeal for the law, but solely from greed, in the expectation of obtaining money for commuting the punishment. These infamous proceedings caused many evils, the worst of them being that the people became impoverished without being corrected, and that then the stronger among them tried to make good their losses by plundering the weaker. This gave rise to all the evils of which we have spoken above and for which the prince is solely responsible....

...

Chapter XXXI

Great men and powerful republics preserve an equal dignity and courage in prosperity and adversity.

Among the admirable sayings and doings of Camillus as told by our historian, Titus Livius, for the purpose of showing how a great man conducts himself, he puts the following words into his mouth: "My courage has neither been inflated by the dictatorship nor abated by exile."[1] These words show that a truly great man is always the same under all circumstances, and if his fortune varies, exalting him at one moment and oppressing him at another, he himself never varies but always maintains a firm courage, which is so closely interwoven with his character that everyone can readily see that the fickleness of Fortune has no power over him. The conduct of weak men is very different. Made vain and intoxicated by good fortune, they attribute their success to merits they do not possess, and this makes them odious and insupportable to all around them. And when they later have to meet a reverse of fortune, they quickly fall into the other extreme and become abject and vile. Thus it is that princes of this character think more of

---

1 See Livy 6.7.

escaping in adversity than of defending themselves, like men who, having made a bad use of prosperity, are wholly unprepared for any defence against reverses.

These virtues and vices are found in republics as well as in individuals. Rome and Venice furnish us an example of this. No ill fortune ever made the former abject, nor did success ever make her insolent. This was clearly shown after the defeat of the Romans at Cannae[1] and after their victory over Antiochus.[2] For this defeat, although most alarming, being the third, never discouraged them: they put new armies into the field and refused to violate their constitution by ransoming their prisoners. Nor did they sue for peace with either Hannibal or Carthage; and repelling all such base suggestions, they thought only of fighting anew and overcame their lack of soldiers by arming their old men and slaves.... On the other hand, they were not made insolent by prosperity, for when Antiochus, before engaging in the battle with them, in which he was defeated, sent messengers to Scipio[3] to ask for peace, the latter named the conditions on which he was willing to grant it, which were that Antiochus should retire beyond Syria and leave the rest of the country to the control of the Romans. Antiochus declined these terms but accepted battle and was defeated, whereupon he sent his messengers back to Scipio with orders to accept whatever conditions Scipio offered. Scipio added no further conditions to those which he had named before his victory, saying: "The Romans do not lose their courage in defeat, nor does victory make them overbearing."[4]

The conduct of the Venetians was exactly the opposite of this, for in good fortune, which they imagined entirely to be the result of a skill and valour which they did not possess, they carried their insolence to the degree that they called the King of France a son of St. Mark.[5] They had no respect for the Church, nor for any other power in all Italy, and had the presumption to think of creating

---

1 The Romans were defeated by Hannibal (247–c. 181 BCE), who commanded an army comprising African, Gallic, and Celtiberian forces, at the Battle of Cannae in 216 BCE, during the second Punic War between Rome and Carthage.

2 Rome's war against the Seleucid Empire (192–188 BCE) marked the second victory of Rome against a successor state of Alexander the Great's empire (Macedon being the first).

3 Scipio Africanus (236–183 BCE) was a celebrated Roman general. The battle mentioned was fought at Magnesia in 190 BCE.

4 See Livy 37.45.

5 The patron saint of Venice.

another empire similar to that of the Romans. Afterwards, when their good fortune abandoned them and they suffered a partial defeat at Vailà at the hands of the King of France,[1] they not only lost the greater part of their state by a rebellion, but, under the influence of their cowardly and abject spirit, they actually made large concessions of territory to the Pope and the King of Spain, and were so utterly demoralized that they sent ambassadors to the Emperor and made themselves tributary to him; and by way of moving the Pope to compassion, they sent him the most humiliating letters of submission. And to this wretchedness were they reduced within the short space of four days and after but a partial defeat. For their army, after having sustained a fight, retreated in part and about half of it was attacked and beaten; however, one of their proveditori[2] saved himself and reached Verona with over twenty-five thousand men, on horse and foot. If there had been but one spark of true valour in the Venetians, they could easily have recovered from this defeat and faced Fortune anew, for they would still have been in time either to have conquered or to have lost less ignominiously, or to have concluded a more honourable peace. But their miserable baseness of spirit, caused by a wretched military organization, made them lose at a single blow their courage and their state. And thus it will always happen to those who are governed in the same way that the Venetians were, for insolence in prosperity and abjectness in adversity are the result of habit and education. If this is vain and weak, then their conduct will likewise be without energy. But if the education be of an opposite nature, then it will produce men of a different character; it will enable them to know the world better, and will teach them to be less elated in good fortune and less depressed by adversity. And what we say of individuals applies equally to the many who constitute a republic, and who will form themselves according to the manners and institutions that prevail there.

Now, any republic that adopts the military organization and discipline of the Romans, and strives by constant training to give her citizens and soldiers experience and to develop their courage and mastery over Fortune, will always and under all

---

1 The Battle of Agnadello (1509) between Venice and the League of Cambrai, consisting of Louis XII of France, Pope Julius II, Ferdinand II of Aragon, and the Holy Roman Emperor Maximilian I. Machiavelli also mentions this event in *The Prince*, chapter 12, and *Florentine Histories* 1.29.

2 A quartermaster.

circumstances find them to display a courage and dignity similar to that of the Romans. But a republic which lacks such military force, and which relies more upon the chances of Fortune than upon the valour of her citizens, will experience all the vicissitudes of Fortune and its citizens will always behave similar to the Venetians.

...

Chapter XXXVI

The reason why the French have been and are still looked upon at the beginning of a combat as more than men, and afterwards as less than women.

The audacity of that Gaul who challenged to single combat any Roman of the army on the Arno, and his subsequent combat with Titus Manlius,[1] reminds me of the saying of Titus Livius, "that the French at the beginning of a battle are more than men, but in the course of combat they become less than women." In reflecting upon the causes to which this is attributed, I believe the general opinion to be true, that it is because of their natural temperament. But we must not infer from this that this temperament, which makes them so ferocious in the beginning, may not be so disciplined by training that they will preserve their valour up to the very end of the fight. And to prove this I maintain that there are three different characters of troops. One combines warlike ardor with discipline: this produces true valour, like that of the Romans. All history shows that a proper discipline prevailed in their armies and had done so for a long time. For in a well-ordered army no one should do anything except in accordance with the regulations; and accordingly we find that the Roman armies (which having vanquished the world may well serve as an example to all others) neither ate nor slept, nor performed any other act, military or civil, unless according to the order of the consul. And armies that do not observe such a system cannot in reality be called armies; and if nevertheless they sometimes seem to deserve the name, it is more by their ardor and a sort of blind impulse than by their steady valour. But where that ardor is properly disciplined, it employs its impetuosity at the right time and with moderation, and no difficulties can abate or unsettle it. For good order sustains

---

1 See Livy 7.10.

courage and reanimates that ardor with the hope of victory, which will never fail if discipline is preserved. The opposite happens in armies that have ardor without discipline: such was the case with the French, who were wholly lacking in discipline during combat. For if they did not overthrow the enemy by their first furious onset, upon which they relied for victory, not being sustained by a well-regulated valour and having nothing besides their impetuosity to give them confidence, they failed when that first ardor was cooled. But with the Romans it was very different; less mindful of danger because of the good order which they preserved during battle, they felt assured of victory and continued the fight with firm and obstinate courage, and manifested the same valour at the end of the battle as they did at the beginning, the heat of the contest inflaming their courage rather than otherwise. The third kind of armies are such as have neither natural ardor nor discipline. Of this kind are the Italian armies of our time, which are entirely useless. Unless they fall upon an enemy that by some accident has retreated, they are never victorious. Without citing any special instances, we have daily proofs of their total lack of valour....

...

Appendix B: Selections from Tercets on Fortune[1]

[A tercet is a three-lined verse, or a group of such verses, often rhyming internally or with surrounding verses. The exact date of composition remains unknown, but Machiavelli likely wrote the *Tercets on Fortune* sometime in the latter half of 1506. He dedicated the poem to Giovan Battista Soderini (1484–1528), who was the nephew of Piero Soderini, the gonfalonier for life and Machiavelli's boss during his career serving the Florentine Republic. This dedication is the second notable direct link between Machiavelli and the younger Soderini, the first being a letter Machiavelli wrote to him in September 1506, referred to by scholars as the *Ghiribizzi* letter (Letter 121), in which Machiavelli outlines several key ideas which would later appear in both *The Prince* and the *Tercets on Fortune*. At a minimum, the existence of the *Ghiribizzi* letter establishes that Machiavelli had already conceived of these ideas in 1506.

Several key political themes are developed in this poem: Fortune is elevated from the status of a raging river or a woman to a goddess; likewise, her power has grown to the point where no individual escapes her influence, and she is depicted as cruel and unfair by human standards. She and the others in her palace drive the rise and fall not only of individuals but also of states, alluding to the cyclical conception of history that Machiavelli discusses openly in the *Discourses on Livy* (3.1) and the *Florentine Histories* (5.1). Building on existing imagery concerning the Roman goddess, Machiavelli creates a mythology around her, depicting her palace as filled with numerous wheels of changing speeds and direction, and he introduces Laziness, Necessity, and Opportunity as personifications of the forces which drive events in one direction or another. The moral of the poem is that the only way to succeed is to be in concert with Fortune's whims, that is, for the individual to jump from wheel to wheel in the hopes of maintaining a position on one with a favourable motion.]

---

1 Translated by Kirsty Jane Falconer for this volume.

… Many call her omnipotent; for whoever comes into this life will feel her power, either sooner or later.

She often tramples the good beneath her feet and raises up the dishonest; and if ever she makes you a promise, she never keeps it.

She turns states and kingdoms on their heads, according to her whim; and she deprives good men of those benefits she gives generously to the unjust.

This fickle Goddess, this changeable deity often seats the unworthy on a throne that he who is worthy of it never attains.

She spends her time as she wills; exalting and undoing us without mercy, law, or reason.

She does not like to favour one man in all seasons, nor does she always go on crushing him who lies beneath her wheel.

Whose daughter she is, from what seed she sprang nobody knows; but we know for sure that even Jove[1] fears her power.

She rules over a palace laid open on all sides; she does not stop anyone from entering, but leaving is uncertain.

Everyone gathers there, eager to see new things and filled with ambition and desire.

She dwells at the highest point, denying no man the sight of her; but in a short time she turns and moves her aspect.

And this ancient witch has two faces, one fierce and the other gentle; and as she turns, she now does not see you, now threatens, now entreats.

She graciously hears all who want to enter, but she becomes enraged with anyone who wants to leave, and often he is deprived of his way out.

Inside her palace, as many wheels turn as there are different ways of reaching those things all living men set out to attain.

Sighing, blasphemy and insults are heard all around from those Fortune harbours within her bounds.

And the richer and more powerful they are, the more discourtesy they show, and the less conscious they are of her benevolence.

For all the evil that comes upon us we blame on her; and if anything good befalls a man, he believes that he got it by his own ability (*virtù*).

Among the singular and varied crowd of fellow servants within that place, Audacity and Youth make the best showing.

---

1 Jove, also referred to as Jupiter, is the supreme god of the Roman pantheon. He is associated with the sky and corresponds to Zeus from the Greek pantheon.

We see Fearfulness prostrate upon the ground, so filled with
doubts that he does nothing at all; Envy and Penitence wage
war on him.

There Opportunity disports herself alone; this simple, tousled
girl goes gambolling among the wheels around.

And those wheels turn day and night, because Heaven (which
is not to be opposed) wills it that Idleness and Necessity spin
them around.

The latter repairs the world and the former ruins it. In every
hour, in every season we see Patience's worth, and how much
she can endure.

Rich and powerful, Usury and Fraud revel with their crew; and
among the company is Liberality, ragged and broken.

Luck and Happenstance, without eyes or ears, are seated above
the gates it's said are never locked.

Power, Honour, Wealth and Health stand ready as rewards;
Servitude, Infamy, Disease and Poverty as punishment and
affliction.

Fortune vents her passionate fury with the latter group; she gives
the former to those she loves.

Among all the others in that place, he is luckiest in his decision
who picks a wheel befitting her desires; because the humours
that move you are what bring you good or ill, according to
how well they suit her.

Therefore you cannot trust in her, nor have faith that you will
avoid her hard bite, her harsh, cruel and impetuous blows.

Because while you are being spun on the rim of a wheel that,
for the moment, is a good and lucky one, Fortune is prone to
reverse its direction halfway round;

and since you cannot change your person or forsake the disposition Heaven gave you, she abandons you in the middle of your
journey.

And so, if he knew and understood this, a man would always
be blessed and fortunate who could jump from one wheel to
another.

But since we are denied this ability by the occult force (*virtù*) that
governs us, our condition changes with the wheel's course.

Nothing is eternal in the world; Fortune wills it thus so that she
can increase her splendour by it, making her power clearer to
see.

That is why we should take her as our guiding star and every
hour, so far as we can, adapt ourselves to her variations.

The whole of her domain is decorated, inside and out, with narrative paintings of those victories of which she is proudest.

First of all we see, in vivid colours, how Egypt[1] conquered and subjugated the world, and kept it under control for a long time through lasting peace; and how it was there that the beauty of nature was first described in writing.

Then we see the Assyrians[2] ascend to the high throne, when Fortune no longer wanted Egypt's rule to prevail.

After that, we see her turn happily to the Medes,[3] from the Medes to the Persians;[4] and with the diadem she took from the Persians, she crowned the locks of the Greeks.[5]

Here we see Memphis and Thebes crushed, and Babylon, Troy and Carthage along with them, Jerusalem, Athens, Sparta and Rome.

Here we see how splendid, exalted, rich and powerful they were and how, at last, Fortune gave them over to their enemies.

Here we see the divine and noble deeds of the Roman Empire, and then how all the world was shattered when it fell.

As a swift, fierce torrent, wherever its current reaches, smashes everything around—building up one place and eroding another, shifting its banks, its bed and its base, and making the earth tremble where it passes—so does Fortune often go changing the things of the world, now here and now there, with her furious impetus.

Look further, and you will see Caesar[6] and Alexander[7] in one panel among those who prospered in life.

From their example we clearly see how pleasing, how acceptable to Fortune is he who pushes her, shoves her, drives her away.

But nonetheless, one of them did not reach his longed-for harbour; and the other died, riddled with wounds, in the shadow of his enemy.

---

1 Egypt dominated much of the Mediterranean region from 3100 BCE, until it was conquered by the Macedonians in 332 BCE.
2 The Assyrian Empire thrived from 1365 to 609 BCE.
3 The Median Empire lasted from c. 625 to 550 BCE.
4 The Medes fell to Cyrus the Great of Persia in 550 BCE.
5 Greek civilization arose in the wake of, and possibly contributed to the decline of, the Mycenaean civilization in 1200 BCE, and lasted until the death of Alexander the Great in 323 BCE.
6 Julius Caesar (100–44 BCE) emerged victorious from the civil war which marked the end of Rome's republican phase.
7 Alexander the Great (356–323 BCE) built upon his father's conquest of the Mediterranean region by conquering Persia.

After these two come infinitely many who rose with Fortune to a
   tremendous height, so as to fall to earth with a greater crash.
Among these, Cyrus[1] and Pompey[2] lie captive, dead and broken,
   Fortune having carried each of them as high as the heavens.
Have you ever seen in some place a furious eagle fly, driven on by
   hunger and fasting? And how she carries a tortoise up high so
   that the impact of the fall shatters it, and she can feed off its
   dead flesh?
So Fortune carries a man up high, not so he may remain there,
   but so she may feast on him at his ruin; and he may weep as
   he falls.
Looking at those who come next, we see how men rise high from
   the basest state, and how changeable life is.
We see how she afflicts Tullius[3] and Marius;[4] many times she
   grows the splendid horns of their glory, then cuts them off.
Finally, we see that in past days few have prospered; and those
   few died before their wheel reversed its course, or before its
   turning bore them down to the depths.

---

1 Cyrus the Great (c. 590/80 BCE–c. 529 BCE), also known as Cyrus
   II, was born Persian but became ruler of the Medes. He was lauded in
   Xenophon's *Cyropaedia* as a great and tolerant monarch. Cyrus had
   many military successes, but he was eventually executed by the queen of
   the Massagetai, a nomadic people whose land he was trying to capture.
2 Gnaeus Pompeius Magnus (106–48 BCE), also known as Pompey the
   Great, was a Roman statesman and military commander who opposed
   Julis Caesar during the civil war. Despite outnumbering Caesar's
   forces, Pompey suffered a decisive defeat against Caesar at the Battle of
   Pharsalus in Greece. He fled to Egypt in hopes of securing aid but was
   betrayed and killed by Ptolemy XIII (r. 51–47 BCE), who at that time
   wanted to maintain good relations with Caesar.
3 Servius Tullius (r. 578–535 BCE), the sixth king of Rome. He was considered a benevolent ruler, although he was plagued by speculation of a
   lowly birth and the fact that he was the first Roman king who was not
   elected to the position. He was murdered by one of his daughters and
   his son-in-law, Lucius Tarquinius Superbus (d. c. 495 BCE), who succeeded him as king and who would be the last king of Rome.
4 Gaius Marius (c. 157–86 BCE) was a Roman politician and general
   who reformed the Roman military and served as consul a remarkable
   seven times; despite his many successes, his ambitions were repeatedly
   thwarted.

Appendix C: On Opportunity[1]

[The poem *On Opportunity* is not an original work by Machiavelli but an adaptation of the twelfth epigram of Ausonius, a fourth-century Latin grammarian, poet, and rhetorician from Gaul. Machiavelli dedicated the work to Filippo de' Nerli, a Medici partisan and participant in the humanist gatherings in the Orti Oricellari. The date of the poem is unknown, but given the dedication it is likely to have been composed during Machiavelli's time with this group.

The poem is significant for fleshing out themes found in *The Prince*, chapters 6 and 26, the *Discourses on Livy* 2.29, and the *Tercets on Fortune*. The poem takes the form of a brief dialogue between the poet and Opportunity (sometimes translated as "Occasion"), who runs free in Fortune's palace, is needed by even the greatest of individuals in order to succeed, and is frustratingly elusive.]

Who are you, who seem no mortal lady; with such grace Heaven
    endows and adorns you.
Why don't you rest? Why do you have wings on your feet?
"I am Opportunity, known to few; and the reason I am always
    restless is that I keep one foot upon a wheel.
My running is incomparably faster than flight; and so I keep
    these wings on my feet, so that everyone is bedazzled as I run.
I wear my sparse hair forward and use it to cover my breast and
    face, so that nobody can recognise me as I approach.
At the back of my head every hair is removed, so that anyone will
    strive in vain [to catch me] if I happen to pass him by or turn
    against him."
And tell me, who is she who goes with you?
"That's Penitence: now note and understand, who cannot seize
    me will end up grasping her.
And while you spend your time talking and busy with idle
    thoughts, lax creature, you don't realise or understand that
    I've already slipped through your hands."

---

1   Translated by Kirsty Jane Falconer for this volume.

Appendix D: Selections from Tercets on Ambition[1]

[The exact dating of the *Tercets on Ambition* remains elusive. However, while on a mission to Verona, Machiavelli makes references in reports to his superiors dated November and December 1509, which suggest he was working on the poem around this time. The poem is dedicated to Luigi Guicciardini (1478–1551), brother of the historian Francesco Guicciardini (1483–1540), who was both a friend and critic of Machiavelli.

Many of the themes in the poem recur in his other works, such as human nature (*The Prince*, chapters 17 and 18), the importance of education and discipline in military engagements (*Discourses on Livy* 2.2, 2.16, and 3.36), and the contrast between ancient and contemporary political and military successes (throughout *The Prince*, the *Discourses on Livy*, and *The Art of War*). Additionally, Machiavelli's poetic talents are on full display as he describes the horrors of war, a reality which is often glossed over in his other discussions of warfare.]

... Ambition and avarice get in everywhere.
When man was born into the world, so too were they; and if not
    for them, our state would be a very happy one.
God had just made the stars, heaven, the light, the elements and
    man—the master of so many beautiful things—and had bro-
    ken the pride of the angels, and exiled Adam and his lady from
    Paradise for tasting the apple;
and then, when Cain and Abel[2] had been born and were living
    happily from their labour in their poor dwelling with their
    father, an occult power that is nurtured in heaven, among
    the stars that revolve within it—a power none too friendly to
    human nature—sent two furies to live on earth to deprive us
    of peace and set us at war, and take from us all tranquillity and
    all well-being.

---

1   Translated by Kirsty Jane Falconer for this volume.
2   Cain and Abel were the children of Adam and Eve. Genesis 4:1–16
    recounts how Cain killed Abel out of jealousy, committing the first
    recorded murder in the Bible.

These two are nude, and each of them appears with such grace
that, to many people's eyes, they seem graceful and abounding
in delight.
But each has four faces and eight hands, and these let them grasp
you, and see wherever they turn.
Envy, Sloth and Hate go with them, filling the world with their
pestilence, and along with those go Cruelty, Pride and Deceit.
They drive Concord down to the depths; and to show their
infinite desire, they carry a bottomless urn in their hands.
Because of these two, the quiet and sweet life that once filled
Adam's dwelling has fled, along with Peace and Love (*carità*).
With their pestiferous poison they armed Cain against his good
brother, filling his gut, breast and heart with it.
And they showed their great power because they could create an
ambitious heart, an avaricious heart even in the earliest times,
when men lived naked and innocent of all riches, and when
there were as yet no examples of poverty or wealth.
O insatiable human spirit, arrogant, shifty and mutable, and
above all else malign, cruel, impetuous and savage; for through
your ambitious desire, the first violent murder was done in the
world, and the first grass bloodied.
Now the bad seed has ripened and the causes of evil multiplied,
there is no longer any reason to repent of wrongdoing.
This is why one man falls and another rises; on this the variation
of every mortal state depends, without law or covenant.
This has brought the King forth from France several times; this
has unmade the states of King Alphonse,[1] and Louis,[2] and
Saint Mark.[3]
Every man values not only whatever good his enemy has, but
also what he appears to have (and so was the world ever made,
both modern and ancient); every man aspires to climb higher
by oppressing now this one, now that one, rather than by some
excellence (*virtù*) of his own.
To each of us, the success of another is always vexatious; and that
is why, with anxiety and effort, we always remain vigilant and
alert for other people's trouble.
We are driven to this by natural instinct, by our own impulse and
our own passion, unless some law or greater force restrain us.

---

1 Probably King Alfonso II of Naples (r. 1494–95).
2 Louis XII of France (r. 1498–1515), whose incursions into Italy were all
repelled.
3 Saint Mark is the patron saint of Venice.

But if you want to know why it is that one people prevails and
    another weeps, while Ambition rules over all;

and why France continues victorious, and why, on the other
    hand, a stormy sea of suffering shatters all Italy, and why these
    lands bear the affliction of that bad seed ripened by Ambition
    and Avarice—[I say that] if Ambition is joined together with a
    fierce heart and well-armed prowess (*virtù*), then a man rarely
    fears that evil will befall him.

When a land lives unbridled by its own nature, and then happens
    to be schooled and brought into order by good laws, then
    Ambition turns against foreign peoples that wrath that neither
    law nor King permit her to use at home; and this means that
    domestic trouble almost always ceases, but Ambition will
    continue to disrupt other sheepfolds wherever her wrath has
    planted its flag.

In the opposite way, that land where the people are ambitious
    and cowardly is a servile one, exposed to every harm and every
    insult.

If Cowardice and Bad Order are seated alongside Ambition, then
    every disaster, every failure, every other ill will soon come.

And if anyone says that it is Nature's fault that in much-suffer-
    ing, weary Italy, men are not born so fierce and hardy, then I
    say that this does not justify or excuse our cowardice, because
    discipline can supplement where Nature is lacking.

In the past, this made Italy flourish; ferocious discipline embold-
    ened her to conquer all the world.

Now we live, if life it is to live weeping, beneath the ruin and the
    fate merited by her great idleness.

This idleness is equal to Cowardice and its companions; the
    wounds that killed the Italian provinces come from Ambition.

…You will see that Ambition gives rise to two types of action:
    one man steals, and the other laments his torn and scattered
    fortunes.

Let him turn his eyes here who wishes to see the struggles of
    other men; let him consider whether the sun has ever beheld
    such cruelty before.

One weeps for his dead father, another for her husband; another
    is dragged, miserable, from his own dwelling, naked and
    beaten.

O, how many times has a father clutched his son in his arms, and
    a single blow has pierced both their breasts!

Another man leaves his ancestral land with his sorrowing brood,
    accusing the cruel and ingrate gods.

O, things such as have never happened in the world! Every day,
many babies are born by a slash to the mother's belly.
The mother says to her woe-filled daughter: "To what unhappy
nuptials, to what cruel husband have I delivered you!"
The ditches and streams are filthy with blood, full of heads, legs,
hands, and other torn and severed parts.
Birds of prey, wild beasts and dogs are now their ancestral
tombs—O cruel, terrible, unnatural sepulchres!
Their faces are always dark and grim, like that of a man horrified
and stunned by new injuries or sudden terrors.
Wherever you look, you see the earth drenched in blood and
tears and the air thick with screams, sobs and sighs.
If anyone deigns to learn from others how Ambition should be
used, then their sad example will teach him.
Since man cannot drive her out of himself, then she must be
accompanied by judgement and sound intellect, with order
and with ferocity.
... I see Ambition flying over the Tuscan mountains with that
swarm Heaven allotted her when the world began;
and she has already sown so many sparks among those people
soaked in envy that she will burn their lands and their home-
steads, unless grace or better government extinguish her.

Appendix E: Selections from
The Golden Ass[1]

[The title *The Golden Ass* was taken from a prose narrative of
the same name by Apuleius of Madauros (second century CE),
a Roman philosopher and rhetorician. The dating of the poem
is uncertain, although its negative themes suggest it was written
between the disinterested reaction of the Medici to *The Prince*
in 1515 and the start of Machiavelli's restoration in 1520. These
were the darkest days of Machiavelli's life, days spent looking longingly at the world of Florentine politics from the outside, bereft of all hope that he would ever be allowed to meaningfully serve Florence again. The poem was never completed
by Machiavelli, so it has no dedicatee, a fact which has spurred
much speculation among scholars. Amidst the dark leitmotifs of
the poem, Machiavelli vented his anger with numerous unflatter-
ing allusions to contemporary figures he despised, making this
a particularly dangerous work which, if released to the public,
would have undoubtedly caused him personal and professional
problems. The combination of darkness, anger, and hopelessness
that characterize the poem provide the most likely explanation for
why Machiavelli stopped working on it: when the Medici Pope
Clement VII (r. 1523–34) began to show signs of being amicable
toward Machiavelli and commissioned him to write the *Florentine
Histories*, Machiavelli then had reason to believe not only that he
could be restored to the world of Florentine politics but that his
advice would be heeded by his superiors. The prospect of political redemption was enough to assuage Machiavelli's personal
grudges and fill him with confidence that Fortune was beginning
to favour him.

The poem's first chapter includes what is widely accepted as
an autobiographical story by Machiavelli of a Florentine youth
possessed by a madness which compels him to run through the
streets, just as Machiavelli cannot keep himself from discussing
politics. From there, the themes of the poem reflect Machiavelli's
bleak perspective in the wake of being shut out of Florentine
political circles. The narrator finds himself terrified and lost in
a dark forest, only to be seemingly rescued by a beautiful young

---

1   Translated by Kirsty Jane Falconer for this volume.

woman herding animals. She introduces herself and informs him that he has stumbled into the domain of Circe (Fortune by another name), a goddess of such power that even Jove, the male head of the Roman pantheon, fears her. Circe is hostile to all men and lies in wait for them to arrive here, where she turns them into animals. Escape is impossible, just as no one escapes Fortune's influence, but Circe's servant eases the narrator's transition by taking the time to explain what his fate will be and giving him time to accept it. Pretending to be one of her animals, the narrator follows her into Circe's encampment and there is hidden by the young woman, who comforts him with intimacy when she is not tending to her flock. In her absence, the narrator reflects on his own situation, how Fortune has treated him, and her role in worldly affairs, including the cyclical conception of history which appeared in both the *Discourses on Livy* 3.1 and the *Florentine Histories* 5.1. As part of the process of reconciling him to his fate, the young woman takes him on a tour of the various animals Circe keeps, all men who have wandered into her domain and have been transformed into animals indicative of their true natures. The tour reaches a climax in which the narrator is permitted a discussion with a boar covered in mud and excrement. The narrator, presumptuous about his own status as human, offers to have the boar transformed back into human form during their discussion, only to be reprimanded by the boar in what becomes a scathing monologue on the human condition, and, by means of contrast, how exalted animals are in their circumstances.]

From the Second Chapter [Circe's servant speaks]

... But since you cannot know about our circumstances, I'll tell
    you in what desolate place you find yourself, and in what
    lands.
When in times past Circe[1] had to flee her ancient nest, back
    before Jove seized power, she found no safe refuge and none
    who would take her in, so loud was the clamour of her infamy;
she made her home in these dense, shadowed woods, fleeing all
    human company, and here she fixed her seat.

---

1 A goddess in Greek mythology, the daughter of the sun god Helios
   and the ocean nymph Perse, said to be powerful with magic and able
   to transform men into animals. In Book 10 of Homer's *Odyssey* she is
   depicted as living on the island of Aeaea, where she ensnares Odysseus's
   crew and turns them into swine.

And so she dwells here among these lonely crags, an enemy of
man, nourished by the sighing of this flock.
Since nobody who comes here ever leaves again, no news of her
has been heard, or is heard still....

From the Fifth Chapter [The narrator contemplates the rise and fall of states]

... And since one thought answers another, my mind flew to past
events that time has not yet hidden from us;
and darted here and there, reflecting on how often Fortune
would now caress, now bite those noble and renowned ancient
peoples.
This all seemed so wondrous to me that I decided to work out for
myself what causes the variation of worldly affairs.
The one thing, more than anything else, that can send a kingdom
tumbling from the highest peak is the fact that the powerful
are never sated by the power they hold.
This means that those who lose are ill content; and the urge
arises to ruin the winners.
This is why one man soars and another perishes; and he who
soars is ever more consumed by new ambition and fear.
This appetite destroys states; and what's stranger still is that
everyone knows about this error, but none avoid it.
Impetuous, importunate Saint Mark[1] did not care if he ruined
everyone else, because he thought the wind would be always at
his back;
he did not see that too much power was harmful, and that it
would be better to keep his tail and rump below water.
A man has often mourned the domain he once had, and real-
ised only afterwards that he expanded it to his own ruin and
detriment.
Athens and Sparta, whose names were once great the world over,
came to grief only when they had conquered all the surrounding powers.
But in the present day, every German city lives securely because
its territory extends less than six miles around.
When our own city's confines lay close to her walls, she did not
even fear Henry with all his might;[2]

---

1 Saint Mark is the patron saint of Venice.
2 Emperor Henry VII (r. 1312–13) unsuccessfully laid siege to Florence in
1312.

but now that she has spread her power all around and grown great and vast, she is frightened of everything, not just large armies.

The strength (*virtù*) sufficient to support a single body is not enough to bear a greater weight.

He who wants to extend his reach from pole to pole finds himself broken on the ground, like Icarus[1] did after his mad flight.

In truth, a power will generally endure for more or less time, according to how good or bad its laws and civic orders are.

The kingdom driven to action by excellence (*virtù*) or by necessity will rise and keep rising.

And on the contrary, the city with good laws and bad customs will be full of brushwood and thorns, and will change her rule from summer to winter until, of necessity, in the end she is reduced to nothing; and her aim will always be off.

If you read about past events, you know that empires begin with Ninus and end with Sardanapalus.[2]

The former was held to be a divine man; the latter was found in among the maidservants, dispensing flax, like a woman.

Excellence (*virtù*) makes regions tranquil; and from tranquillity then results idleness; and idleness burns towns and villages.

And then when a province has been caught up in disorder for a time, excellence usually returns to live there again.

She who rules us permits this sequence and wills it, so that nothing under the sun is or can ever be constant.

It is, always has been and always will be the case that evil follows good, and good evil; and that one is always cause of the other....

...The belief that God will fight for you without your doing anything, while you are idle upon your knees, has ruined many kingdoms and governments.

Prayers are indeed necessary; the man who denies the people ceremony and bans them from their devotions is entirely mad; in fact, it seems that good order and union may be reaped from these, and good, happy fortune depends on them.

---

1   In Greek mythology, Icarus was the son of the master craftsperson and inventor Daedalus. While fleeing justice for a crime he committed, Daedalus and his son were held captive by king Minos on Crete. To escape, Daedalus fashioned two pairs of wings made out of feathers and wax. As they made their escape, Icarus flew too close to the sun, the wax melted, the wings failed, and he plummeted into the sea and drowned.

2   The legendary first and last rulers of the Assyrian Empire. The founding of the city of Nineveh is attributed to Ninus, while Sardanapalus' rule ended with the Assyrian Empire falling to the Medes.

But nobody should be so lacking in brains as to believe that, if his
    house is collapsing, God will save it without any other support;
    for he will die beneath the wreckage....

From the Eighth Chapter [The narrator's discussion with the filth-covered boar]

... When we arrived, the pig raised his snout, all smeared with
    mud and filth; it nauseated me to look at him.
And since he had known me long ago, he turned to me and
    showed me his teeth, but otherwise stayed quietly where he
    was.
In gracious tones I said to him: "May God grant you a better fate,
    if you wish—may He keep you, if you be content. If you would
    like to talk with me, then I shall be happy....
She who showed me this desert path gave me her permission to
    speak to you freely and honestly....
She also asked me to tell you on her behalf that she will free you
    from this great evil, if you want to return to your old form."
Hearing this, the Boar stood up straight on his hind legs, all agi-
    tated and muddy, and replied:
"I don't know from where you've come or from what shore, but if
    you came for no other reason than to take me away from here,
    then you can go right back again.
I don't want to live among you. I refuse. And I clearly see that
    you are in that same error that long had hold of me, too.
So badly does your self-love deceive you that you think there is
    no other good than human life and its merit;
but if you set your sights on me, then I shall make sure you are
    disabused of this error before you leave my presence.
Let me start with prudence: an admirable virtue through which
    men increase their excellence.
They use it best who know—for themselves, without other
    instruction—how to pursue their own well-being and avoid
    harm.
But without any doubt I state and affirm that we are superior;
    and shortly, not even you will deny it.
What preceptor shows us which plant is which, whether benign
    or harmful?
We don't study these things; we aren't ignorant like you.
We move our dwelling-place from shore to shore, and it never
    pains us to leave one abode, so long as we live happily and
    well.

One flees the frost and another the sun; we seek the climate most
    hospitable to us, as Nature wills who teaches us.

You, unhappier than I can say, go searching this place and that;
    not to find a cool or pleasant climate, but because your brazen
    greed does not allow your spirit to keep to a frugal, modest
    and civil way of life;

you often leave a good climate and move where the air is rotten
    and sick, and not as a way of protecting your lives.

We only flee the climate, but you flee poverty, seeking wealth
    among dangers; and this has barred your path to well-doing.

If we are to talk about strength, then how far we exceed you is as
    clear to see as is the sun by its brightness.

The Bull, the proud Lion, the Elephant—there are infinitely
    many of us in the world to whom man cannot hold a candle.

And if it's fitting to talk about spirit, you will see that we are more
    liberally endowed with invincible, generous, strong hearts.

Among us, brave deeds are done without hope of a triumph or
    some other glory; just like those once-famous Romans.

You will see that the Lion is greatly proud of a noble deed, and
    wants to stamp out the memory of a shameful one.

There have yet been beasts among us who, by dying, escape their
    prison shackles and gain freedom and glory; and such cour-
    age dwells in their breasts that, having lost their liberty, their
    hearts cannot bear living in servitude.

And if you turn to temperance, you will see that we beat you at
    that game, too.

We spend but a little brief time on Venus;[1] but you, without mod-
    eration, follow her always and everywhere.

Our species does not care for other food than heaven makes with-
    out artifice; but you want food that Nature cannot create.

You are not content with just one food, as we are; but better to
    satisfy your gluttonous desires, you travel as far as the Eastern
    kingdoms[2] for them.

The food you can gather on land is not enough for you; you will
    plunge into the Ocean's bosom to sate yourself with its spoils.

If I tried to show how unhappy you are above all other animals
    on earth, I would never finish talking.

We are greater friends to Nature; to us she dispenses more of her
    vigour (*virtù*), making you beg for every benefit she endows.

---

1 Goddess of love in the Roman pantheon, often equated with her Greek
    counterpart, Aphrodite.

2 Kingdoms in Asia.

If you want to see this, use your senses, and you will easily come
   to believe what you now, perhaps, reject.
The eagle's eye, the dog's nose and ear, and taste, too—we can
   show these to be superior, though the sense of touch is more
   properly left to you; and this is given not to honour you, but
   only so that the appetite of Venus may better trouble and
   afflict you.
Each animal among us is born clothed, and this protects it from
   cold, cruel weather under every sky, on every shore.
Man alone is born naked of all protection, with no hide, no
   spines, feathers or fleece, no bristles or scales to shield him.
His life starts with crying, and in such a hoarse, painful voice that
   he is a pitiful sight;
and as he grows, his life is small indeed compared to that of a
   stag, a crow or a goose.
Nature gave you hands and words, but along with these she gave
   you ambition and avarice, which cancel out that benefit.
To how many ills are you subjected—first by Nature, then by
   Fortune! How much good does Fortune promise you to no
   effect!
Yours are ambition and lust and sorrow and avarice, which
   devour like mange the life you prize so dear.
No other animal has a life so fragile and so much will to live,
   more bewildered fear or stronger rage.
One pig does not hurt another pig, or one stag another stag; only
   man murders another man, crucifies him, robs him.
Now ask yourself: why should I go back to being human, since I
   am free from every misery I bore as a man?
And if anyone among men seems god-like, joyful and content,
   don't give him too much credence; I live more happily here in
   this mud, where I wallow and roll without a care."

Appendix F: Selections from Florentine Histories[1]

[Machiavelli received a commission from Pope Leo X (Giovanni de' Medici, 1475–1521) in 1520 to write the *Florentine Histories*. In 1525 he travelled to Rome to present the work in eight books to Pope Clement VII (Giulio de' Medici, 1478–1534); unlike his presentation of *The Prince* to Lorenzo de' Medici in 1515, the *Florentine Histories* was favourably received by the Medici pope and represents the apex of Machiavelli's elusive reinstatement into Florentine politics.

Machiavelli wrote in the humanist tradition, which differs significantly from modern approaches to history. Humanist historiography did not value historical accuracy in the way modern historians do, and it had no problem distorting or sacrificing it for the sake of producing a desired message. Consequently, the work is not a history in the current sense of the word but rather, like almost everything else Machiavelli wrote, a political treatise. Whereas *The Prince* was presented to a new ruler who was insecure and consumed with his own interests and survival, Machiavelli had been commissioned to write this work by a pope who was interested in reforming the Florentine government. In this work, Machiavelli argues, along the lines he did in his *Discourse on Florentine Affairs* (late 1520 or early 1521), that Florence should ultimately be constitutionally transformed into a genuine republic.

Many of the themes present in his other political works are discussed in the *Florentine Histories* as well, including factionalism (1.5, 3.5, and 7.1), religion (1.5), the Polybian cycle of history (5.1), the decadence of sixteenth-century Florence (3.5), the political problem of the papacy (3.7), as well as criticisms of mercenaries (3.7), the aristocracy, and monarchies. Despite this being a commissioned work, Machiavelli is careful to distance himself from direct criticism of the Medici, typically placing disapproval of their actions in the reported words of their opponents.]

---

1 Translated by Kirsty Jane Falconer for this volume.

1.5 [Factions and Religion]

And indeed, if any time was miserable in Italy and in these provinces overrun by the barbarians, it was the time from Arcadius and Honorius[1] to Theodoric.[2] For if we consider how much damage is done to a kingdom or to a republic by a change of ruler (*principe*) or government, not through any external force, but through civil discord alone—which shows how just a few changes have caused every republic and every kingdom, even the most powerful, to collapse—we can easily imagine how badly Italy and the other Roman provinces suffered in that time, since not only their governments and their princes changed but also their laws, their customs, their ways of life, their religions, languages, clothing and names.... This gave rise to the destruction, creation and growth of many cities.

... Among these ruins and these new peoples emerged new languages, such as we see in the habitual speech of France, Spain and Italy; this, mixed together with the native language of these new peoples and that of ancient Rome, creates a new way of speaking. Furthermore, not only the provinces have changed their names, but also the lakes, the rivers, the seas and the men; France, Italy and Spain are all full of new names, entirely different from the ancient ones.... But in the midst of all these changes, the change of religion was no less important. For combatting the tradition of the old faith with the miracles of the new created great turmoil and discord among men. And had the Christian religion been united, this would have led to less upheaval; but since the Greek, the Roman and the Ravennate churches[3] were all fighting with one another—and the heretical sects with the catholic ones—they inflicted suffering on the world in many ways. One witness to this is Africa, which suffered far more on account of the Arian sect in which the Vandals believed than of any avarice or natural cruelty

---

1   Arcadius and Honorius co-ruled the Roman Empire, with Arcadius serving as the Eastern Roman emperor from 383 to 408 and Honorius serving as the Western Roman emperor from 393 to 423.

2   Theodoric the Great (454–526) founded the Ostrogothic kingdom of Italy, making the city of Ravenna his capital.

3   Schisms in the Church were not uncommon and were rooted in differences of language, personal ambitions of clergy, and claims about political authority, as much as they were about theological concerns. Even after the Great Schism between East and West in 1054 that separated the Catholic Church from the Orthodox Church, further schisms occurred within both churches.

of theirs. Living in the midst of so much persecution, the terror of men's souls was written in their eyes. For apart from the infinite evils they endured, many of them were unable to flee to God's aid, in which those who are miserable are used to hope. Since most of them were unsure to which god they were supposed to turn, lacking all help and all hope, they died miserably.

3.5 [Factions and Decadence in Florence]

And so a great number of citizens, moved by love for their country, assembled in the church of San Pier Scheraggio. After discussing these troubles extensively among themselves, they went to see the Signoria, to whom one of them—who bore greater authority than the rest—spoke in these words:

... "The love we bear our native city, Magnificent Signori, first made us come together, and now makes us come to you to discuss that evil that is already so great and that continues to grow in this republic of ours—and to offer ourselves ready to help you stamp it out. This you could manage to do (even if it seems a difficult undertaking), so long as you are willing to leave private considerations aside and exert your authority with the public forces.

"Magnificent Signori, the corruption that afflicts every city in Italy has corrupted and continues to corrupt your own. Because after this province extracted itself from Imperial control, its cities—without a powerful restraining force to correct them—organised their states and their governments, not as free, but as split into factions. This is the root of all the other evils, all the other disorders that emerge in these cities. Firstly, there is no union or friendship among their citizens; except among those who are party to some wicked scheme, whether against their native city or against private persons. And since religion and the fear of God are extinguished in everyone, vows and promises are kept for as long as they are profitable; and so men do not make them in order to keep them, but as a means of deceiving people more easily; and the easier and more secure the deception, the more praise and glory it brings. This is why evil men are praised as clever and hard-working, while good men are condemned as fools. And truly everything that can be corrupt, and corrupting to others, is concentrated in the cities of Italy. The young are lazy and the old lascivious, and both sexes and all ages are full of foul habits; which good laws cannot cure, since they have been ruined by bad customs.

"From this comes the avarice we see in our citizens, and their hunger, not for true glory, but for infamous honours; which are the basis of hatreds, enmities, quarrels, factions. And these result in deaths, banishments, the affliction of the good and the advancement of the wicked. Because the good, trusting in their own innocence, do not seek out someone who will defend and honour them by illegal means, as the wicked do; and so, defenceless and unhonoured, they descend into ruin. This is what creates loyalty to the factions and brings them influence: for the wicked adhere to them out of avarice and ambition, and the good out of necessity. And what is yet more sickening is to see how the agents and founders of these factions dress up their intentions and their ends in pious words. Because they are all hostile to liberty, they always oppress her, under the guise of defending an aristocratic government or a popular one. For the prize they want for victory is not the glory of having liberated the city, but the satisfaction of having defeated all others and taken over her rule. Having got so far, there is no act so unjust, so cruel, so avaricious that they dare not carry it out. And so they make statutes and laws, not for the public benefit, but for their own. Wars, peace treaties and alliances are decided upon, not for the glory of all, but for the satisfaction of the few.

"If other cities are full of such disorders, ours is tainted by them more than any other, because our laws, our statutes, our civil ordinances are and always have been set out, not so as to live in freedom, but in accordance with the ambition of the winning faction. And this means that whenever one faction is driven out and one division suppressed, another emerges. Because when a city prefers to govern by factions rather than laws, and one of those factions is left unopposed, that city must by necessity divide within herself; those private measures she originally put in place for her own good cannot now protect her. The divisions in our city, both ancient and modern, show that this is true. When the Ghibellines were destroyed, everyone believed that the Guelphs[1] would live happily and honoured for a long time. Nevertheless, a short time later the Guelphs split into Black and White.[2] Once the

---

1 The Guelphs and the Ghibellines were factions in Germany and Italy during the thirteenth and fourteenth centuries which politically supported the pope and the Holy Roman emperor, respectively. The tension between these two factions was felt keenly in Florence, where the distinction between them overlapped with other existing tensions such as family histories and economic interests, with the merchant bankers supporting the Guelphs and the noble families of Florence supporting the Ghibellines.

2 By the early 1300s, infighting among the Guelphs in Florence led to a

Whites were defeated, the city was never free of factions; we were constantly fighting, now in support of the exiles, now on account of the hostilities between the people and the aristocracy (*popolo e grandi*). And so as to give to others what we could not or did not want to possess by agreement among ourselves, we subjugated our freedom now to King Robert,[1] now his brother, now his son,[2] and finally to the Duke of Athens.[3]

"... Nonetheless, as soon as [the Duke of Athens] was driven out, we took up our arms and fought one another with more hatred and greater rage than we had ever fought at any other time; and so our old nobility was defeated and left at the mercy of the people's will (*popolo*). Few believed that there would ever again be cause for scandal or division in Florence, since those had been reined in who seemed to have brought it about through their pride and their insufferable ambition.

"But we can now see from experience how fallacious men's opinions are and how false their judgement. The pride and ambition of the aristocracy (*grandi*) were not extinguished; rather, they were taken from them by our commoners (*popolani*), who now—as ambitious men do—seek to achieve first rank in the republic. Since they have no other way to achieve it than discord, they have once again divided the city and revived the names of Guelph and Ghibelline—which had been snuffed out, and it would have been a good thing had they never existed in our republic. It is ordered from on high (so that nothing in human affairs should ever be lasting or peaceful) that all republics have fatal families who are born for their ruin. Our own republic has abounded in these more than any other. Not one family, but many have disturbed

---

split in their ranks. The Black Guelphs supported the pope, while the White Guelphs opposed interference from the pope in Florentine affairs.

1 King Robert of Naples (1278–1343) was invited to rule Florence from 1313 to 1322, so that the city might receive his military protection. See *Florentine Histories* 2.24–25.

2 Charles, Duke of Calabria (1298–1328) was elected by Florence to lead them in 1326. He overtaxed the population, and despite some initial military success, left for Naples the following year when King Louis the Bavarian entered Italy to march on Rome. See *Florentine Histories* 2.30.

3 Walter VI of Brienne (1302–56) was also known as the duke of Athens due to his family heritage in that city. He was invited by the noble families of Florence to rule the city in 1342, with the hope that he would help the Florentines in war efforts against Pisa and deal effectively with a number of other social and economic problems. The nobility soon found his rule tyrannical, and within a year they conspired against him, forcing him to resign and flee the city. See *Florentine Histories* 2.33–37.

and afflicted her; as first did the Buondelmonti and the Uberti, then the Donati and the Cerchi, and now (O shameful, ridiculous thing!) the Ricci and the Albizzi unsettle and divide her.

... And our republic especially (notwithstanding ancient examples to the contrary) cannot only be maintained united, but reformed with good customs and civil methods; so long as you Signori will resolve to act. And we, moved by love for our native city rather than any private passion, encourage you to do so. Although she has been greatly corrupted, stamp out at once the sickness that infects her, the rage that consumes her, the poison that kills her. Do not blame the old disorders on the natures of men, but on the times—and since those have changed, you may hope that better laws will bring our city better fortune. The malignity of Fortune can be overcome with prudence, by reining in those men, annulling the laws that breed factions and choosing those that conform with a truly free and civil way of life. And content yourselves to do this now, with the benign aid of the law, rather than put it off and so compel men to do it by force of arms."

3.7 [Mercenaries are Untrustworthy; Love of Soul vs. Love of the Patria]

On the pontifical throne at that time was Pope Gregory XI.[1] Since he was in Avignon, he governed Italy by way of Legates, as his predecessors had; and these Legates, being full of pride and avarice, had caused affliction to many cities. One of them, who was then in Bologna, decided to become master of Tuscany, taking the opportunity of the famine in Florence that year. Not only did he provide no sustenance to the Florentines, but—so as to deprive them of the hope of future harvests—he attacked them with a great army at the very start of spring, hoping to find them unarmed and starving and thus to overcome them easily. And perhaps he would have succeeded, had the forces he used to assault them not been faithless and venal. For the Florentines, since they had no other remedy, paid his soldiers a hundred and thirty thousand florins and got them to abandon the undertaking. Wars begin when men will them, but they do not end at their will. This war, which began by the Legate's ambition, was

---

1 Pierre Robert de Beaufort was elected Pope Gregory XI (c. 1329–78) in 1370. He ruled from Avignon, where the papacy was located from 1309 to 1377; the Legates he appointed were from France and were despised by the Italians.

continued by the Florentines' resentment. They formed a league with Messer Bernabò [Visconti, of Milan] and all the cities hostile to the Church; and they appointed eight citizens to direct the war, who had the authority to act without appeal and spend without account.

... The war lasted three years and ended only with the death of the Pope; and it was run with such skill and such satisfaction to all that the magistracy[1] of the Eight was extended every year. They were called Saints, although they cared little for the censures against them, and stripped the churches of their property, and forced the clergy to celebrate the divine offices. So greatly did these citizens then value their native city above their souls. They showed the Church that, just as they had defended her as friends, so they could afflict her as enemies; for they made the whole of the Romagna, Marche and Perugia rebel.

5.1 [The Cycle of History]

When provinces[2] undergo change, they usually go from order to disorder and then back again from disorder to order. Because Nature does not allow the things of the world to stand still, when they reach their ultimate perfection—since they cannot ascend any further—they have to descend. And in the same way once they have descended, and their disorders have brought them to their lowest point, they cannot descend any further and so by necessity must ascend; and so they always descend from good to bad, and ascend from bad to good. For excellence (*virtù*) creates serenity, serenity creates idleness, idleness creates disorder and disorder, ruin; and in the same way, from ruin comes order, from order comes excellence, and from excellence glory and good fortune. Therefore wise men have observed that literature comes after warfare and that, in cities and in provinces, commanders are born before philosophers. Because once good, well-ordered armies have brought about victory, and victory brought about serenity, the fortitude of the martial spirit cannot be corrupted by any more honourable idleness than that of literature; nor can this idleness enter into well-instituted cities by any bigger or more dangerous deceit. Cato[3] recognised this very well when the philosophers

---

1 Their term in office.
2 A region or territory.
3 Cato the Elder (234–149 BCE), Roman orator, censor, and statesman. See *Discourses on Livy* 3.1.

Diogenes and Carneades[1] came to Rome as ambassadors sent by Athens to the Senate. Seeing that the Roman youth were beginning to admire and follow them, and knowing the harm that could result to his homeland from this honourable idleness, he saw to it that no philosopher would be received in Rome. And so provinces come to ruin by these means; and having arrived there, and once their men have grown wise through the blows they have suffered, they return to order—as I have said—unless stifled by some extraordinary force.

These causes made Italy happy and wretched by turns; first through the ancient Tuscans, then through the Romans. And it so happens that afterwards, nothing was built upon the ruins of Rome that could redeem her from them, enabling her to pursue a glorious course under outstanding (*virtuoso*) rule. Nonetheless, in some of the new cities and states that came forth from the Roman ruins, such prowess (*virtù*) emerged that although one did not dominate the others, they were so harmonious and well-ordered that they liberated and defended Italy from the barbarians. Among these states, the Florentines ...

Therefore if the times that resulted from the prowess (*virtù*) of these new principalities were not quiet through prolonged peace, nor were they made dangerous by the brutality of war. One cannot call it peace when principalities frequently attack one another with weapons; but neither can one call it war when men are not killed, cities are not sacked, principalities are not destroyed. These wars became so enfeebled that they were started without fear, conducted without danger, and finished without damage. And so that vigour (*virtù*) that is usually extinguished in other provinces by a prolonged peace, was extinguished in Italy by the cowardly nature of those wars; as will be clear from the events we shall describe from 1434 to 1494. Here we will see how, in the end, the way was laid open to the barbarians once again; and, once again, Italy placed herself in bondage to them.

---

1 Diogenes and Carneades were heads of prominent philosophical schools in Athens. Diogenes of Babylon (c. 230–150 BCE) was head of the Stoic school of philosophy and Carneades (214–c. 129 BCE) was a sceptical philosopher who became the leader of Plato's Academy. They were sent along with Critolaus (c. 200–c. 118 BCE), the head of the Peripatetic school of philosophy in Athens, to Rome in 155 BCE to represent Athens in a petition before the Roman Senate. It is said that while in Rome, Carneades gave a public lecture defending justice only to give a second lecture the following day in which he critiqued justice and demolished his previous defence of it.

... And if my description of the events that took place in this rotten world tells nothing of the soldier's fortitude, the commander's prowess (*virtù*), the citizen's love for his native land, you shall see by what deceptions, by what tricks and artful means princes, soldiers and the heads of republics contrived to maintain a reputation they did not earn. These are, perhaps, no less useful to know than the things of the ancient world; for if the latter inspire liberal minds to imitation, the former will inspire such minds to avoid and stamp them out.

5.8 [Necessity, Especially in Defence of the Patria, Justifies Violence]

The princes of Italy had initially been dismayed, fearing that the Duke [Filippo Maria Visconti, Duke of Milan] would become too powerful. But these events, managed in such a way, gave them hope (in view of the outcome) that they could hold him in check. Notwithstanding the league recently formed, the Florentines and Venetians formed an alliance with the Genoese. And so Messer Rinaldo degli Albizzi and the other leading Florentines in exile, seeing that everything was in upheaval and that things now looked very different, began themselves to hope that they might be able to persuade the Duke to engage in open war against Florence. Going to Milan, Messer Rinaldo addressed the Duke as follows:

"If we, who were once your enemies, now put our trust in you and ask you to help us return to our homeland, then neither you nor anyone else should wonder at it; not if you consider the course of human affairs, and the changeability of Fortune. That said, the reasons for our past and present actions—how we formerly acted towards you, and how we now act towards Florence—are clear and abundant. No good man will ever reproach someone who is attempting to defend his native city, however it be defended. And it was never our aim to harm you, only to preserve Florence from harm. The proof of this is that in the course of our league's greatest victories, when we found you disposed to make a true peace, we wanted that peace even more than you did. So we believe firmly that we have never done anything to cast doubt on our obtaining some grace from you.

"Not even our native Florence can reproach us for asking you now to take up arms against her, those same arms from which we so stubbornly defended her before. For a state deserves to be loved by all who loves all her citizens equally, not one who venerates a very few and casts all the rest from her. Nor should those be condemned who take up arms in any way against their city. Cities are made of many bodies, but they resemble a single body. Just as bodies are often afflicted by disease that cannot be cured without applying fire or steel, so often in cities, too, such problems arise that a good, pious citizen errs far more by leaving them untreated than he does by curing them, even if he must cure them with steel. And what graver sickness than servitude can afflict the body of a republic? What medicine is more necessary to employ than that which relieves it of this sickness? The only just wars are necessary ones, and arms are merciful when there is no other hope. I cannot imagine a need greater than ours, or a mercy exceeding that which frees one's native city from servitude. It is, therefore, absolutely certain that our cause is both pious and just. That must be considered by you as it is by us....

"What stubbornness do you expect to find in a people disunited by such diverse and new enmities? This disunity is the reason why even such wealth as is left there cannot be spent now as it could be back then. For men will happily spend away their inheritance when they believe they are doing so for glory and for their own honour and standing, hoping to reacquire in peacetime those assets taken from them by war; but not when they see themselves oppressed in war and in peace alike, having to endure the insults of their enemies in the former and the insolence of their rulers in the latter. And the people are harmed much more by the avarice of their own citizens than by the rapacity of their enemies, because one may hope eventually to see an end to the latter; but to the former, never.

"And so, in past wars, you deployed your weapons against an entire city; now you deploy them against the slightest part of her. You came to deprive many good citizens of sovereignty; now you come to deprive a few wicked ones. You came to deprive a city of her liberty; now you come to return it to her.... In other times this conquest would have been judged ambitious and violent, but now it will be judged right and merciful. So do not let this opportunity go by, and bear in mind that if your other excursions against this city brought you difficulty, expense and infamy, this one will easily bring you the greatest benefit and most honourable reputation."

7.1 [Factions]

... But first I want to explain to some degree ... why those who hope that a republic can be united are greatly deceived in that hope. It is true that some divisions harm republics, and some help them. Those divisions cause harm that bring with them factions and partisans. Those help that are maintained without factions or partisans. Therefore, since the founder of a republic cannot make sure that there will be no enmities within it, he must at least make sure that there are no factions. And so he needs to know that the citizens of a city acquire standing in one of two ways: by public paths, or by private methods. Standing is acquired publicly by winning a battle, acquiring a territory, conducting a legation carefully and prudently, being a wise and successful advisor to the republic. In private, it is acquired by benefitting this and that citizen, defending him against the magistrates, aiding him financially, winning him undeserved honours, and winning favour with the common people through games and public endowments. This way of proceeding gives rise to factions and to partisans. And to the same extent that standing earned in this way is harmful, so it is beneficial when it is not mixed with factionalism, because it is founded on a common and not a private interest. And although there is no way to ensure that no strong hatreds will arise between citizens who are made in this way, yet if they have no partisans who follow them out of their own interests, then these men cannot harm the republic; rather, they must help it. For in order to succeed, they must direct their efforts to exalting the republic, and especially watch one another to make sure that the bounds of civil law are not transgressed.

Enmities in Florence were always factional, and therefore always damaging; and no winning faction was ever united, except for as long as the enemy faction survived. But once the defeated faction was extinguished, the ruling faction would split within itself, since there was no longer any fear to restrain it or any internal discipline to hold it back. Cosimo de' Medici's faction was the winning one in 1434; but fear kept it united and humane for a time, since the defeated faction was large and full of very powerful men. During that time no errors were made within Cosimo's faction, and they did nothing wicked to make the people hate them.

Appendix G: Selections from The Art of War[1]

[*The Art of War* was published in Florence in 1521. It is the only political text by Machiavelli that was published in his lifetime, with the exception of his play *Mandragola*. The book is in the form of a fictional dialogue taking place in 1516 at the Orti Oricellari among several of Machiavelli's contemporaries: the condottiere Fabrizio Colonna, who largely serves as the voice for Machiavelli's ideas; Cosimo Rucellai, who hosted the gatherings in the Orti Oricellari; and Luigi Alamanni, Battista della Palla, and Zanobi Buondelmonti, who were participants in the discussions. Machiavelli dedicated the work to Lorenzo di Filippo Strozzi, a participant in the Orti Oricellari who was related through both career and marriage to the Medici, and whom Machiavelli acknowledged as having helped him.

While the main topic of the text is clearly military organization and tactics, Machiavelli includes many aspects of his political philosophy that he discusses in both *The Prince* and the *Discourses on Livy*. His critique of mercenaries and the need for a militia are on display throughout the text, as are his critique of Italy's princes (Book 7), his insistence on the importance of training and discipline (Books 2 and 6), his pragmatic use of religion (Books 4 and 6), and the importance of oratory (Book 4); even his cyclical account of history is acknowledged by Fabrizio (Book 1).]

Dedication

... But if we were to consider the ancient ways, then we would find nothing more cohesive, nothing more regular, nothing of which one by necessity so loves the other as these. For all the arts instituted in a given state for the common good of men, all the statutes created in it so that men live in fear of God and the law would be in vain unless provided with defences; which, when well-ordered, preserve these arts and statutes even if they are not themselves well-ordered. And so also in reverse, good customs fall into disorder without military support, just like the rooms of a splendid and royal palace, even one adorned with gold and

---

1 Translated by Kirsty Jane Falconer for this volume.

jewels, fall into disorder if they are not covered and have nothing to protect them from the rain. And if every diligent effort was once made in cities and in kingdoms to keep the men of every other order loyal, peaceful and God-fearing, then this effort was redoubled in the military. For in what man should his country seek to find greater faith than in he who must promise to die for her? Who should love peace more than he who can only be injured by war? Who should fear God more than he who, subjecting himself to infinite dangers every day, has greater need of His help? This necessity was well considered both by those who gave laws to the empires and by those in charge of military training, and this meant that the soldier's life was praised by other men and was followed and imitated with every care. But since military customs are [now] entirely corrupt and very far separated from the ancient ways, they have given rise to those malign opinions that make men despise soldiering and flee the company of those who engage in it. Yet I consider, on the basis of what I have seen and read, that it is not impossible to bring the military back to the ancient ways and restore some aspects of its former excellence (*virtù*). And so I decided, rather than spend this idle period of mine without doing anything, to write down what I understand of the art of war for the enjoyment of those who admire the ancient deeds. And while it is daring of me to treat matters that other men have made their profession, nonetheless I do not think it wrong to hold in words a rank that many others, with greater presumption, have held in deeds. For any mistake I make while writing can be corrected without harm to anyone; but the mistakes other men make in their deeds are discovered only with the fall of their empires....

Book 1 [Mercenaries Are More Costly than Militias; the Cyclical Account of History]

... FABRIZIO: I do not believe that you believe that everyone has his place in time of peace. Even if we suppose that no other reason can be adduced, the small number of all those who remain in the places you mentioned would rebut your claim. What is the proportion of infantry required in wartime compared to those employed in peacetime? For those cities and fortresses that are guarded in peacetime are much more heavily guarded in wartime; and to this we must add the soldiers stationed in the field—a large number—who are all dismissed in time of peace. And concerning state guards—a small number—you and Pope Julius have shown everyone just how much are to be feared those men who do not want to pursue any other occupation than war. On account of their insolence, you removed them from your garrisons and installed Switzers,[1] as they are born and raised under the law and chosen by true selection by their sovereign states. So do not say any more that there is a place for everyone in peacetime. As for men-at-arms, since these continue to receive their pay in time of peace, this seems a more difficult question to solve. But he who considers it all thoroughly will see that the answer is simple, because this way of keeping men-at-arms is not a good one, but corrupt. This is because these men make a profession of war; and, if they had sufficient company around them, they would create a thousand problems every day in the states where they are based. But since there are only a few of them, and they cannot form an army by themselves, they cannot inflict serious damage all that often....

... COSIMO: Would you want to do without them? Or, if they are to be kept, how would you want to keep them?

FABRIZIO: By way of the citizen army. Not like that of the King of France, which is dangerous and insolent like our own; but like that of the ancients, who raised cavalry from among their subjects and then, in peacetime, sent them back to their own homes to live by their own occupations. I shall speak on this at greater length before this discussion is over. And so if this part of the military is currently able to live by military activity even when there is peace, this is the result of corrupt method. As for the wages reserved to me and the other commanders, I tell you that, in the same way, this is a greatly corrupt method. A wise republic should not be paying these to anyone. Rather, it should deploy its own citizens as commanders in wartime, and in peacetime have them return to their occupations. Neither should a wise king pay these wages; or if he does, it should either be as a reward for some outstanding deed, or because he wants to make use of a given man in peace as well as war. And since you mentioned me, I want to use myself as an example. I tell you that I have never made war my profession, because my profession is to govern my citizens and defend them; and, so that I can defend them, to love peace and know how to wage war. My king rewards and esteems me not so much because I know about war, but because I also know how to advise him in

---

1 Swiss mercenaries.

peacetime. And therefore no king, if he is wise and means to act prudently, should want anyone near him who is not made as I am. For if he has men around him who love peace too much, or love war too much, they will cause him to err....

Book 2 [The Importance of Training and Discipline]

FABRIZIO: ... Going on with this subject of training, I say that in order to make good armies, it is not enough to have hardened your men, to have made them bold, swift and dexterous. They must also learn to stay in their ranks, to obey signals, sounds and their leader's commands; and they must know how to keep their ranks while at halt, retreating, advancing, fighting and marching. Because there was never a good army without this discipline, respected and implemented with all diligence and precision. And fierce but disorderly men are without a doubt much weaker than timid but orderly ones; because order drives the fear out of men, but disorder lessens their ferocity....

Book 4 [The Importance of Oratory and Religion]

... FABRIZIO: To persuade or dissuade a few people of a given thing is very easy, because if words are not enough, you can use authority and force. The difficulty is to eliminate a malevolent opinion from a multitude of people—it being contrary either to the common good or to your own opinion—when you can use nothing but words; and those words need to be heard by everyone, since you want to persuade everyone. This is why all the great commanders [once] had to be orators, because it is hard to put anything good into effect unless you know how to speak to the whole army; something that is entirely neglected in our own time. Read the life of Alexander the Great, and you will see how often he had to assemble the army and speak to it publicly. Otherwise, since it had become rich and heaped with spoils, he would never have been able to lead it into India and through the deserts of Arabia where they encountered so much difficulty and distress. Infinitely often, matters arise that would lead to an army's ruin if their commander either did not know how to speak, or was not in the habit of speaking to them; because this speech relieves fear, fires up spirits, increases determination, unveils deceptions, promises rewards, points out dangers and how to flee them, reproaches, entreats, threatens, fills with hope, praises, condemns, and does all those things that either extinguish human passions or inflame them. And so any prince or republic that desires to create a new army and win it a reputation should accustom the soldiers to hearing their commander speak, and the commander to knowing how to address the soldiers. Religion was also of great value in keeping soldiers of ancient times in order, as was the oath they took when they began soldiering. For in every transgression they were threatened, not only with those punishments they could fear from men, but also those they could expect from God. Combined with the other religious customs, this made easy all sorts of enterprises for the commanders of the ancient world, on many occasions; and so it always shall, wherever religion is feared and followed. Sertorius made use of it by affecting to speak with a deer,[1] which promised him victory on God's behalf. Sulla used to say that he spoke with an image he had taken from Apollo's temple. Many have said that God appeared to them in a dream, admonishing them to fight. King Charles VII of France in our fathers' time, in the war he fought against the English, claimed to be advised by a girl sent from God, whom everyone called the Maid of France;[2] and this was the cause of his victory....

Book 6 [The Importance of Training, Discipline, and Religion]

FABRIZIO: ... And because neither fear of the law nor fear of men is enough to restrain armed men, the ancients added the authority of God to these; therefore they made their soldiers swear, with tremendous ceremonies, to obey military discipline so that if they acted against it, they had to fear not only men and laws but God, too; and they did everything possible to imbue them with religion....

... The commanders of antiquity had one worry from which present ones are virtually free: how to interpret sinister auguries to

---

1 Quintus Sertorius (123–72 BCE) was a Roman statesman and military commander. The deer was a white fawn which Quintus Sertorius received as a gift from a pleb named Spanus. Sertorius tamed it and created a religious mythos around it by claiming it was a gift from the goddess Diana and that the deer sent him messages in his dreams. When agents informed him of victories by his generals, he would conceal their presence, dress the deer up with garlands for receiving good news, and present it to his troops as evidence that they would soon learn of a victory.

2 Joan of Arc (1412–31).

their own advantage. If a lightning bolt fell within the ranks of an army, if there was an eclipse of the sun or moon, if there was an earthquake, if the commander fell while mounting or dismounting his horse, the soldiers interpreted this as a bad sign; and it created such fear in them that, had they gone into battle, they would easily have lost. And so, as soon as an incident of this kind occurred, the ancient commanders would either explain the reason behind it, attributing it to natural causes, or else interpret it to their own ends. Caesar, falling over as he disembarked in Africa, said: "I have got you, Africa"; and many have explained the cause of a lunar eclipse or an earthquake. These things cannot happen in our day, both because our men are not so superstitious and because our religion entirely rejects such views. But if they should occur, then we must imitate the ways of the ancients.

Book 7 [Critique of Italy's Princes]

FABRIZIO: ... And so that you understand this aspect better, you must know that commanders are lauded in one of two cases. One case is those who achieved great feats with an army that was organised by its own natural discipline. Such were the majority of Roman citizens and others who have commanded armies. Their only challenge was to keep them good, and to make sure of leading them safely. The other case is those who not only had to vanquish the enemy, but who had to make their own army a good and well-organised one before they could get so far. Without any doubt, these commanders deserve far more praise than those who have worked skilfully (*virtuosamente*) using old-and-good armies. Pelopidas and Epaminondas,[1] Tullus Hostilius,[2] Philip of Macedonia father of Alexander,[3] Cyrus King of the Persians,[4] and Gracchus the Roman[5] are all of this type. All of them first had to make their

---

1 Both Pelopidas (c. 410–364 BCE) and Epaminondas (c. 418–362 BCE) served Thebes as statesmen and generals. They defeated Sparta at the battle of Leuctra (371 BCE), freed Thebes from Spartan rule, and made it a dominant power in the region.
2 Tullus Hostilius, legendary third king of Rome who succeeded Numa Pompilius, reigned from 672 to 641 BCE. The reorganization of the Roman army was one of many achievements with which he is credited.
3 Philip II of Macedonia (382–336 BCE). See *The Discourses on Livy* 1.20 and 1.26.
4 Cyrus II, also known as Cyrus the Great (c. 590/80–529 BCE).
5 Tiberius Sempronius Gracchus (d. 212 BCE) was a Roman consul who defeated Hanno during the Second Punic War.

army good, and then use it to fight. All of them were able to do so, both on account of their prudence and because they had subjects whom they could put through this kind of training. It would never have been possible for any of them, be they ever so good and full of excellent qualities, to do any praiseworthy work in a foreign land full of corrupt men unused to any honest obedience....

... But let us return to the Italians. Since they have not had wise princes, they have not taken on any good customs; and since they have not been subject to the same necessity as the Spanish, they have not taken these on by themselves, and so they remain the disgrace of the world. The peoples of Italy are not to blame for this; but their princes certainly are, and they have been punished for it. They have borne the just penalties for their ignorance, ignominiously losing their states, and without producing any outstanding (*virtuoso*) example. Do you want to see whether what I say is true? Think how many wars there have been in Italy from the passage of King Charles[1] until today; and while wars usually make men bellicose and win them renown, the bigger and fiercer these wars have been, the more they have caused both the limbs and the heads to lose their standing. This had to happen, because the customary methods were not and are not good; and there is nobody among us who has known how to adopt new methods. Nor should you ever believe that Italian arms will win repute by any way but the one I have shown you, and by means of those who maintain great states in Italy; for this form can be imposed on simple, rough and local-born men, but not on malign, poorly governed and foreign ones. You will never find a good sculptor who thinks he can make a beautiful statue from a badly hewn piece of marble; but from a rough piece, he certainly can. Before they got a taste of the blows of Transalpine war, our Italian princes believed that it was enough for a prince to know how to invent a subtle answer in writing, to display wit and dexterity in his words and sayings, to know how to weave a deception, to adorn himself with gold and jewels, to sleep and to eat in greater splendour than the rest, to surround himself with great licentiousness, to behave proudly and avariciously towards his citizens, to rot in idleness, to award military ranks by grace, to despise anyone who shows him some laudable course of action, to expect his words to be received as the words of an oracle; and the wretches did not realise that they were setting themselves up to be the prey of anyone who attacked them. From this

---

1 Charles VIII of France (1470–98), who invaded Italy in 1494.

came the great terrors, sudden flights and miraculous losses of the year 1494; and so three tremendously powerful Italian states were repeatedly sacked and laid waste.[1] But what is worse is that those that remain persist in the same error and live in the same disorder. They do not consider that, in ancient times, those who wished to keep hold of their states did, and made to be done, all those things I have discussed here; that their work was to prepare the body to endure discomfort and the spirit not to fear danger. This is why Caesar, Alexander, and all those other excellent men and princes were first into battle, going in armour and on foot; and if they lost their states, then they wanted to lose their lives as well. So outstandingly (*virtuosamente*) did they live and die. And if in those men—or in some of them—we could condemn too much ambition for power, yet we shall never find any softness to condemn in them, or any quality that might render their men delicate or cowardly. If these princes [of ours] read and believed these things, then it would be impossible for them not to change their way of living, and for the provinces they rule not to change their fortunes....

---

1   Milan, Florence, and Venice.

Appendix H: Selections from
The Life of Castruccio Castracani[1]

[*The Life of Castruccio Castracani* was written in 1520 during a mission to recover monies owed to Florentine business interests in Lucca. The mission was significant for Machiavelli, as it was backed by Cardinal Giulio de' Medici (1478–1534), who would go on to become Pope Clement VII and who had taken over as representative of the Medici in Florence after the death of Lorenzo de' Medici (1492–1519). Some of these debts were owed to members of the Medici and their friends, imbuing this mission with an indication of trust in Machiavelli's abilities and signalling the first concrete sign that his restoration was a real possibility. Machiavelli dedicated the work to Zanobi Buondelmonti and Luigi Alamanni, whom he described as friends.

While the work is based upon a historical figure, the Lucchese condottiere Castruccio Castracani (1281–1328), the work is thoroughly fiction and Machiavelli merely uses Castruccio as a character to tell a story and continue to expound his messages regarding political and military matters. Thus, contrary to historical fact, Castruccio's origins are depicted as similar to other legendary leaders such as Romulus and Remus, as well as Moses, with Machiavelli claiming Castruccio was adandoned as an infant and adopted. The point of creating such an origin story is to reiterate the message of the *Discourses on Livy* 2.29 and chapter 6 of *The Prince* that even the most able prince still needs Fortune to give him the opportunity to display his *virtù*. The final line of the work stresses this, claiming that had Castruccio been born in a city more fertile for his talents, he would have accomplished more than Philip of Macedon or Scipio of Rome.

Castruccio is described as having *virtù* in every respect—he is masterful with arms, a brilliant tactician, learns from every turn of events, takes a hands-on approach to all matters, which leaves little to chance, and while he is capable of being a diplomat and gentleman, he is both cunning and ruthless when he has to be in order to secure his position. His meteoric rise to power involves him seizing opportunity after opportunity, with his successes including becoming ruler of Lucca, leader of the

---

1 Translated by Kirsty Jane Falconer for this volume.

Ghibelline faction in the area, the capture of several towns, and the repeated defeat of Florentine (and Guelph) forces. He does everything correctly by Machiavellian standards and yet still dies, and without his *virtù* all his gains are vulnerable. His death from a fever and illness caught while overseeing his troops return from battle mirrors that of Cesare Borgia, who fell seriously ill at the same time as his father Alexander VI, in that there was little either could do to guard against such an occurrence. On his deathbed, Castruccio laments to his ward, Paolo Guinigi, that had he known Fortune would end his life so early, he would have devoted himself to establishing a more secure, even if smaller, state to leave his successor. This reiterates two messages from the *Discourses on Livy*. First, if someone stands in Fortune's way, no matter how much *virtù* he possesses, she will incapacitate him or remove him (2.29). Second, republics are longer lived than princedoms because the *virtù* of a prince dies with him, and it is rare that his heir will possess the same ability as the departed prince, but a republic has many individuals of *virtù* to call upon to lead it (1.11, 19–20). Rome could survive rapid expansion because it was a republic, but for a princedom to do so it is much more difficult.]

To those who consider it, my dearest Zanobi and Luigi, it will seem an astonishing thing that all those—or the majority of those—who have effected great things in this world, and who excelled among the others of their age, have had an obscure birth and beginnings, or else have been afflicted by Fortune beyond all measure. For all of them were exposed to the wild beasts, or had so wretched a father that, being ashamed of him, they made themselves out to be sons of Jove or some other god. It would be tiresome to repeat who these were, since many of them are known to all, and it would scarcely be satisfactory to the reader; and so we shall set it aside as superfluous. I believe that this happens because Fortune—wanting to show the world that she, and not Prudence, is the one who makes men great—begins to display her powers in a time when Prudence cannot play any part; rather, she herself must be given credit for everything. And so Castruccio Castracani of Lucca was one of those who, by the standards of the time in which he lived and the city in which he was born, did tremendous things; and, like the others, he did not have a happier or more glorious birth, as shall become clear as we reflect on the course of his life ...

... But when it was time to give him life, Fortune, hostile to his glory, took it from him and cut short those plans he had long since intended to put into effect, in which death alone could have stopped him. Castruccio had been fighting hard in the battle all day. When it was over, he stood at the gate of Fucecchio, all sweaty and exhausted, to wait for his men as they returned from victory and to welcome and thank them in person; he was ready, too, to tackle any further movement on the part of the enemy, who might have amassed some forces somewhere—for he believed that it was the duty of a good commander to be first to mount up and last to dismount. This meant that he was exposed to a wind that usually rises from the Arno around midday, and is almost always pestiferous, and so he was chilled to the core. This was the cause of his death, since he paid it no heed, being used to such discomforts. The following night he was assailed by a very high fever, which kept rising all the time—all the doctors judged it to be fatal. When Castruccio became aware of this, he called for Paolo Guinigi and spoke these words to him:

"My son, had I believed that Fortune meant to cut short midway my path to the glory promised by my many happy achievements, then I would not have worked so hard; and I would have left you, if a smaller state, then also fewer enemies and fewer who envy you. Being content with ruling Lucca and Pisa, I would not have subjugated the Pistoiese, or irritated the Florentines with so many affronts; rather, I would have befriended both of these two peoples and led, if not a longer life, then certainly a quieter one. And I would have left you a state, though smaller, but without a doubt more secure and stable. But Fortune, who wants to be the arbiter of all human affairs, did not grant me enough judgement to know her from the start, or enough time to overcome her.... Therefore I leave you a large state, and with that I am very content; but I am greatly sorry because I leave it to you weak and infirm. You have the city of Lucca, which will never be happy to live under your rule. You have Pisa, where the men are changeable and deceitful by nature; and although the city was accustomed to servitude at various times, she will always resent having a Lucchese as ruler. You also have Pistoia, which is scarcely loyal to you because she is divided, and stirred up against our family by recent affronts. You have the offended Florentines for neighbours, whom we insulted in a thousand ways but never destroyed; and they will be happier at the news of my death than they would be at conquering all Tuscany. You cannot put your trust in the princes of Milan or the Emperor, because they are far away and slow to act, and their help is tardy. Therefore you must not hope in anything but your own ability and the memory of my excellence (*virtù*), and the renown the present victory brings you. If you can use this last wisely, then it will help you in reaching an agreement with the Florentines, who should consent eagerly since this defeat has upset them. Where I set out to make them my enemies, believing their enmity would bring me power and glory, you ought to make every effort to befriend them; their friendship will bring you security and advantage." ...

... Castruccio lived for 44 years, and in every state of fortune he behaved as a prince. And since his good fortune is very often commemorated, so he wanted to commemorate his ill fortune, too. The manacles that bound him in prison can still be seen today hung up in the tower of his dwelling; he put them there himself, so that they would always testify to his adversity. And since in life he was the inferior neither of Philip of Macedonia father of Alexander, nor of Scipio of Rome, he died at the same age as both of them; and without doubt he would have outdone them both, had he been born in Macedonia or Rome instead of Lucca.

Appendix I: Selections from Machiavelli's Personal Correspondence[1]

[In addition to the Legations, the copious reports he wrote to his superiors while on official Florentine state business, Machiavelli maintained a considerable correspondence with many friends and familial relations. Those documents which have survived provide valuable insights into his formal writings, his motivations, his friendships, and his thoughts that sometimes found no place in his public writings. They are also useful sources for dating his various works.

The letters collected here are all addressed to his long-time friend Francesco Vettori (1474–1539). Machiavelli's relationship with Vettori was complicated. It began in anger when aristocratic families rejected Machiavelli for a diplomatic mission to the court of Maximilian I in 1507. Maximilian I was rumoured to be planning a march on Rome, and the aristocrats of Florence argued that a high-born individual—Vettori—was a more appropriate candidate for a mission so important to Florentine interests. Machiavelli felt crushed and betrayed as he was passed over, despite his obvious skills. However, his boss Soderini found Vettori's reports untrustworthy and sent Machiavelli in an official capacity as a backup in case the reports became lost; in reality, Machiavelli was there to ensure that Vettori's reports became more reliable. Once Machiavelli arrived at his destination and began working with Vettori, the two quickly established a friendship that would last the rest of Machiavelli's life.

Of the hundreds of personal letters which are known to scholars, the following three powerfully speak to Machiavelli's personality. The first two letters are from 1513, after Machiavelli's release from prison; in the first he admits (not unlike the youth at the beginning of *The Golden Ass* who cannot stop himself from running) that he is unable to keep himself from thinking about politics, and in the second he describes the intolerable boredom of his exile and the triviality of his day, the sacred attitude he holds for interrogating historical authors about political and military

---

1 Translated by Kirsty Jane Falconer for this volume.

matters in the evening, and the composition of *The Prince*. The third letter is from 1527, shortly before his death, and expresses his devotion and loyalty to his beloved Florence.]

1. Letter 120, to Francesco Vettori [Politics or nothing], 9 April 1513

... If you have grown tired of discussions after seeing, on many occasions, things happen that fall outside the concepts and arguments you form, you are right; something similar has happened to me. But if I could speak to you, I would not be able to help filling your head with castles-in-the-air. Because Fortune has made it so that, since I don't know how to talk about the silk trade or the wool trade, or about profits or losses, I must talk about government; either I must take a vow of silence, or I must talk about it....

2. Letter 137, to Francesco Vettori [Machiavelli's life in exile], 10 December 1513

Magnificent Ambassador:
... Since Fortune wants to do everything herself, she wants us to let her get on with it, to be quiet and give her no trouble, and to wait for the time when she will allow men to do something. And then it will be fitting for you to work harder and keep a sharper eye on things, and for me to leave my farm and say: Here I am. I cannot therefore, since I want to render equal favour,[1] tell you anything in this letter other than how my life is; and if you decide that it should be exchanged for your own, I will be happy to make the change.

I am on my farm; and since those last incidents befell me, I have not been twenty days in Florence if you add them all together.... I rise in the morning with the sun and go into a grove of mine that I am having cut down; I remain there for two hours reviewing the previous day's work and passing time with the woodcutters, who always have some trouble to deal with, either among themselves or with their neighbours. And about this grove, I could tell you a thousand marvellous things that have happened to me in dealing with Frosino da Panzano and others who wanted some of this wood....

---

1   Machiavelli's letter, in part, mirrors Vettori's previous letter, in which his friend complains about boredom and lack of employment.

Leaving the grove, I go to a spring, and from there to one of my fowling-grounds. I have a book with me, Dante or Petrarch, or one of those minor poets like Tibullus or Ovid or similar. I read about their amorous passions, and their loves remind me of my own; I enjoy these thoughts for a while. Then I go up the road to the inn. I talk to those who pass and ask them for news of their villages; I learn various things and take note of the varied tastes and differing fancies men have. In the midst of this comes dinner time, when together with my household I eat such food as this poor farm and scanty holdings provide. Having eaten, I go back to the inn; there is the innkeeper, usually a butcher, a miller, a couple of furnace-men. In their company I debase myself all day playing cricca and trich-trach, and these give rise to a thousand quarrels and boundless teasing with hurtful words; and most of the time we are fighting over a quattrino,[1] but nonetheless we can be heard yelling all the way from San Casciano. So, plunged in among these penny-pinching parasites, I shake the mould from my brain and satisfy the malice of this my fate; I am content to let her beat me along this path, to see if she will be ashamed of it.

When evening comes, I go back to the house and enter my study; and in the doorway I strip off those everyday clothes covered in mud and filth, and put on regal, courtly dress. And, appropriately clad, I enter the ancient courts of ancient men; where, lovingly received by them, I feed on the nourishment that is mine alone and for which I was born. I am not ashamed to speak with them and ask them for the reasoning behind their actions, and in their kindness they answer me. And for four hours I feel no sorrow, I forget all worry, I do not fear poverty, and death does not scare me; I give myself entirely to them.

And since Dante says that no knowledge is produced unless we retain what we have found out, I have noted down everything of value I have gleaned from their conversation, and I have composed a little work called *De principatibus*; in which I go as deeply as I can into thinking about this subject, debating what a principality is, what types there are, how they are acquired, how they are maintained and why they are lost. And if ever any of my wild ideas please you, then this one should not displease you. And it should be appreciated by a prince, especially a new prince; and so I am dedicating it to His Magnificence Giuliano.[2] Filippo Casavecchia[3]

---

1 A quarter of a florin.
2 Giuliano de' Medici (1479–1516).
3 A friend of both Machiavelli and Vettori.

has seen it; he will be able to tell you to some extent both about the thing itself and about the conversations I have had with him, although I continue to fill it out and polish it.

You desire, Magnificent Ambassador, for me to leave this life and come to enjoy yours with you. I will, in any case; but what tempts me right now are certain affairs of mine, which I will have finished within six weeks. What makes me uncertain is that those Soderini are there [in Rome] and if I went there, then I would be forced to visit them and speak with them. I would be afraid that, on my return, I would have no hope of dismounting at home but would dismount at the Bargello.[1] Because although this government has tremendous foundations and a great degree of security, nonetheless it is new, and therefore distrustful. Nor is there any lack of know-it-alls who, like Paolo Bertini, would seat others around the dinner table and leave me to pay. I beg you to relieve me of this fear and then, in any case, I shall come to visit you within the stated time.

I have spoken with Filippo about this little work of mine, whether it would be good to present it or not; and if it is good to present it, whether it is fitting that I bring it or that I send it to you. If I do not present it, I would fear that, if nothing else, Giuliano would not read it; and that man Ardinghelli[2] would reap the honours from this latest labour of mine. I am forced to present it by the necessity that drives me, because I am using up all my money, and I cannot remain like this for long before poverty earns me contempt. This in addition to my desire that our Medici masters put me to work, even if they start by making me roll a stone. For if I could not then win them around, I would be aggrieved at myself; and this thing, if it is read, would show them that for the fifteen years I have been studying the art of government, I have been neither sleeping nor playing; and anyone should be glad to make use of someone who is full of experience at the expense of others. And there should be no doubt of my faithfulness (*fede*) because, having always kept my word (*fede*), I am not about to learn how to break it. He who has been good and faithful for forty-three years, as I have, cannot change his character, and my poverty is witness to my faithfulness and my goodness.

I would, therefore, also like you to write to me what you think about this matter; and I put myself in your hands. Be happy.

---

1 The prison where Machiavelli was held and tortured in 1513.
2 Piero Ardinghelli (1470–1526), secretary to Pope Leo X.

3. Letter 225, to Francesco Vettori [Machiavelli's love of Florence], 16 April 1527

Magnificent etc., Monseigneur de la Motte was today in the Imperial camp with the outcome of the agreement made there: if Bourbon accepts, he must halt his army; if he moves his army, it is a sign that he does not accept. And so tomorrow must be the judge of our affairs. Therefore we have decided here that if tomorrow he moves, we must absolutely think of war, without a hair on our bodies that goes on thinking of peace; if he does not move, we must think of peace and abandon all thought of war. You too must navigate with this north wind and, resolving on war, cut off all negotiations for peace, and in such a way that the members of the League [of Cognac][1] will advance without any hesitation. For here we can no longer limp along but must rush headlong; and often desperation finds remedies that choice was not able to find.

... I love my native city more than my own soul. And I tell you this, by the experience that sixty years have given me, that I do not think harder moments have been struggled with than these: when peace is necessary and war cannot be abandoned, and we have on our hands a prince who with difficulty can deal with peace alone, or with war alone. I send you my greetings.

---

1   The League of Cognac, a political and military alliance to repel the Spanish and limit the influence of Emperor Charles V, was formed in 1526 by Francis I of France, Francesco Sforza of Milan, the Republic of Venice, and Pope Clement VII, with Henry VIII of England joining later. Machiavelli died on 21 June 1527, long before the League was dissolved in August 1529.

Select Bibliography

Biographies

Celenza, Christopher S. *Machiavelli: A Portrait*. Harvard UP, 2015.

de Grazia, Sebastian. *Machiavelli in Hell*. Vintage Books, 1994.

Oppenheimer, Paul. *Machiavelli: A Life Beyond Ideology*. Continuum, 2011.

Ridolfi, Roberto. *The Life of Niccolò Machiavelli*. Translated by Cecil Grayson, U of Chicago P, 1963.

Villari, Pasquale. *The Life and Times of Niccolò Machiavelli*. Translated by Linda Villari, Ernest Benn, 1929.

Viroli, Maurizio. *Niccolò's Smile: A Biography of Machiavelli*. Translated by Antony Shuggar, Farrar, Strauss and Giroux, 2000.

Vivanti, Corrado. *Niccolò Machiavelli: An Intellectual Biography*. Translated by Simon MacMichael, Princeton UP, 2013.

Historical Context

Anglo, Sydney. *Machiavelli—The First Century: Studies in Enthusiasm, Hostility, and Irrelevance*. Oxford UP, 2005.

Baron, Hans. *The Crisis of the Early Italian Renaissance*. Princeton UP, 1966.

Brown, Alison. *The Return of Lucretius to Renaissance Florence*. Harvard UP, 2010.

Brucker, Gene. *Renaissance Florence*. U of California P, 1983.

Burkhardt, Jacob. *The Civilization of the Renaissance in Italy*. The Modern Library, 1954.

Colish, Marcia L. "Cicero's *De Officiis* and Machiavelli's *Prince*." *Sixteenth Century Journal*, vol. 9, no. 4, Winter 1978, pp. 80–93.

Gilbert, Felix. *Machiavelli and Guicciardini: Politics and History in Sixteenth Century Florence*. W.W. Norton, 1984.

Hale, J.R. *Machiavelli and Renaissance Italy*. Pelican Books, 1961.

———. *War and Society in Renaissance Europe 1450–1620*. McGill-Queen's UP, 1988.

Najemy, John M. *A History of Florence: 1200–1575*. Wiley-Blackwell, 2008.

Rahe, Paul. "In the Shadow of Lucretius: The Epicurean Foundations of Machiavelli's Political Thought." *History of Political Thought*, vol. 28, no. 1, Spring 2007, pp. 30–55.

Ruggiero, Guido. *The Renaissance in Italy: A Social and Cultural History of the Rinascimento*. Cambridge UP, 2015.

Schellhase, Kenneth C. *Tacitus in Renaissance Political Thought*. U of Chicago P, 1976.

Skinner, Quentin. *The Foundations of Modern Political Thought*. 2 vols., Cambridge UP, 1996.

Trompf, G.W. *The Idea of Historical Recurrence in Western Thought: From Antiquity to the Reformation*. U of California P, 1979.

Works on *The Prince*

Benner, Erica. *Machiavelli's Prince: A New Reading*. Oxford UP, 2013.

Connell, William J. "Dating *The Prince*: Beginnings and Endings." *Review of Politics*, vol. 75, 2013, pp. 497–514.

Coyle, Martin, editor. *Niccolò Machiavelli's The Prince: New Interdisciplinary Essays*. Manchester UP, 1995.

de Alvarez, Leo Paul S. *The Machiavellian Enterprise: A Commentary on The Prince*. Northern Illinois UP, 2008.

Fuller, Timothy, editor. *Machiavelli's Legacy: The Prince After Five Hundred Years*. U of Pennsylvania P, 2016.

Gilbert, Allan H. *Machiavelli's "Prince" and Its Forerunners: "The Prince" as a Typical Book "de Regimine Principum."* Duke UP, 1938.

Giorgini, Giovanni. "Five Hundred Years of Italian Scholarship on Machiavelli's *Prince*." *Review of Politics*, vol. 75, 2013, pp. 625–40.

Richardson, Brian. "*The Prince* and Its Early Readers." Coyle, pp. 18–39.

Vatter, Miguel. *Machiavelli's The Prince*. Bloomsbury, 2013.

Viroli, Maurizio. *Redeeming* The Prince: *The Meaning of Machiavelli's Masterpiece*. Princeton: Princeton UP, 2013.

General Works

Ascoli, Albert Russell, and Victoria Kahn, editors. *Machiavelli and the Discourses of Literature*. Cornell UP, 1993.

Black, Robert. *Machiavelli*. Routledge, 2013.

Del Lucchese, Filippo. *The Political Philosophy of Niccolò Machiavelli*. Edinburgh UP, 2015.

Femia, Joseph V. *Machiavelli Revisited.* U of Wales P, 2004.

Machiavelli, Niccolò. *Lettere familiari di N. Machiavelli.* G.C. Sansoni, 1883.

Parel, Anthony. *The Machiavellian Cosmos.* Yale UP, 1992

——, editor. *The Political Calculus: Essays on Machiavelli's Philosophy.* U of Toronto P, 1972.

Skinner, Quentin. *Machiavelli: A Very Short Introduction.* Oxford UP, 2001.

Viroli, Maurizio. *Machiavelli.* Oxford UP, 1998.

Influential Interpretations

Althusser, Louis. *Machiavelli and Us.* Translated by Gregory Elliott, Verso, 2000.

Berlin, Isaiah. "The Originality of Machiavelli." In *Against the Current: Essays in the History of Ideas,* edited by Henry Hardy, Oxford UP, 1981, pp. 25–79.

Croce, Benedetto. *Politics and Morals.* Translated by Salvatore J. Castiglione, Philosophical Library, 1945.

Dietz, Mary G. "Trapping the Prince: Machiavelli and the Politics of Deception." *The American Political Science Review,* vol. 80, no. 3, Sept. 1986, pp. 777–99.

Falco, Maria J., editor. *Feminist Interpretations of Niccolò Machiavelli.* U of Pennsylvania P, 2004.

Gramsci, Antonio. "The Modern Prince." In *Selections from the Prison Notebooks of Antonio Gramsci,* translated and edited by Quentin Hoare and Geoffrey Nowell Smith, International Publishers, 1973, pp. 123–43.

Lefort, Claude. *Machiavelli in the Making.* Translated by Michael B. Smith, Northwestern UP, 2012.

McCormick, John P. *Machiavellian Democracy.* Cambridge UP, 2011.

Meinecke, Friedrich. *Machiavellianism: The Doctrine of Raison d'État and Its Place in Modern History.* Translated by Douglas Scott, Routledge and Kegan Paul, 1962.

Negri, Antonio. *Insurgencies: Constituent Power and the Modern State.* Translated by Maurizia Boscagli, U of Minnesota P, 2009.

Pitkin, Hanna Fenichel. *Fortune Is a Woman: Gender and Politics in the Thought of Niccolò Machiavelli.* U of California P, 1987.

Pocock, J.G.A. *The Machiavellian Moment: Florentine Political Thought and the Atlantic Republican Tradition.* Princeton UP, 1975.

Strauss, Leo. *Thoughts on Machiavelli*. U of Chicago P, 1978.

Vatter, Miguel E. *Between Form and Event: Machiavelli's Theory of Political Freedom*. Kluwer, 2000.

Index

Achilles, 43, 98, 105
Aeneas, 137&n2, 138
Aetolian League, 108n1
Africa, 79, 114, 120, 198, 213
Agathocles, 43, 78, 79, 81
Al-Ashraf Qansuh al-Ghawri,
    114n2
Alexander III (the Great) of
    Macedon, 43, 44, 47, 65&n1,
    66n1, 67, 96, 98, 102, 126,
    137&n1, 157&n1, 158, 176n2,
    183nn5&7, 211, 213, 215, 219
Alexander VI (Rodrigo Borgia),
    Pope, 23, 24, 37, 43, 47, 63&n2,
    64, 71n1, 73, 76–77, 79, 80,
    87&n1, 88, 106, 174&n3, 217
Alfonso II, 187n1
Althusser, Louis, *Machiavelli and
    Us*, 33–34
Amboise, Georges d' (Cardinal of
    Rouen), 37, 47, 64n3, 65, 78n5
Anne of Brittany, 64n2
Arcadius, 198&n1
Ardinghelli, Piero, 223&n2
Aristotle, 12, 43
Assyrian Empire, 183&n2, 193n2
Athens, 48, 68n1, 69n1, 137,
    150n2, 163, 183, 192, 201&n3,
    204&n1

Barbiano, Alberigo da, 92&n4
battles, 131; of Agnadello, 177n1;
    of Cannae, 176n1; of Leuctra,
    145n1, 213n1; of Pharsalus,
    184n2; of Ravenna, 38, 131
Beaufort, Pierre Robert de. *See*
    Gregory XI
Bentivoglio, house of, 62, 63n1,
    109, 118&n3, 128n1
Bentivoglio, Annibale, 109
Berlin, Isaiah, "The Originality of
    Machiavelli," 34

Bertini, Paolo, 223
Boccalini, Traiano, 32
Borgia, Cesare, 37, 43, 44, 45, 46,
    63n2, 64, 72, 74n1, 75n1, 79n2,
    80–81, 94, 96n3, 102, 118, 119,
    129n2, 174n3, 217
Borgia, Rodrigo. *See* Alexander VI
Buondelmonti, Zanobi, 133, 208,
    216, 217
Bussone, Francesco (Il
    Carmagnola), 92n1

Caesar, Julius, 43, 98, 101&n3,
    102, 112, 148&n3, 149, 159n1,
    168n2, 183n6, 184n2, 213, 215
Caligula, 148&n2
Calleoni, Bartolomeo (of
    Bergamo), 92&n2
Camillus, Marcus Furius 152&n1,
    154, 175
Cantacuzene, John, 94n3
Caracalla, 110&n1, 112, 113, 115,
    148&n1
Carneades, 204n1
Carthage, 68, 168n1, 176&n2, 183
Castracani, Castruccio, 76n1,
    216–17
Cato the Elder, 168&n2, 203
Cato the Younger, 168&n2
Charlemagne (Charles the Great),
    152&n2, 153
Charles V, 39, 43, 44, 47, 224n1
Charles VII, 43, 95&n3, 96n3, 212
Charles VIII, 13, 14, 24, 37, 44, 46,
    62&n1, 68n3, 87n3, 89&n1,
    95&n4, 214&n1
Charles, Duke of Calabria, 201n2
Chiron the Centaur, 44, 105
Cicero, Marcus Tullius, 27, 44, 143;
    De amicitia, 143n1; *De officiis*,
    27&n2, 44, 105n1
Cincinnatus, Lucius Quinctius, 174

Joan of Arc, 212n2
Julianus, 110n1, 112, 114
Julius II (Giuliano della Rovere),
  Pope, 15, 23, 38, 45, 57n4, 58,
  59n1, 77&n1, 78&n1, 87n2,
  88&n1, 93, 94n1, 101, 118n3,
  120n3, 128&n1, 146n1, 153n1,
  172n2, 177n1, 209
Junius Brutus, 155, 170&nn1&2,
  171, 172–73

Ladislas II, 153n1
League of Cambrai, 15, 38, 45,
  64n1, 146n1, 153n1, 177n1
League of Cognac, 39, 44, 224
League of Venice, 37
Lefort, Claude, *Machiavelli in the
  Making*, 35
Leo III, Pope, 152n1
Leo X (Giovanni de' Medici), Pope,
  15, 38, 39, 45, 57n4, 88&n1,
  130n1, 197, 223n2
Livy (Titus Livius), 12, 136,
  152&n1, 153, 170, 175, 178;
  History of Rome, 121n1, 130n2
Lombardy, 62, 63, 64, 91, 117, 130,
  152, 163
Louis IX, 109n3
Louis XI, 45, 95&n4
Louis XII, 14, 37, 45, 47, 58&n3,
  59&n1, 62&n1, 63, 64&n1,
  73n2, 95n4, 101&n1, 146n1,
  153n1, 177n1, 187&n2
Lucretia, 170&n3
Lucretius, 12, 27&n1, 37, 45
Lycurgus, 139&n1, 147, 150&n1

Macedonian kingdom, 61, 157n1,
  183n1
Machiavelli, Bernardo, 12
Machiavelli, Niccolò: and
  other thinkers, 26–28; and
  Renaissance Florence, 12–16
Machiavelli, Niccolò: some key
  concepts in his thought, 17–26;
  ambition, 62, 63, 65, 83, 88,

91, 107, 109, 110, 141, 147,
  157, 168, 169, 171, 172, 181,
  186–89, 192, 196, 200, 201,
  202, 215;
Christianity (critique of), 23–25,
  133–34;
the Christian religion and
  Christian states, 134, 136,
  152, 198;
the Church, 12, 23–24, 33, 63,
  64, 65, 73, 74, 87, 88, 92,
  130, 151–53, 176, 203;
fear, 11, 21–22, 25, 60, 61, 63,
  66, 70, 77, 78, 80, 81, 83,
  85, 86, 92, 102–05, 107,
  108, 109, 112–13, 114, 118,
  119, 120, 121, 122, 123,
  128, 131–32, 140, 142n1,
  143, 144, 149, 150–51, 152,
  153, 155, 161, 163, 168,
  169, 170n1, 181–82, 187,
  191–92, 196, 199, 204, 205,
  207, 208–09, 210, 211, 212,
  213, 215;
fortresses, 26, 115–19, 209;
Fortune, 17–18, 20, 35, 56, 70,
  71, 72, 73, 96, 117, 126–29,
  133, 134, 162, 166, 175,
  177–78, 180–84, 190, 191,
  192, 196, 202, 205, 216, 217,
  218, 221;
generosity, 22–23, 27, 77,
  100–02;
glory, 21, 27, 72, 98, 104, 119,
  125, 127, 134, 137, 148–49,
  161, 164, 184, 195, 199–200,
  203, 206, 218, 219;
honour, 55, 80, 83, 107, 112,
  119, 122, 129, 130, 131, 148,
  158, 165, 171, 173, 182, 206;
mercenaries, 24, 25–26, 80n1,
  89–93, 94, 95, 96, 116, 202,
  208, 209, 210n1;
necessity, 18, 23, 58, 64, 81,
  89, 95, 99, 121, 123, 125,
  137–41, 146, 161, 172, 180,

About the Publisher

The word "broadview" expresses a good deal of the philosophy behind our company. Our focus is very much on the humanities and social sciences—especially literature, writing, and philosophy—but within these fields we are open to a broad range of academic approaches and political viewpoints. We strive in particular to produce high-quality, pedagogically useful books for higher education classrooms—anthologies, editions, sourcebooks, surveys of particular academic fields and sub-fields, and also course texts for subjects such as composition, business communication, and critical thinking. We welcome the perspectives of authors from marginalized and underrepresented groups, and we have a strong commitment to the environment. We publish English-language works and translations from many parts of the world, and our books are available world-wide; we also publish a select list of titles with a specifically Canadian emphasis.

broadview press